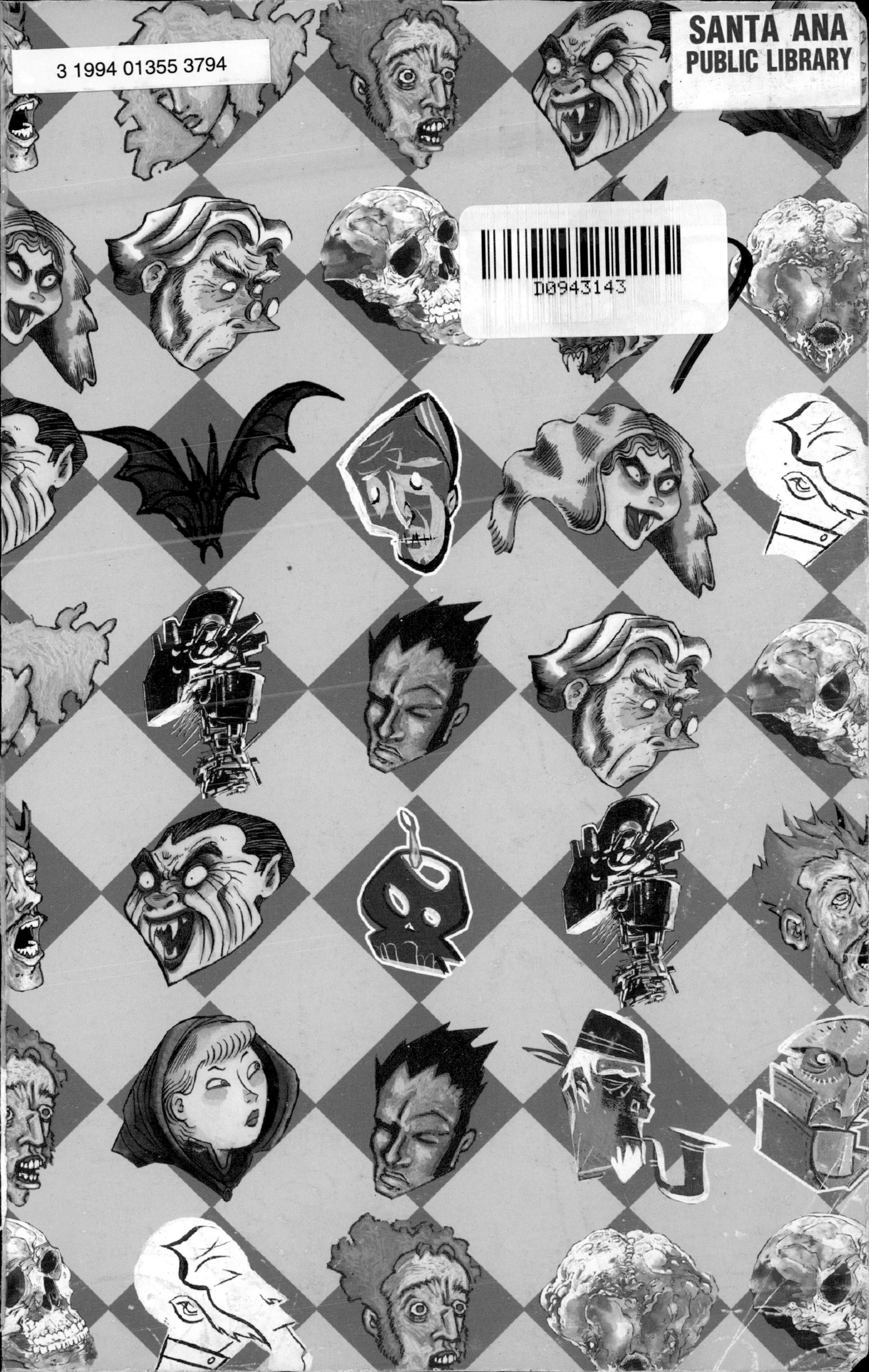

FRANKENSTEIN

Written in 1816 when she was only nineteen, MARY SHELLEY's novel chillingly dramatized the dangerous potential of life begotten upon a laboratory table. A frightening creation myth for any era, *Frankenstein* remains one of the greatest horror stories ever written and is an undisputed classic of its kind.

Frankenstein has been reprinted, reproduced, abridged, and dramatized numerous times, with stage performances beginning as early as 1823. There have been multiple film versions and elaborations, as well as sequels and spoofs. But most of these works deviate from Shelley's original tale, which played more as an update of the myth of Prometheus. The terror evoked by her original patchwork monster has been substituted for a more romanticized version of the creature. IDW's *Little Book of Horror: Frankenstein* presents the creature, and the tale itself, as Shelley originally intended.

H.G. WELLS'S THE WAR OF THE WORLDS

"No one would have believed in the last years of the nineteenth century that this world was being watched keenly and closely by intelligences greater than man's..." Thus begins the all-time classic alien invasion story *The War of the Worlds*, first published by H.G. Wells in 1898. With lethal heat rays and giant death machines, the legendary story of Martian invaders has captured the imagination of readers for over a century.

Since its first publication, *The War of the Worlds* has been presented in numerous adaptations other than print, including film and television, as well as the legendary radio dramatization of 1938 that horrified millions of unsuspecting listeners. IDW Publishing's *Little Book of Horror: The War of the Worlds* presents a new and harrowing re-presentation of Wells's timeless tale of extraterrestrial terror.

BRAM STOKER'S DRACULA

BRAM STOKER's 1897 novel *Dracula* stands out as one of the greatest horror stories in all of literature. More than just a spine-tingling tale of horror, the work boasts one of fiction's most terrifying characters — Count Dracula, Lord of the Undead. In Stoker's novel, Jonathan Harker journeys to Transylvania to conduct business with the mysterious Count Dracula–only to discover a horror that will threaten the very love he left back in England.

Originally published in 1897, Bram Stoker's *Dracula* quickly achieved worldwide fame and has been re-created for the stage and screen countless times—in fact, an estimated 160 films feature *Dracula* in a major role (and 650 movies in total), a number second only to Sherlock Holmes. IDW is proud to present a re-presentation of the harrowing classic with *Little Book of Horror: Dracula*.

BIG BOOK OF HORROR

book design by
Neil Uyetake

collection edited by
Justin Eisinger

IDW PUBLISHING is:
Ted Adams, Co-President
Robbie Robbins, Co-President
Kris Oprisko, Vice-President
Chris Ryall, Publisher/Editor-in-Chief
Neil Uyetake, Art Director
Dan Taylor, Editor
Justin Eisinger, Editorial Assistant
Chris Mowry, Production Assistant
Matthew Ruzicka, CPA, Controller
Alonzo Simon, Shipping Manager
Alex Garner, Creative Director
Yumiko Miyano, Business Development
Rick Privman, Business Development

www.IDWPUBLISHING.com

09 08 07 06   1 2 3 4 5
ISBN10: 1-600100-14-7
ISBN13: 978-1-600100-14-7

FRANKENSTEIN

written by
Steve Niles
painted art by
Scott Morse
lettering and design by
Robbie Robbins
edited by
Chris Ryall
inspired by
Mary Shelley's *Frankenstein*

THE WAR OF THE WORLDS

written by
Steve Niles
painted art by
Ted McKeever
lettering and design by
Robbie Robbins
edited by
Chris Ryall
inspired by
H.G. Wells's *The War of the Worlds*

DRACULA

written by
Steve Niles
painted art by
Richard Sala
lettering and design by
Robbie Robbins
edited by
Chris Ryall
inspired by
Bram Stoker's *Dracula*

LITTLE BOOK OF HORROR™
FRANKENSTEIN

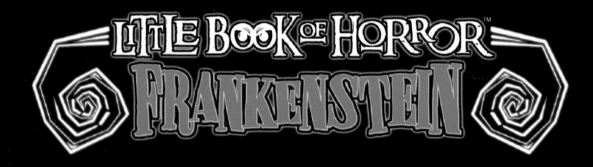

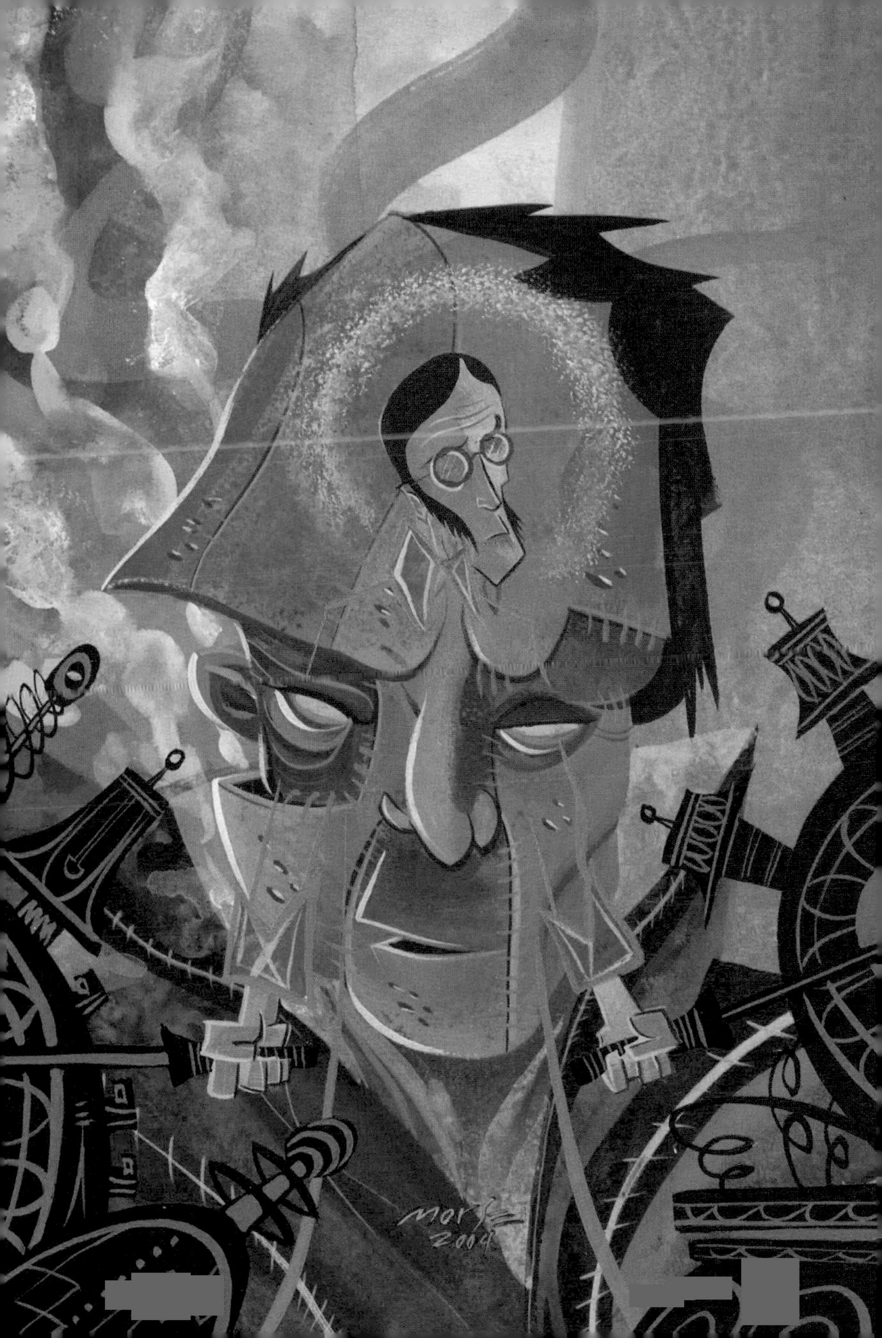

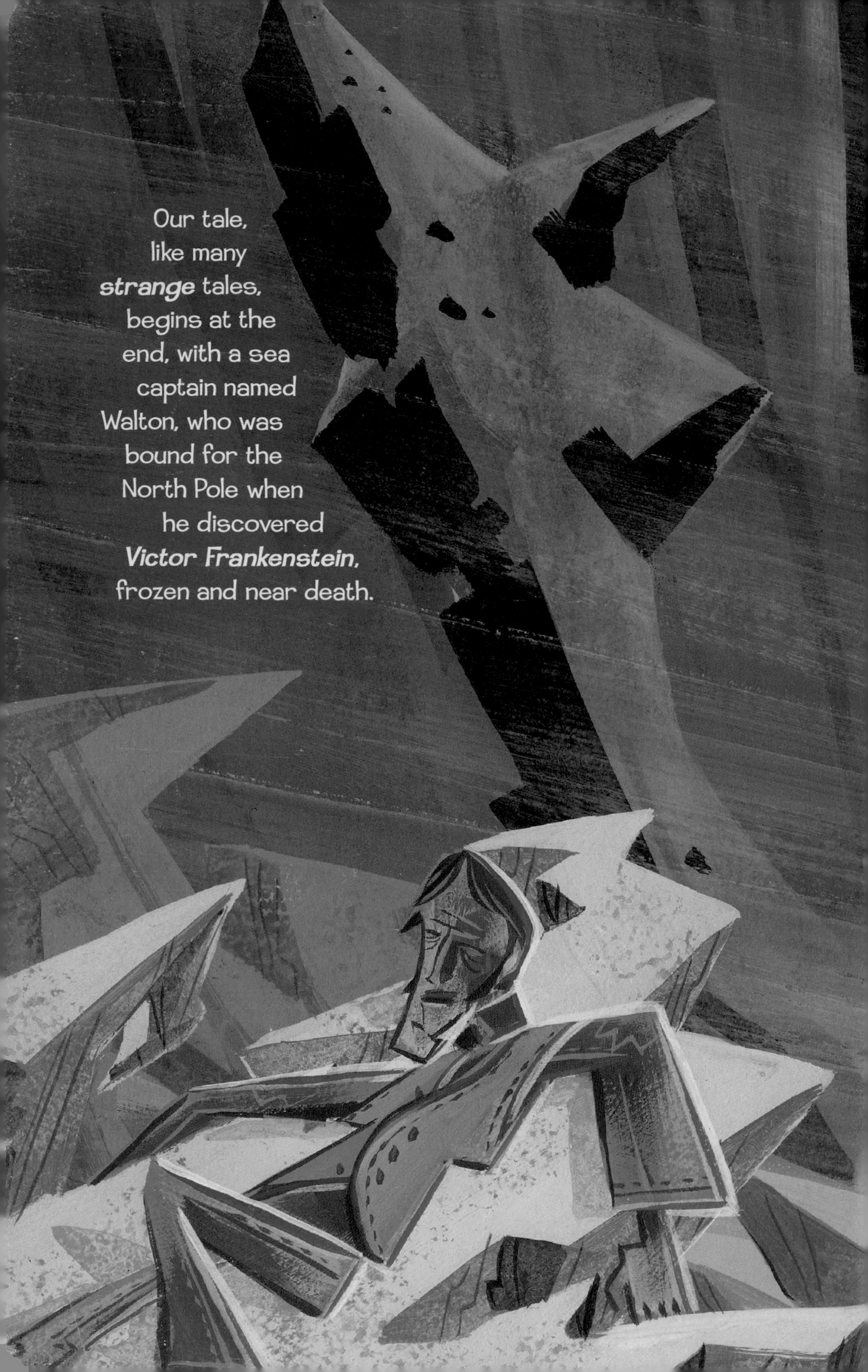
Our tale, like many ***strange*** tales, begins at the end, with a sea captain named Walton, who was bound for the North Pole when he discovered ***Victor Frankenstein,*** frozen and near death.

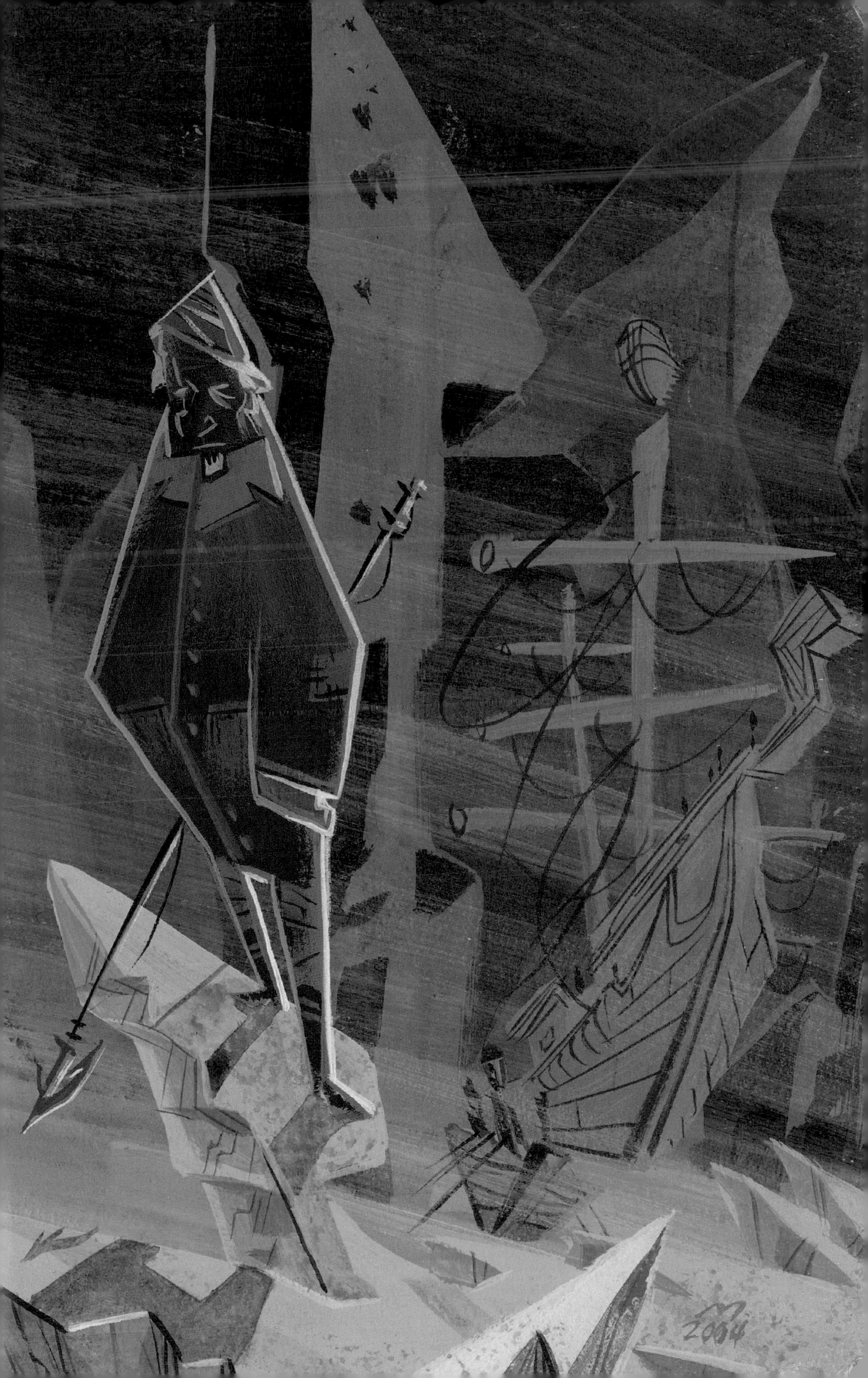

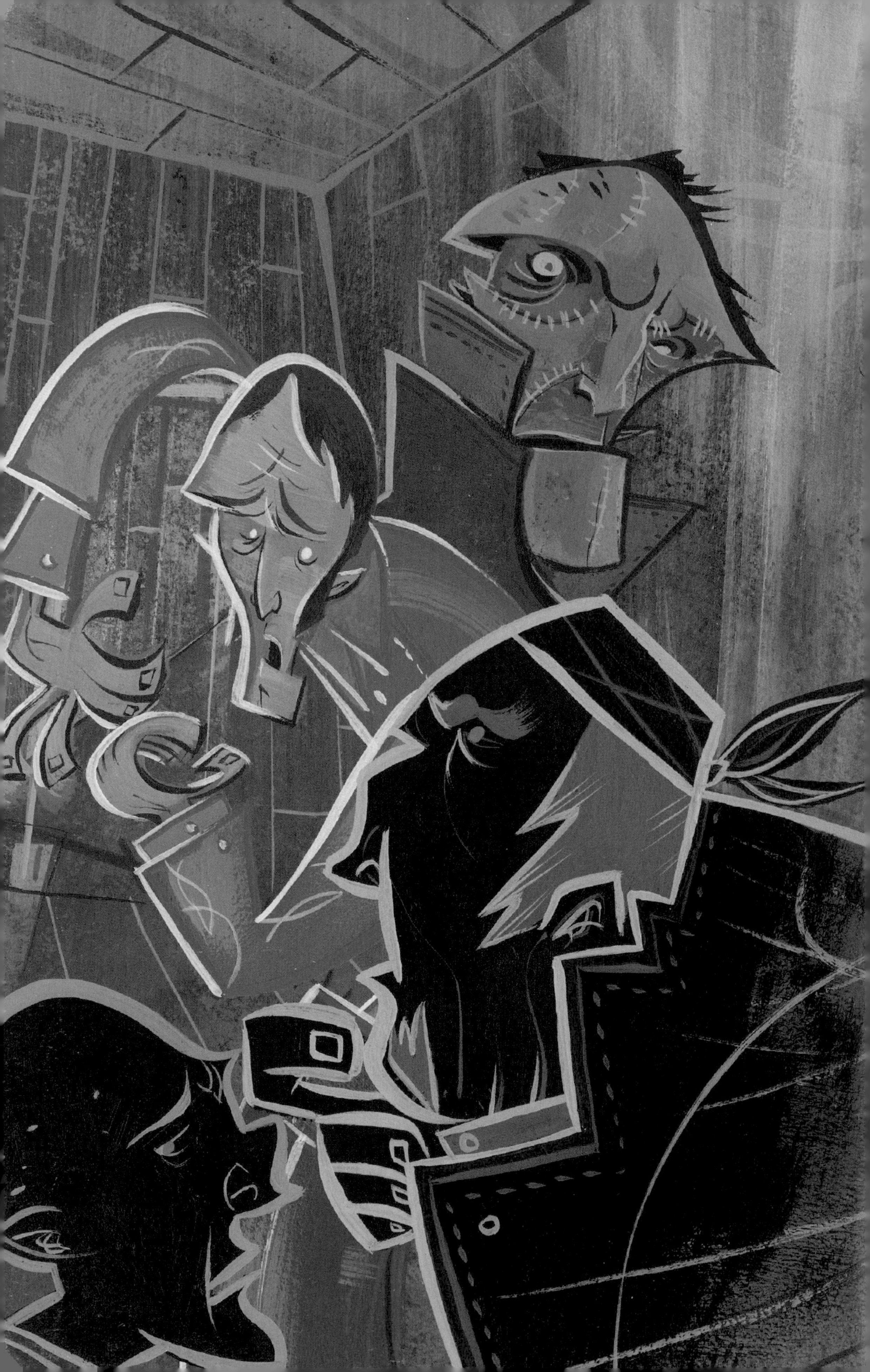

Feverish to the point of madness, Victor tells his story to Walton—the fantastic tale of the ***monster*** which Frankenstein created with his own two hands and the stolen limbs and organs of the dead!

Victor begins his story with a bit of background about his early years in Geneva and a happy childhood with his cousin Elizabeth, whom Victor would grow to love and one day marry.

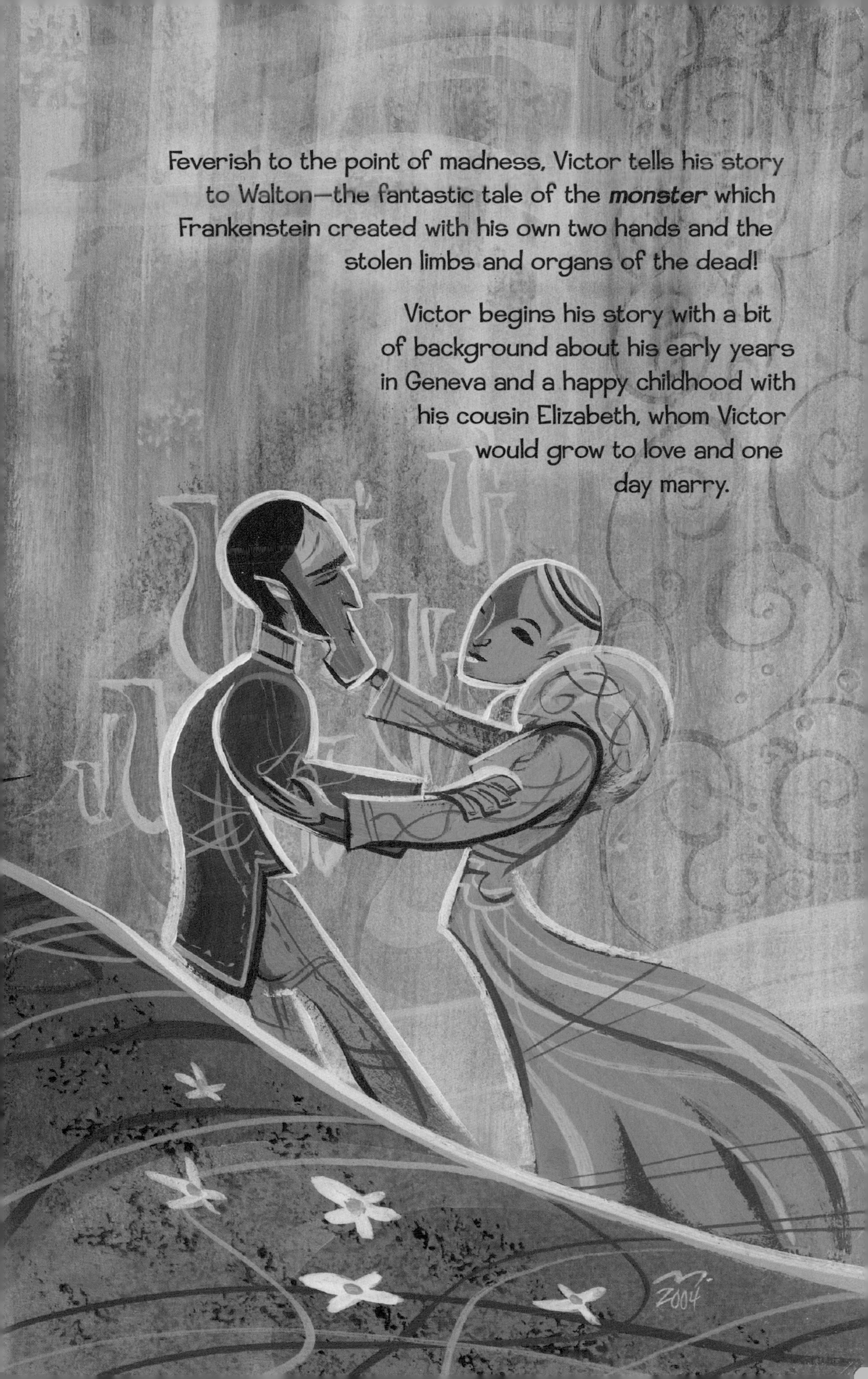

But Victor's first love was knowledge.
He attended university and feverishly,
some say *obsessively*, studied
philosophy, surgery, and chemistry.

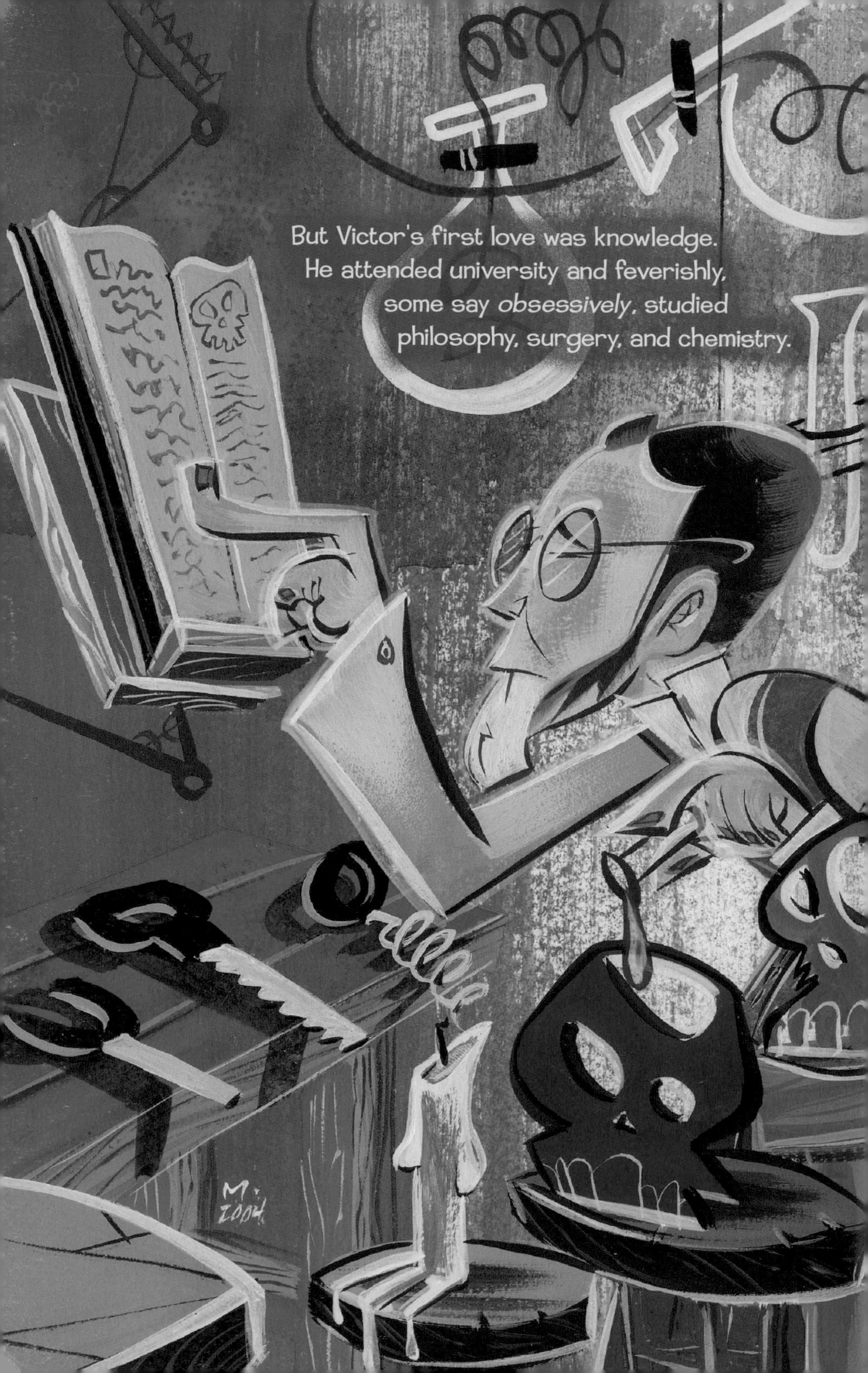

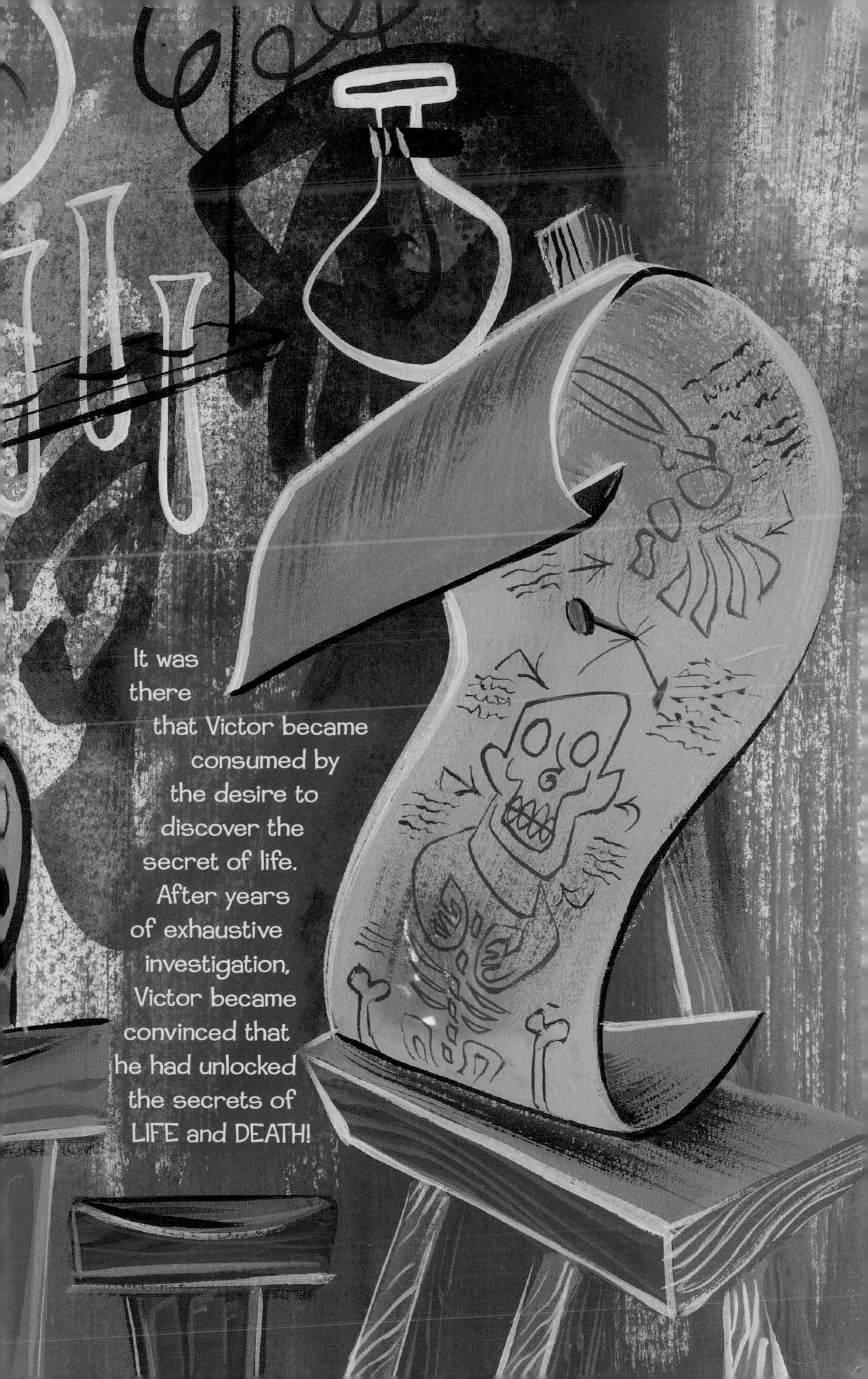
It was
there
that Victor became
consumed by
the desire to
discover the
secret of life.
After years
of exhaustive
investigation,
Victor became
convinced that
he had unlocked
the secrets of
LIFE and DEATH!

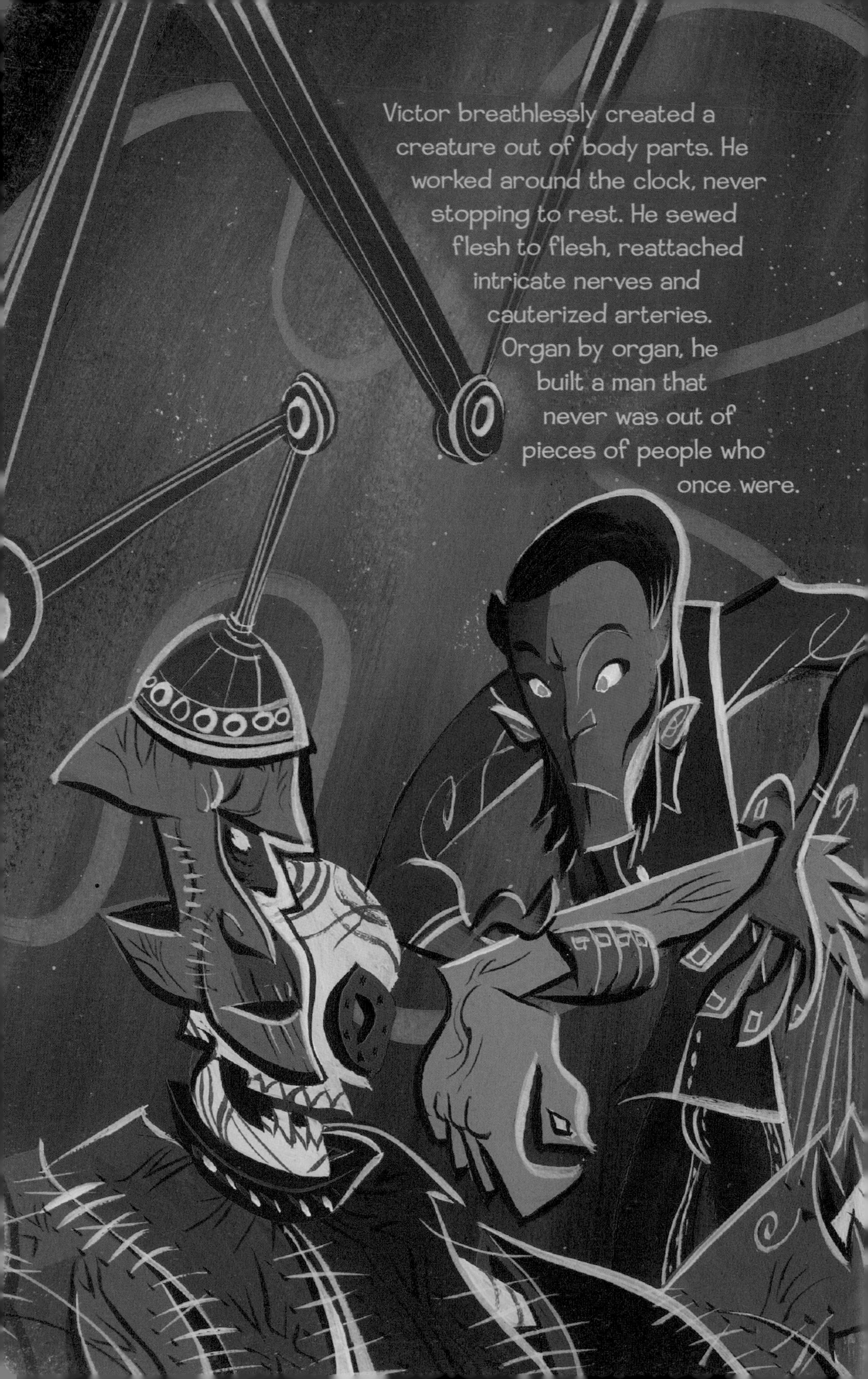

Victor breathlessly created a creature out of body parts. He worked around the clock, never stopping to rest. He sewed flesh to flesh, reattached intricate nerves and cauterized arteries. Organ by organ, he built a man that never was out of pieces of people who once were.

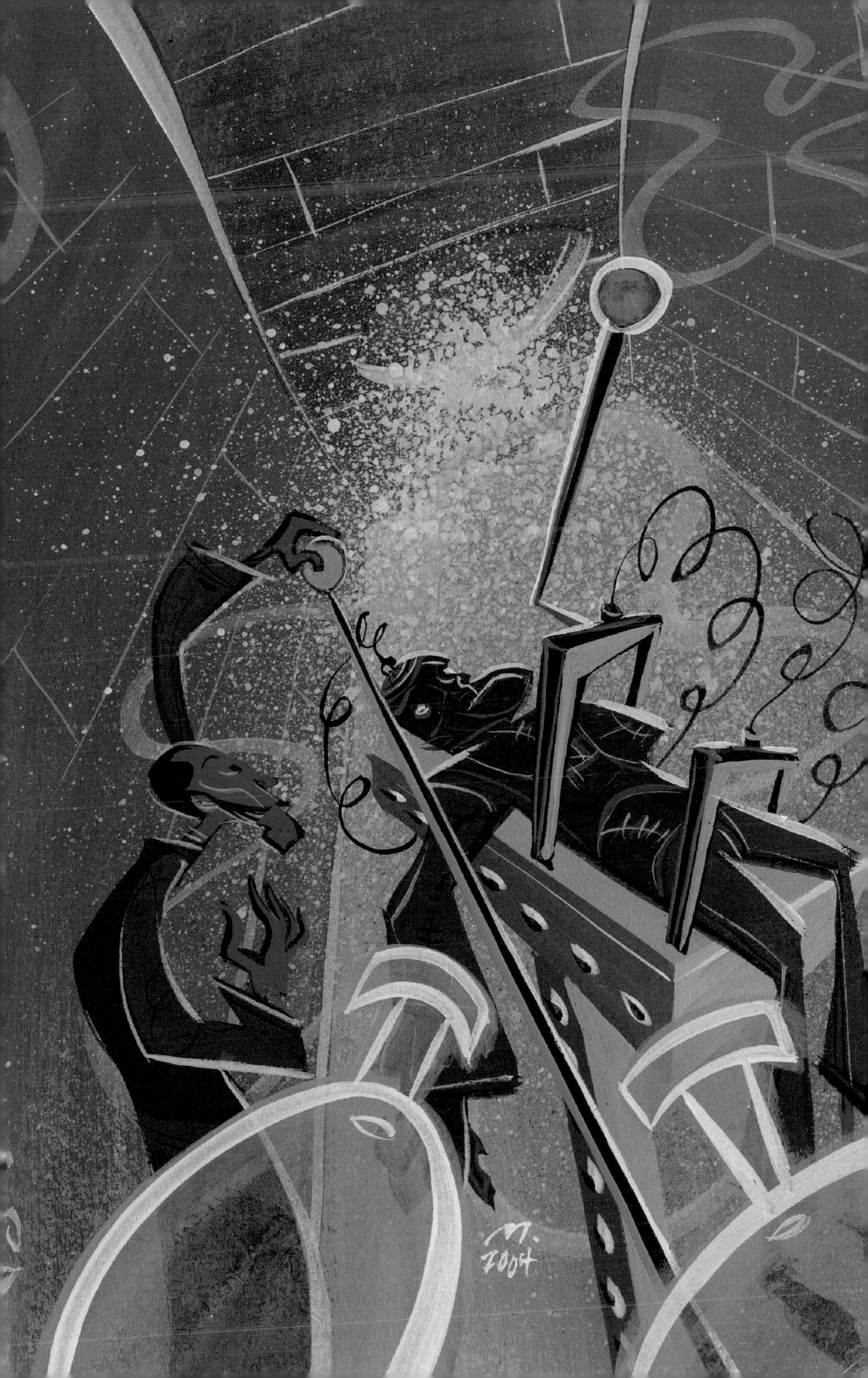

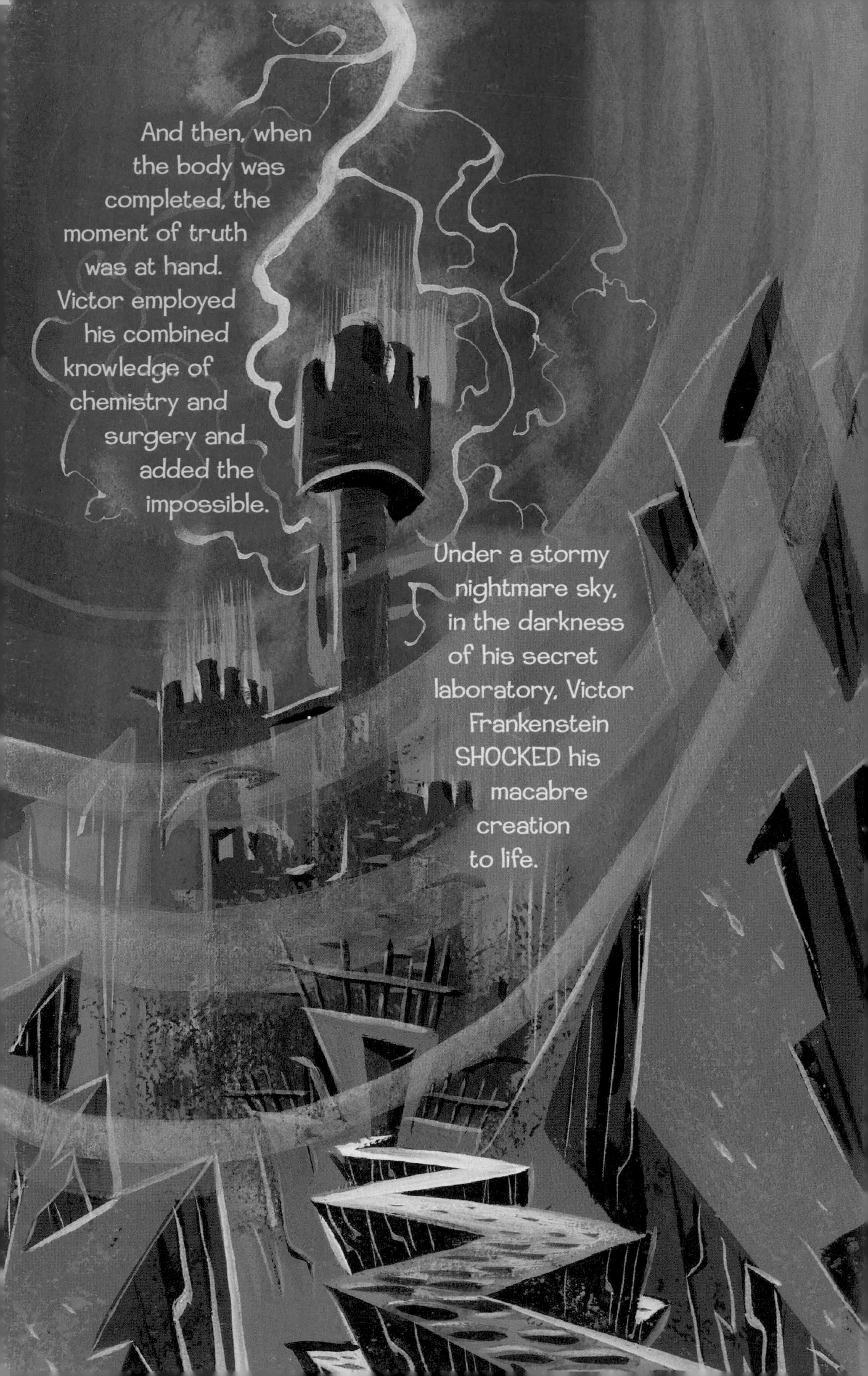

And then, when the body was completed, the moment of truth was at hand. Victor employed his combined knowledge of chemistry and surgery and added the impossible.

Under a stormy nightmare sky, in the darkness of his secret laboratory, Victor Frankenstein SHOCKED his macabre creation to life.

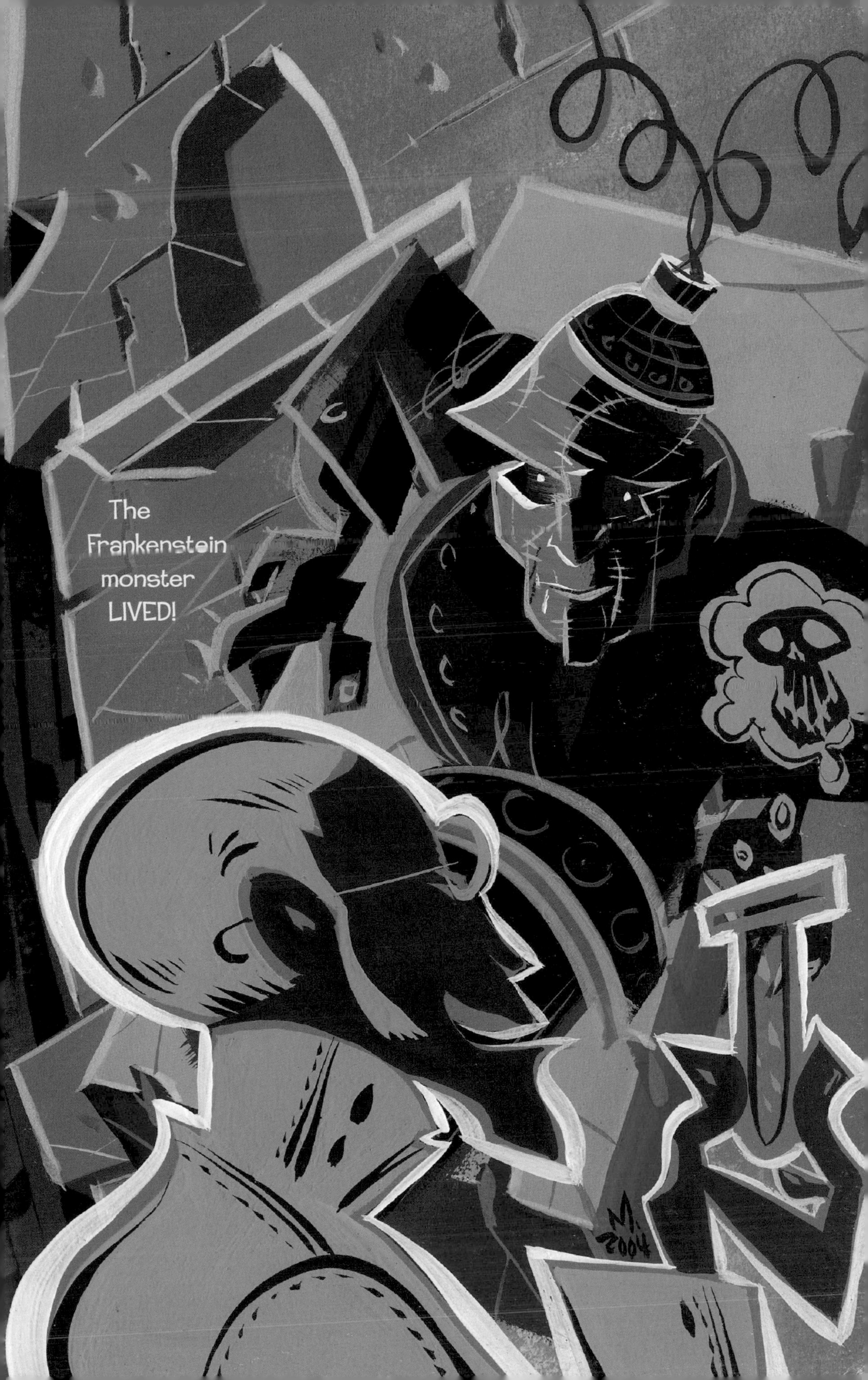
The Frankenstein monster LIVED!

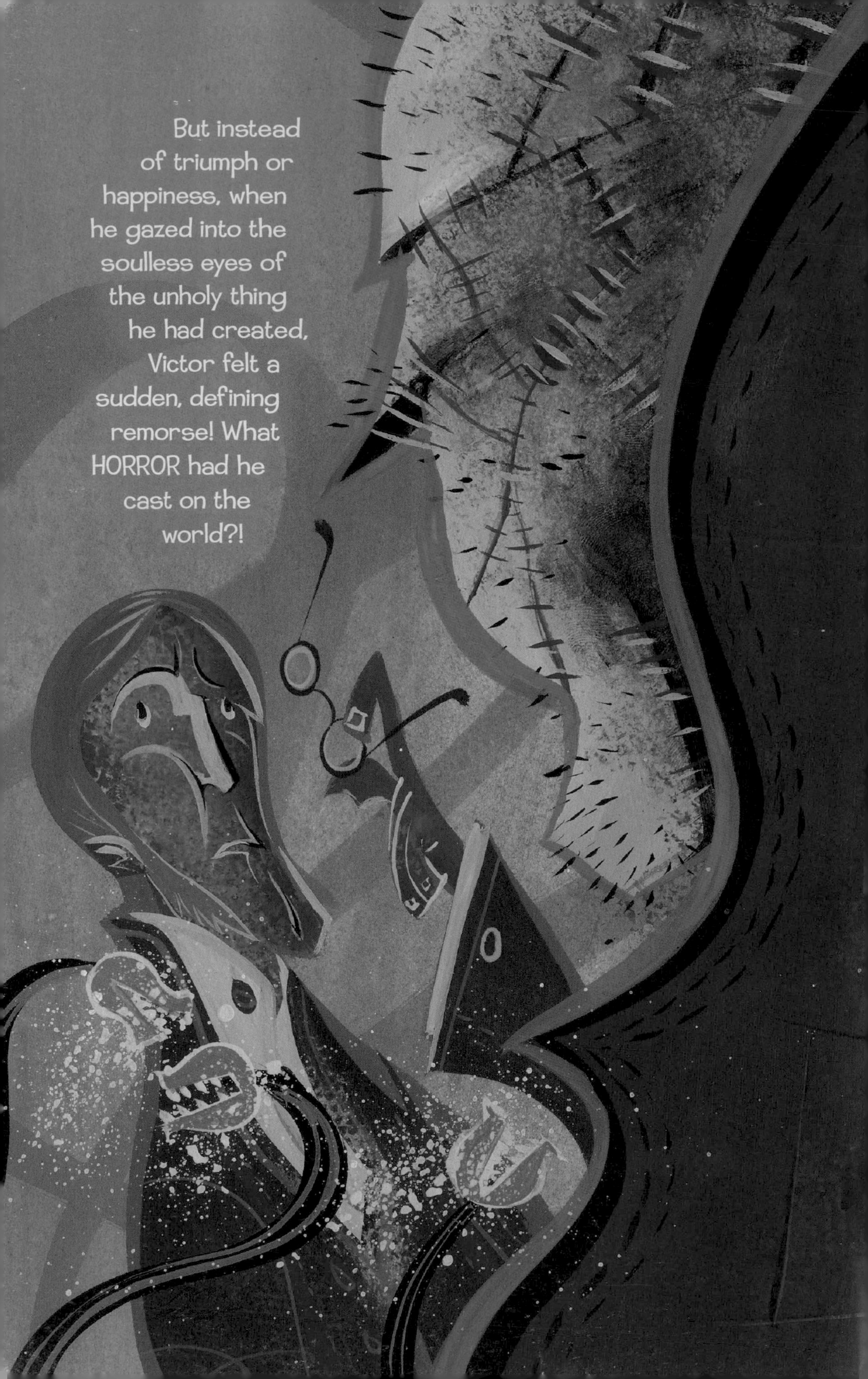
But instead
of triumph or
happiness, when
he gazed into the
soulless eyes of
the unholy thing
he had created,
Victor felt a
sudden, defining
remorse! What
HORROR had he
cast on the
world?!

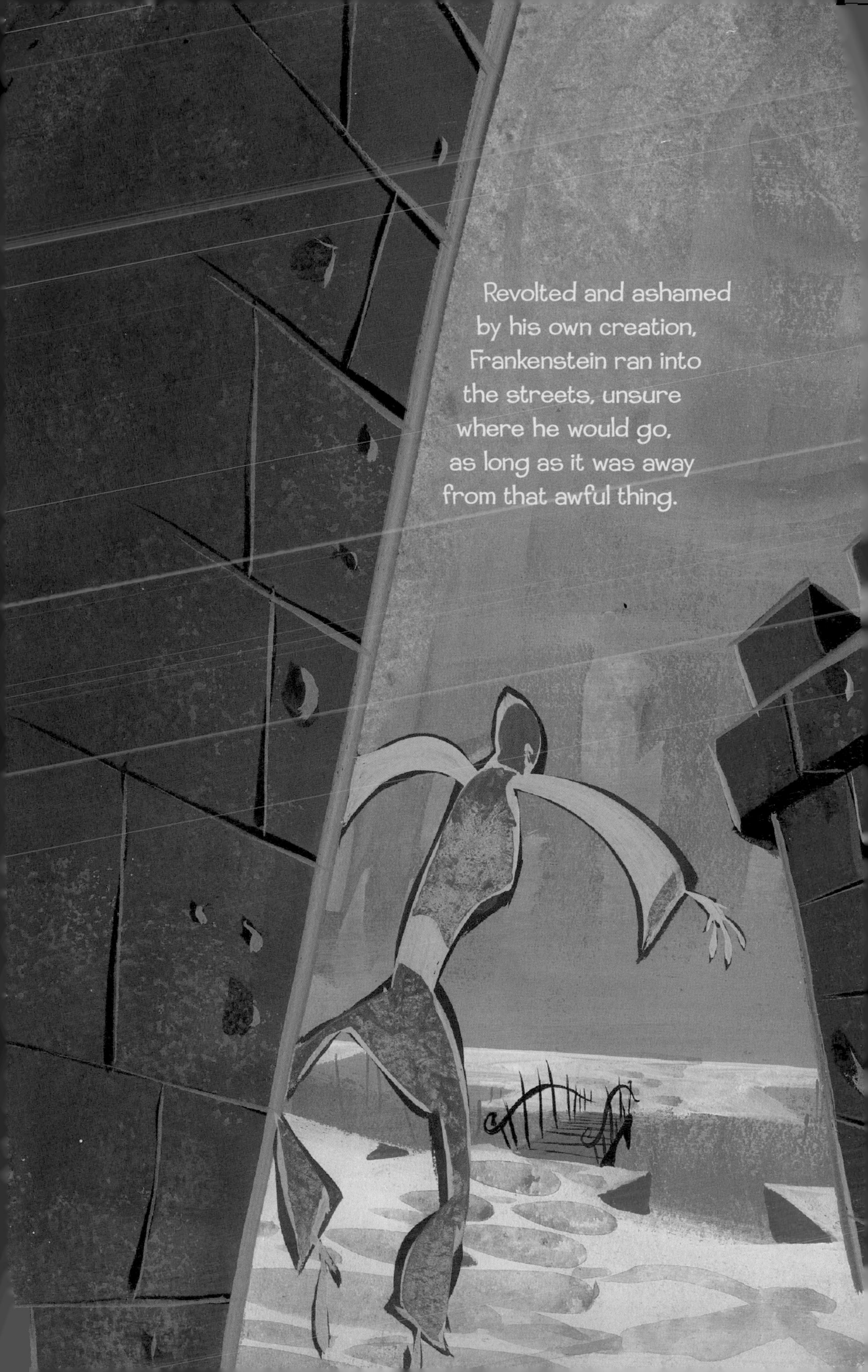

Revolted and ashamed
by his own creation,
Frankenstein ran into
the streets, unsure
where he would go,
as long as it was away
from that awful thing.

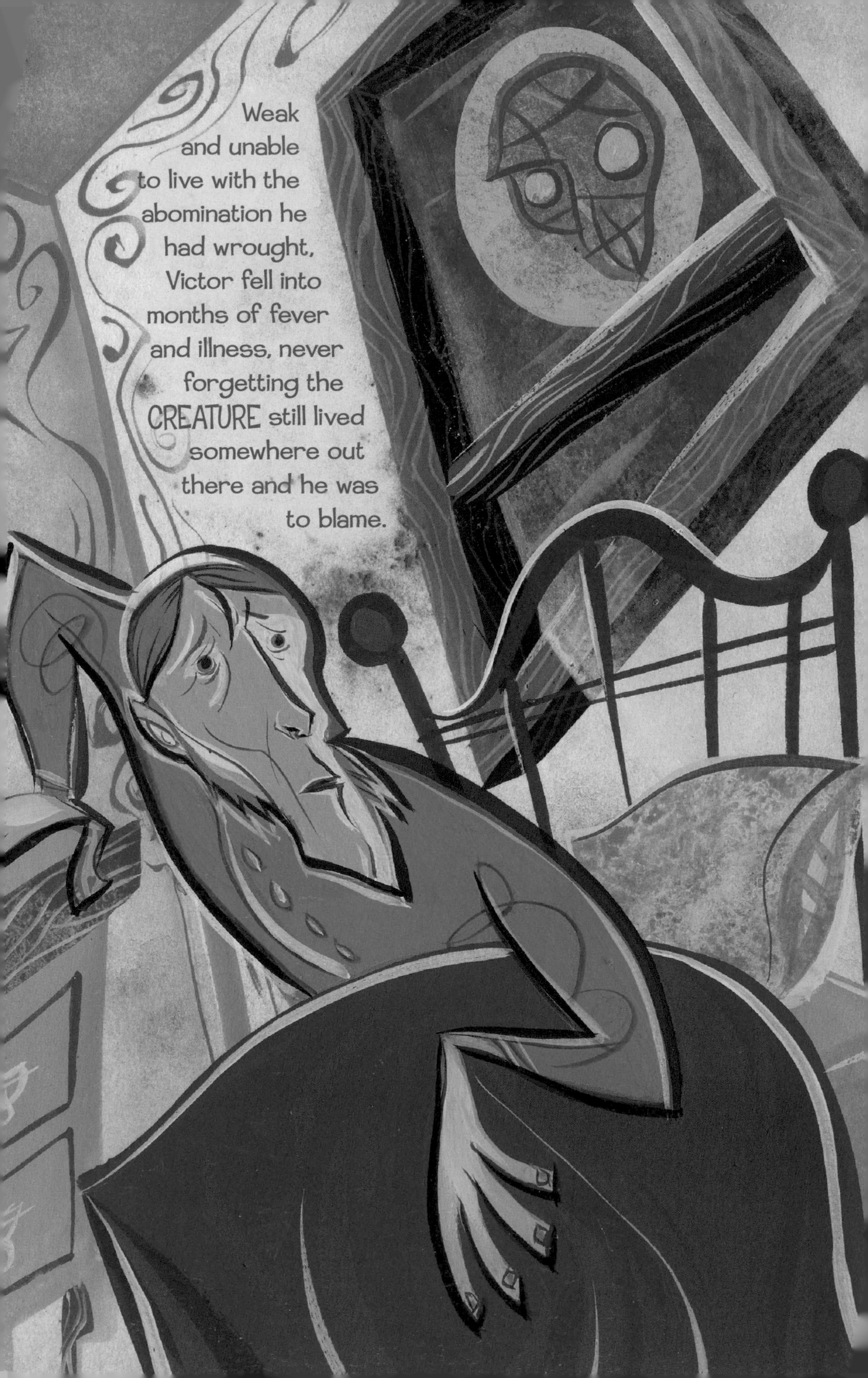
Weak and unable to live with the abomination he had wrought, Victor fell into months of fever and illness, never forgetting the CREATURE still lived somewhere out there and he was to blame.

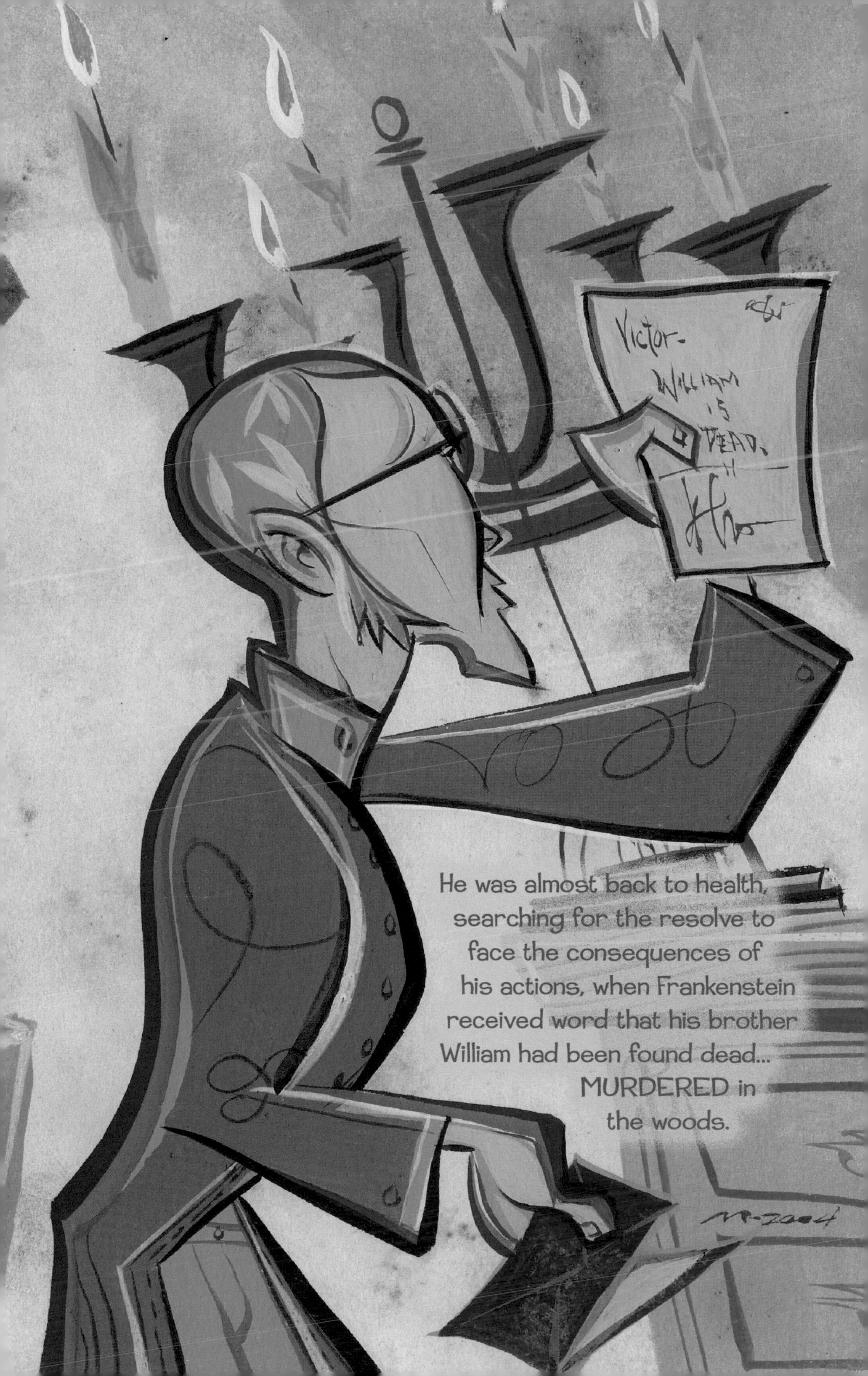
Victor-
William
is
DEAD.
He was almost back to health, searching for the resolve to face the consequences of his actions, when Frankenstein received word that his brother William had been found dead...
MURDERED in the woods.

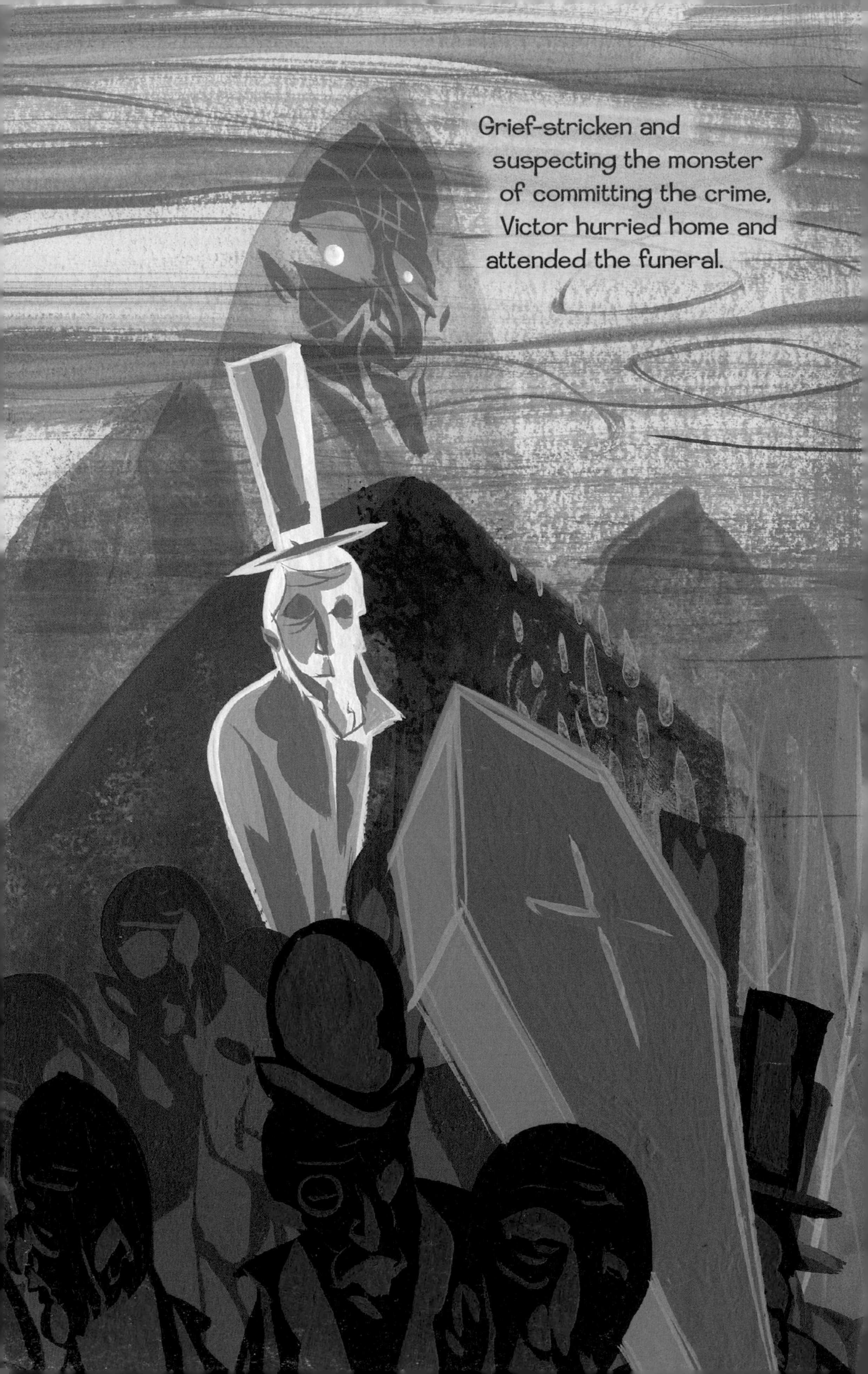
Grief-stricken and suspecting the monster of committing the crime, Victor hurried home and attended the funeral.

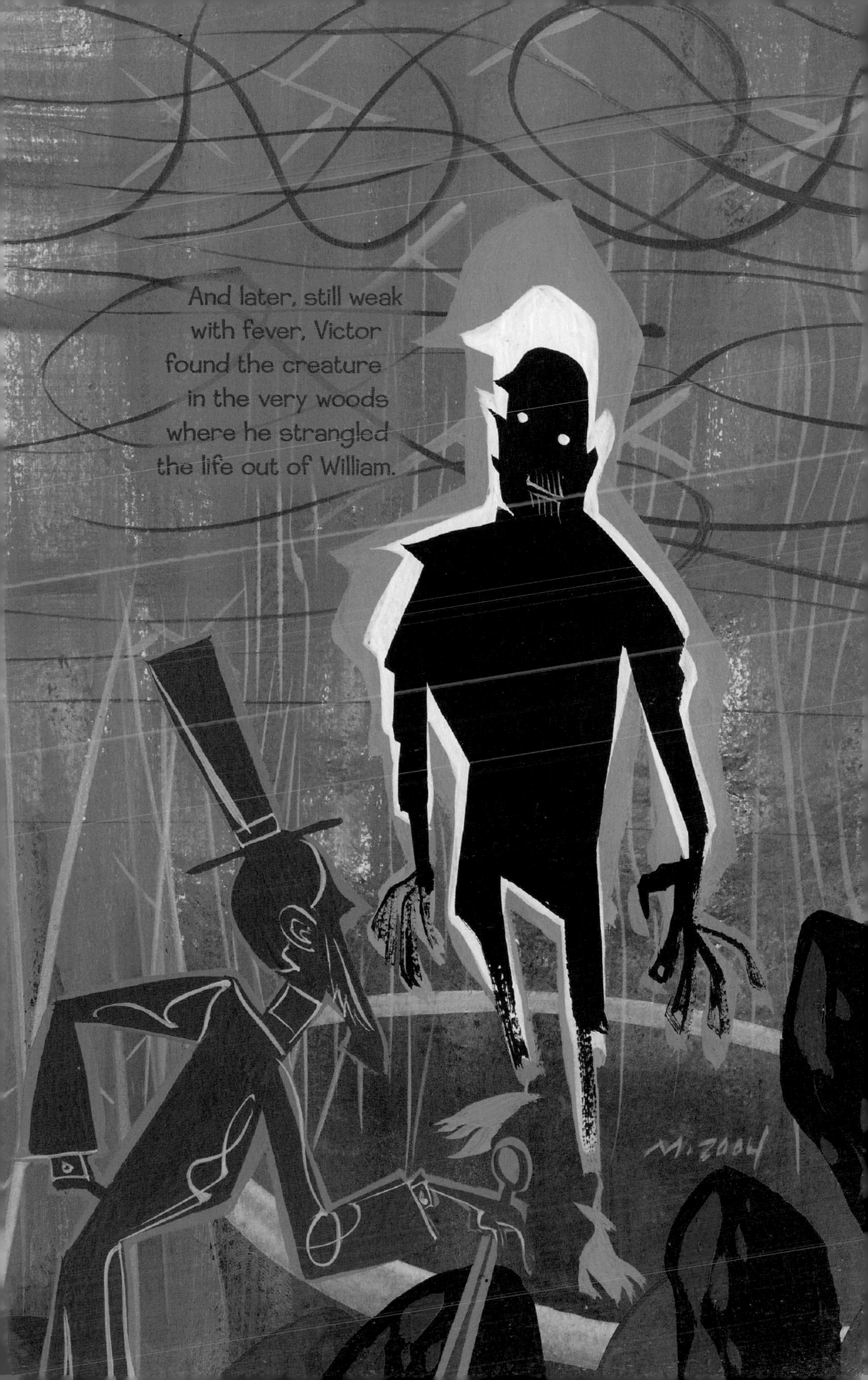
And later, still weak
with fever, Victor
found the creature
in the very woods
where he strangled
the life out of William.

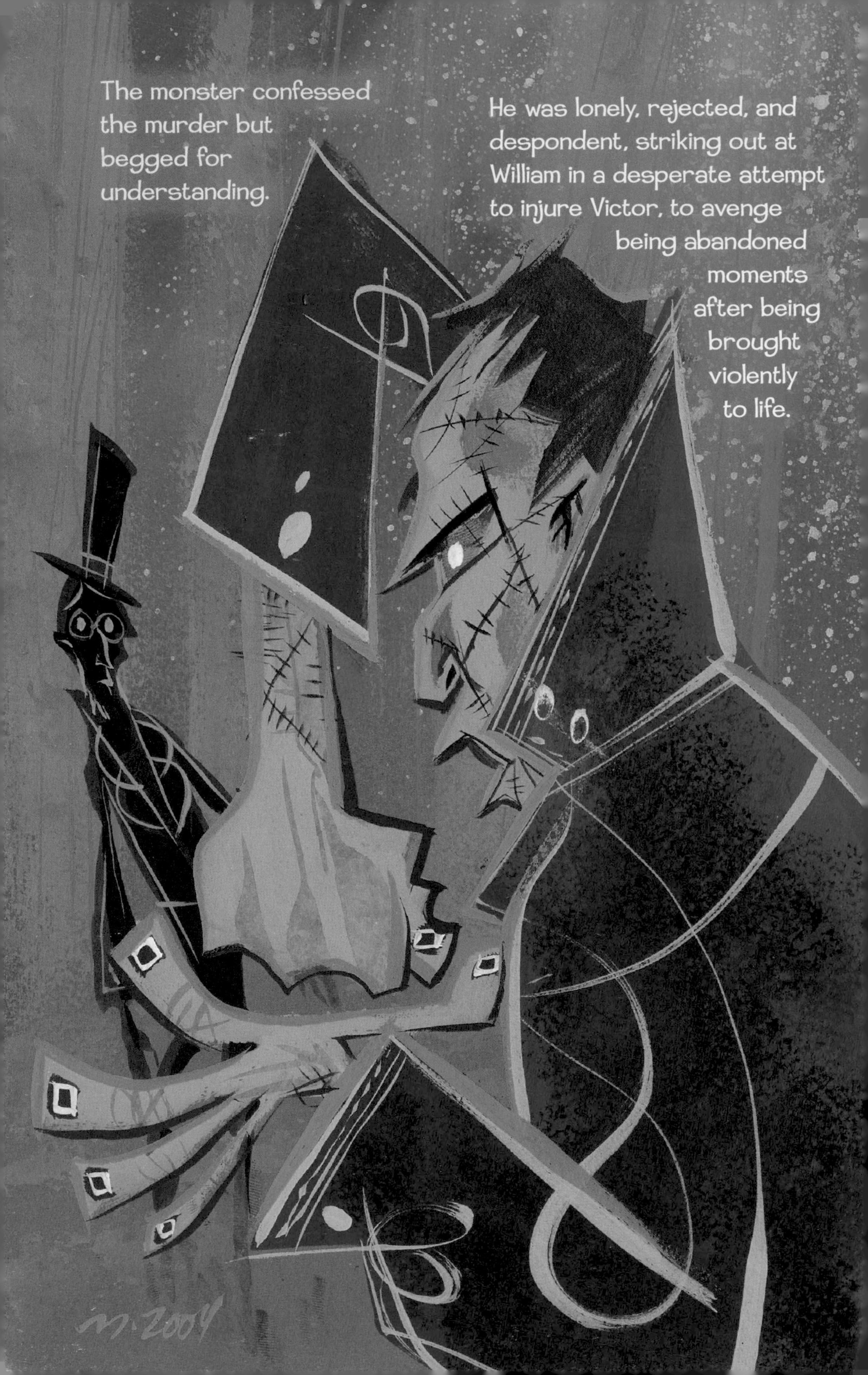
The monster confessed the murder but begged for understanding.
He was lonely, rejected, and despondent, striking out at William in a desperate attempt to injure Victor, to avenge being abandoned moments after being brought violently to life.

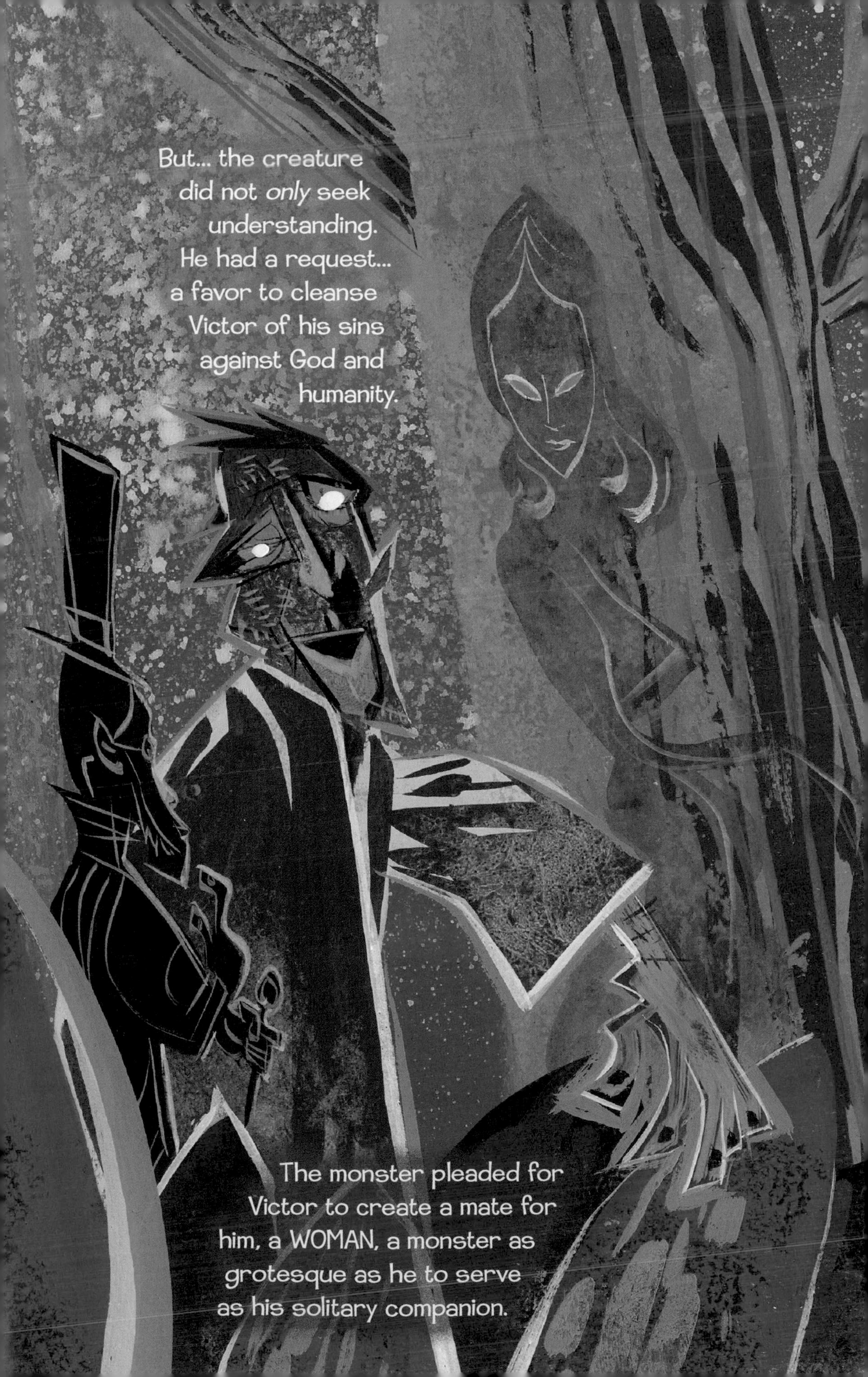
But... the creature did not *only* seek understanding. He had a request... a favor to cleanse Victor of his sins against God and humanity.
The monster pleaded for Victor to create a mate for him, a WOMAN, a monster as grotesque as he to serve as his solitary companion.

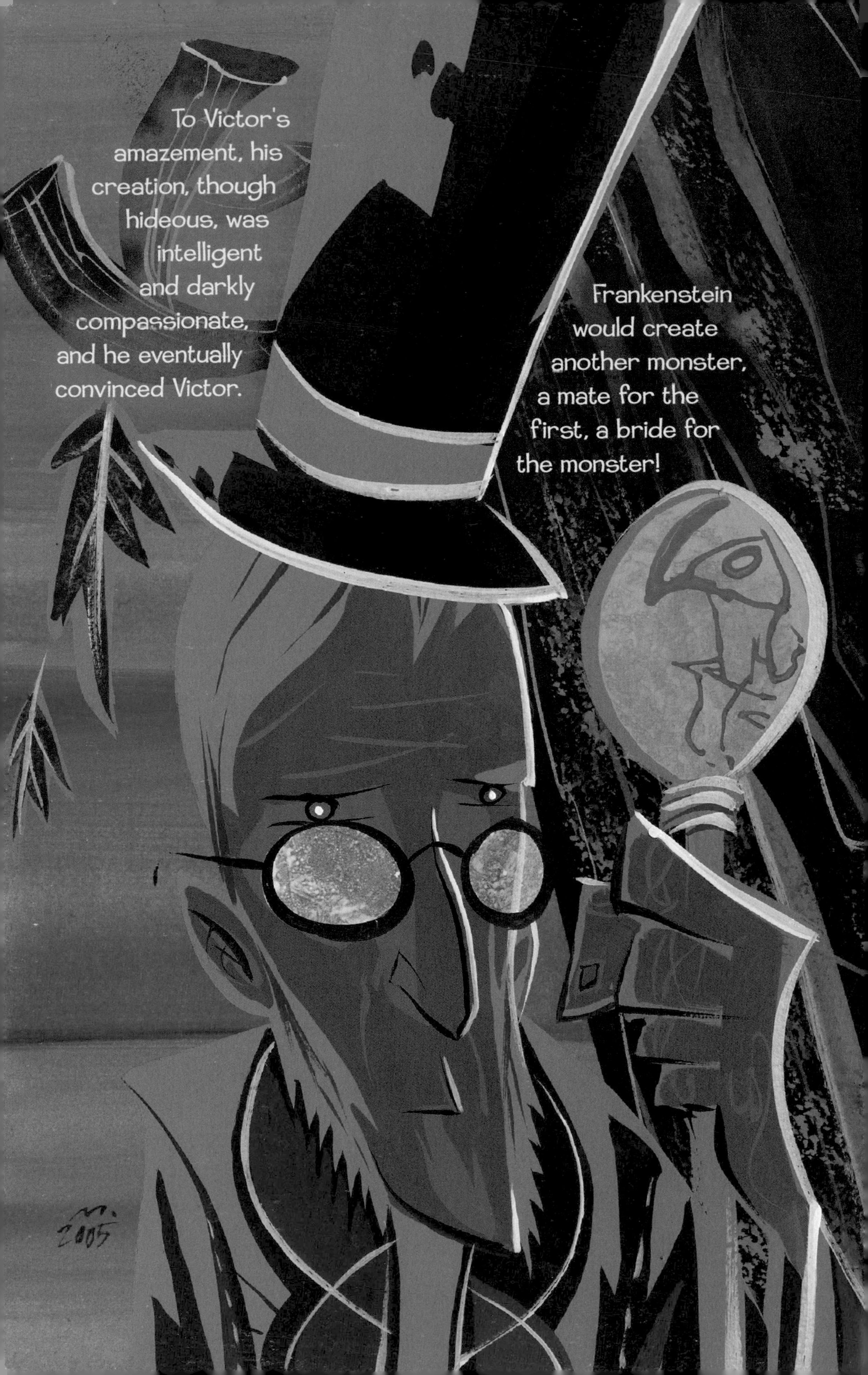
To Victor's amazement, his creation, though hideous, was intelligent and darkly compassionate, and he eventually convinced Victor.
Frankenstein would create another monster, a mate for the first, a bride for the monster!

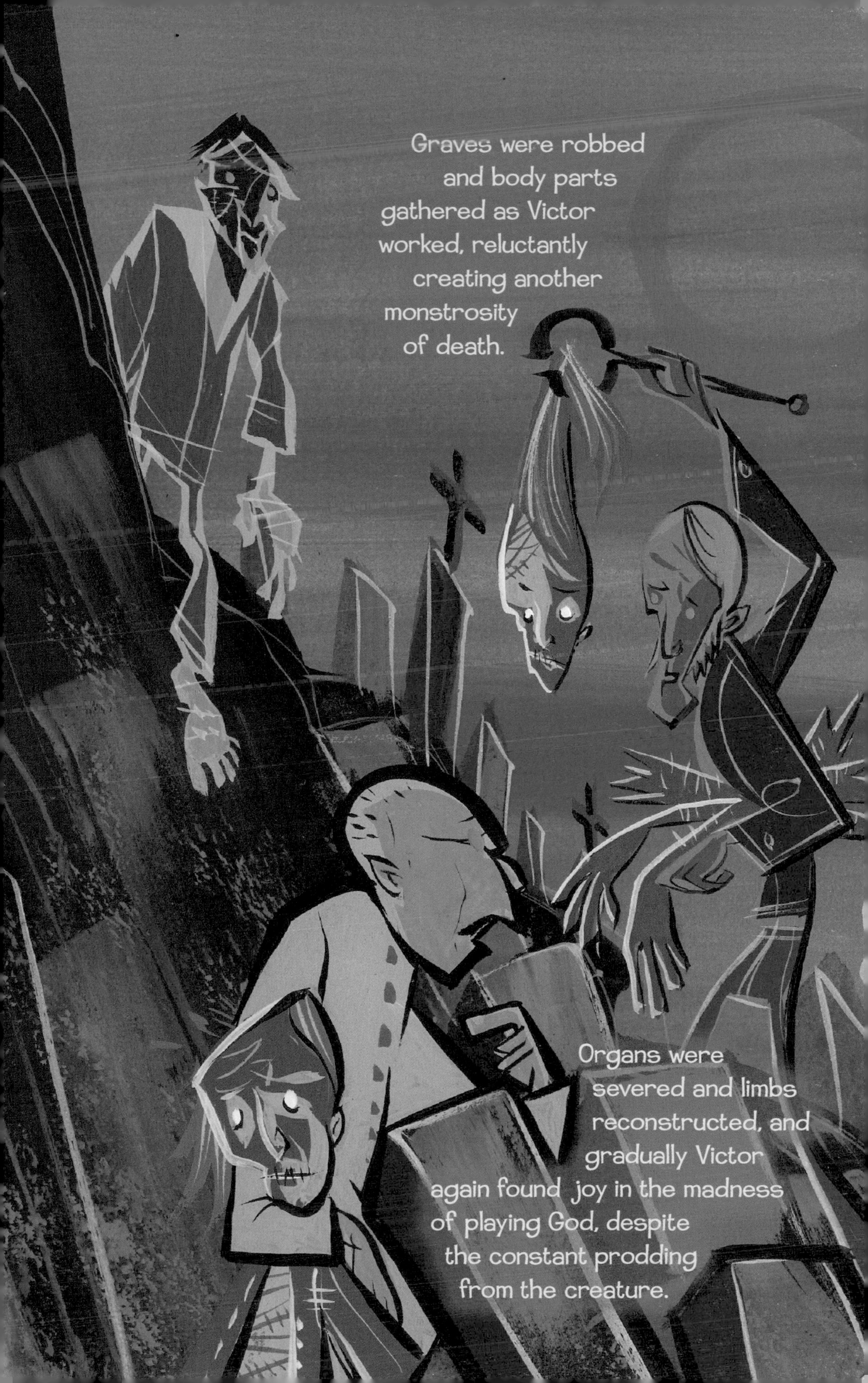
Graves were robbed and body parts gathered as Victor worked, reluctantly creating another monstrosity of death.
Organs were severed and limbs reconstructed, and gradually Victor again found joy in the madness of playing God, despite the constant prodding from the creature.

He would not leave him to work, always prodding, always peering in as he worked and waking him when he attempted to rest. That was the one thing Victor could not return to his creation. It never slept, and so, neither would he.

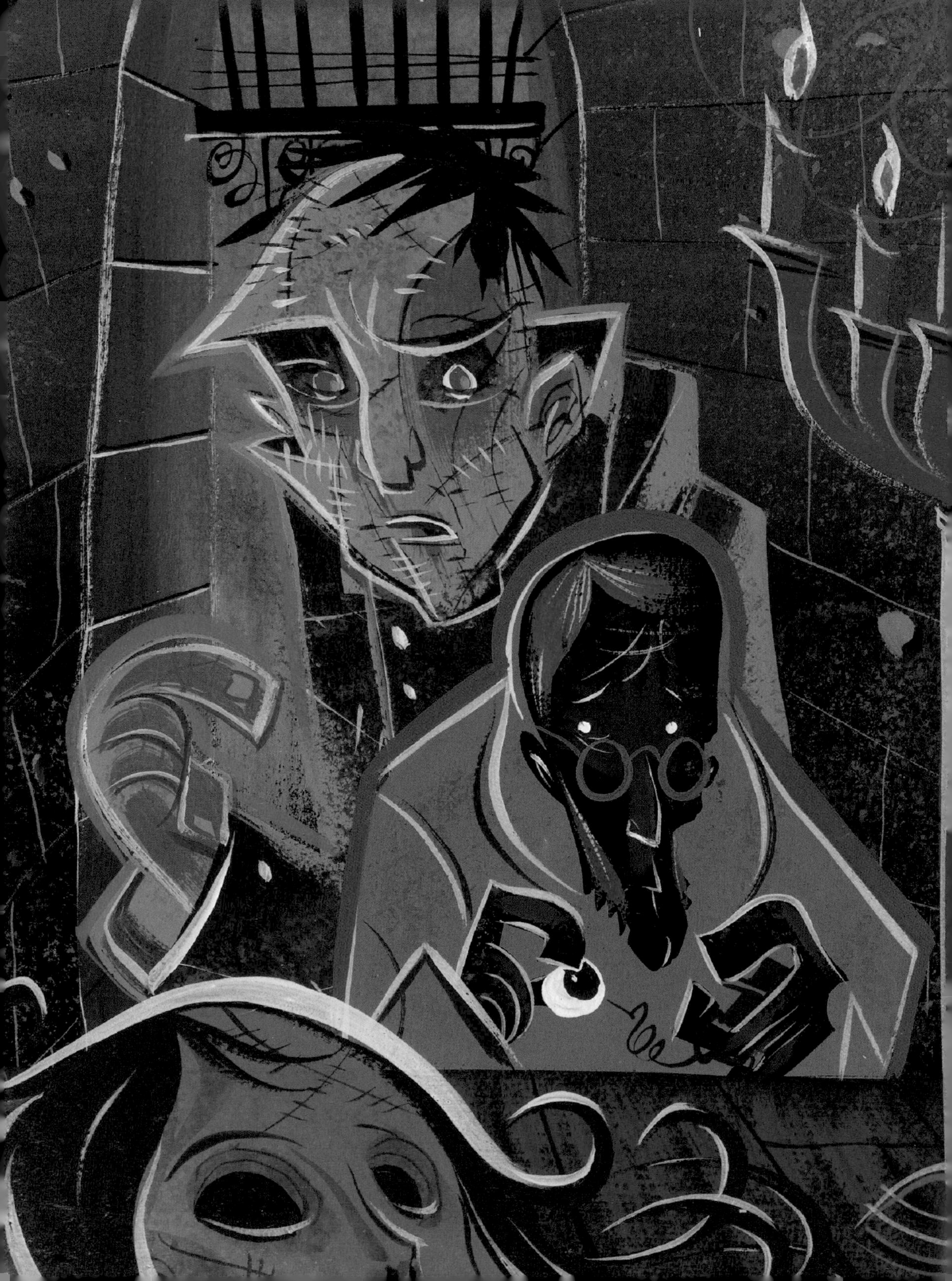

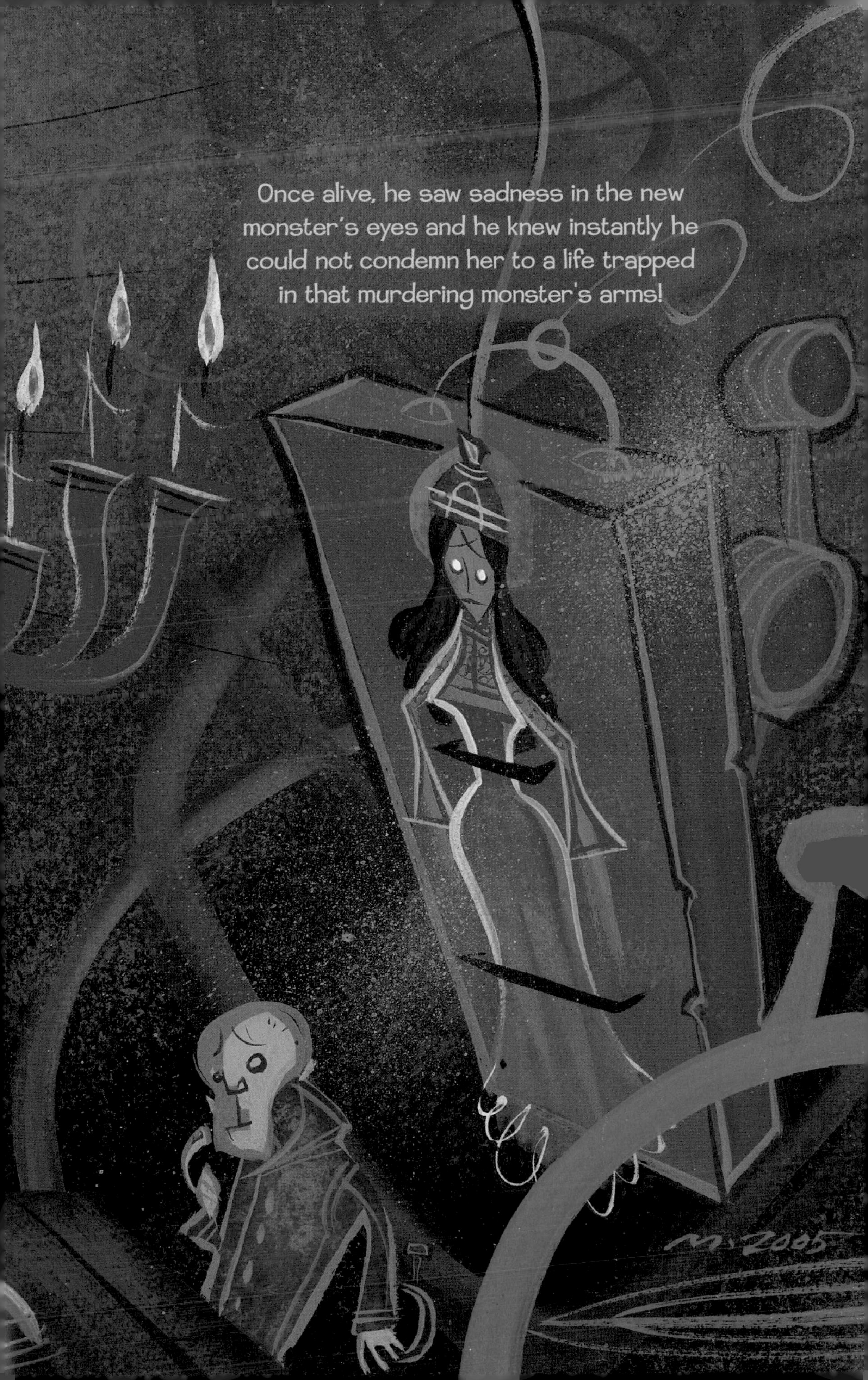
Once alive, he saw sadness in the new monster's eyes and he knew instantly he could not condemn her to a life trapped in that murdering monster's arms!
M. 2005

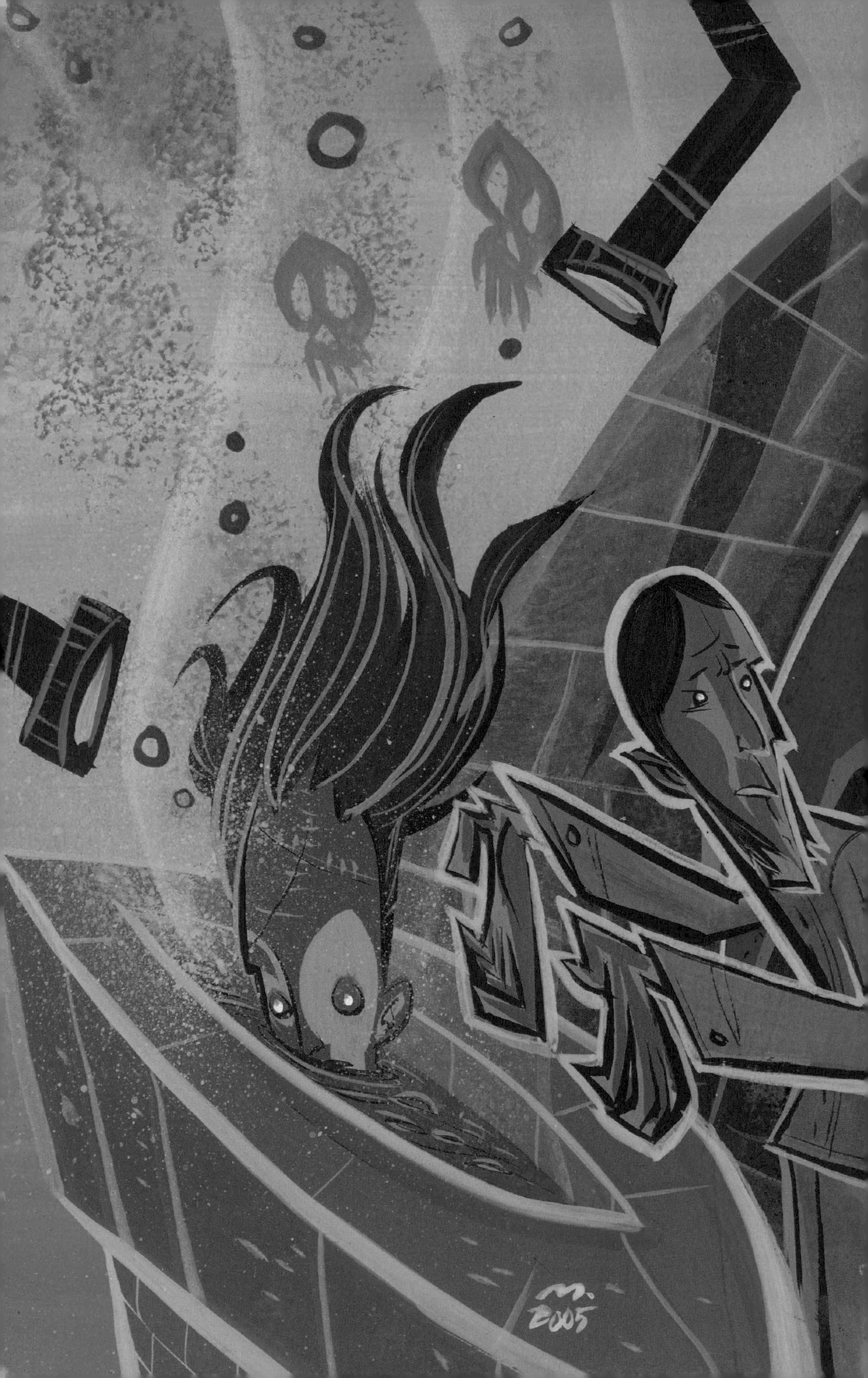

Horrified by the sudden realization of what he had done, Victor destroyed his new creation, immersing her *still-living* form into a tub of ACID right before the monster's eyes!

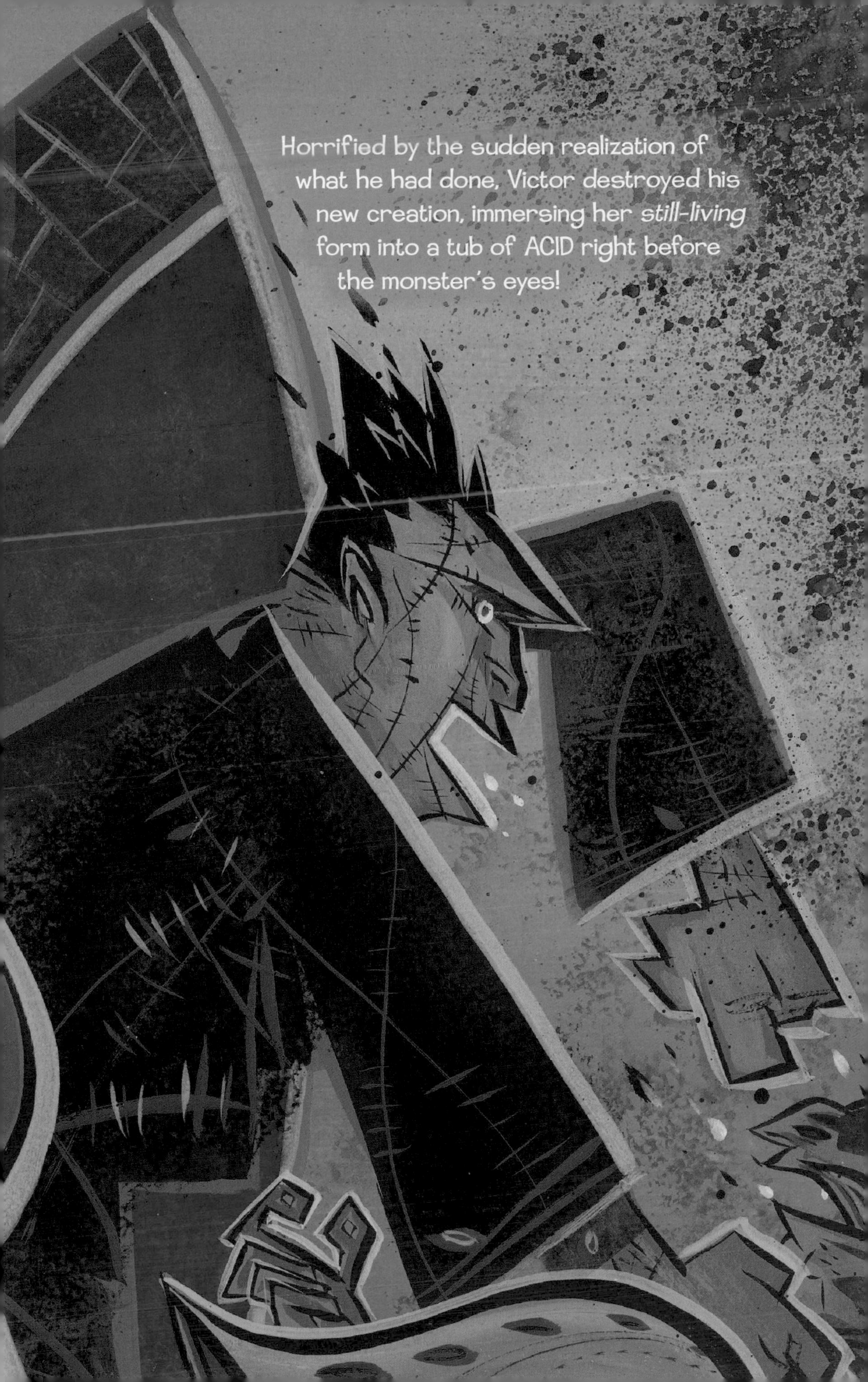

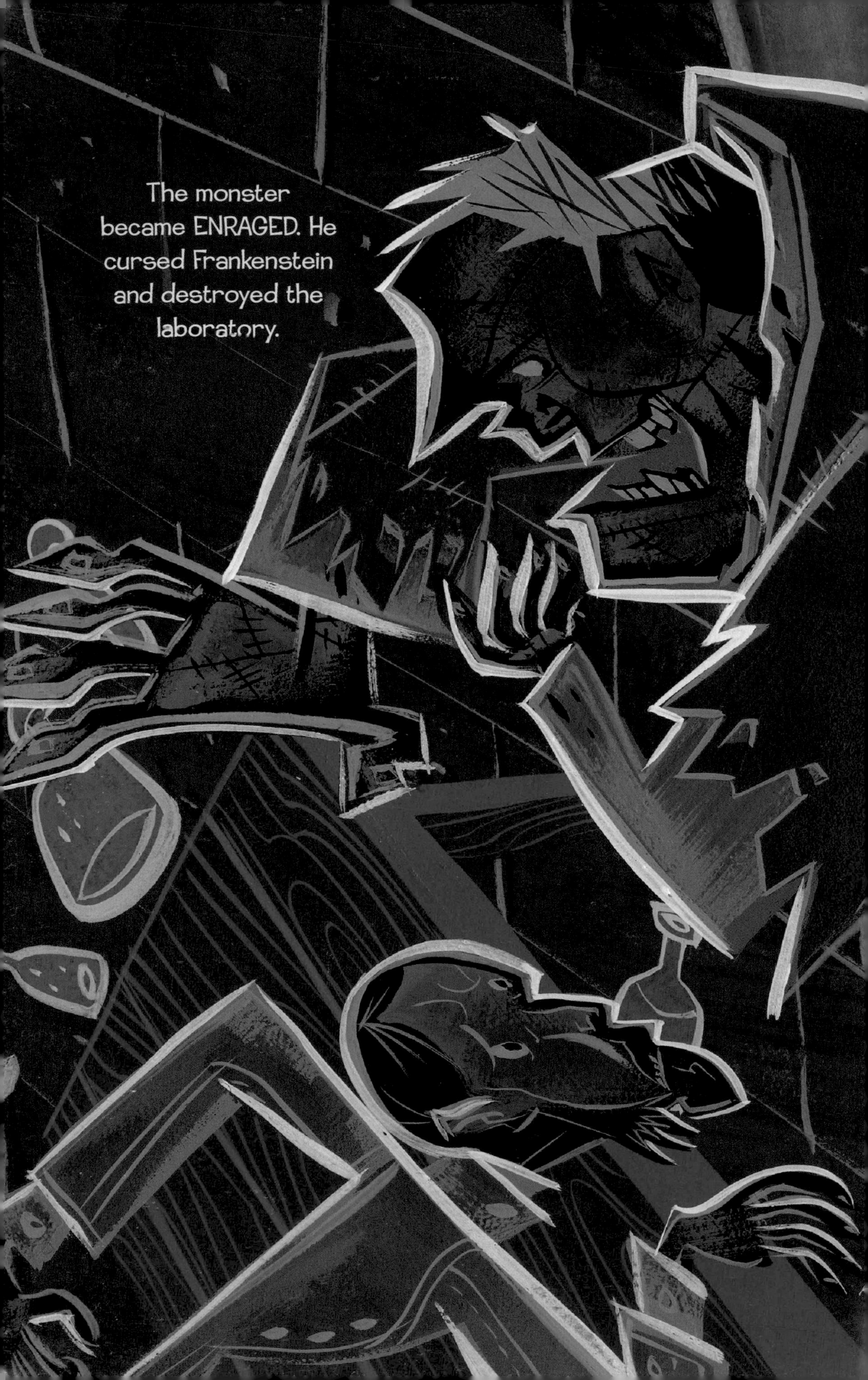
The monster became ENRAGED. He cursed Frankenstein and destroyed the laboratory.

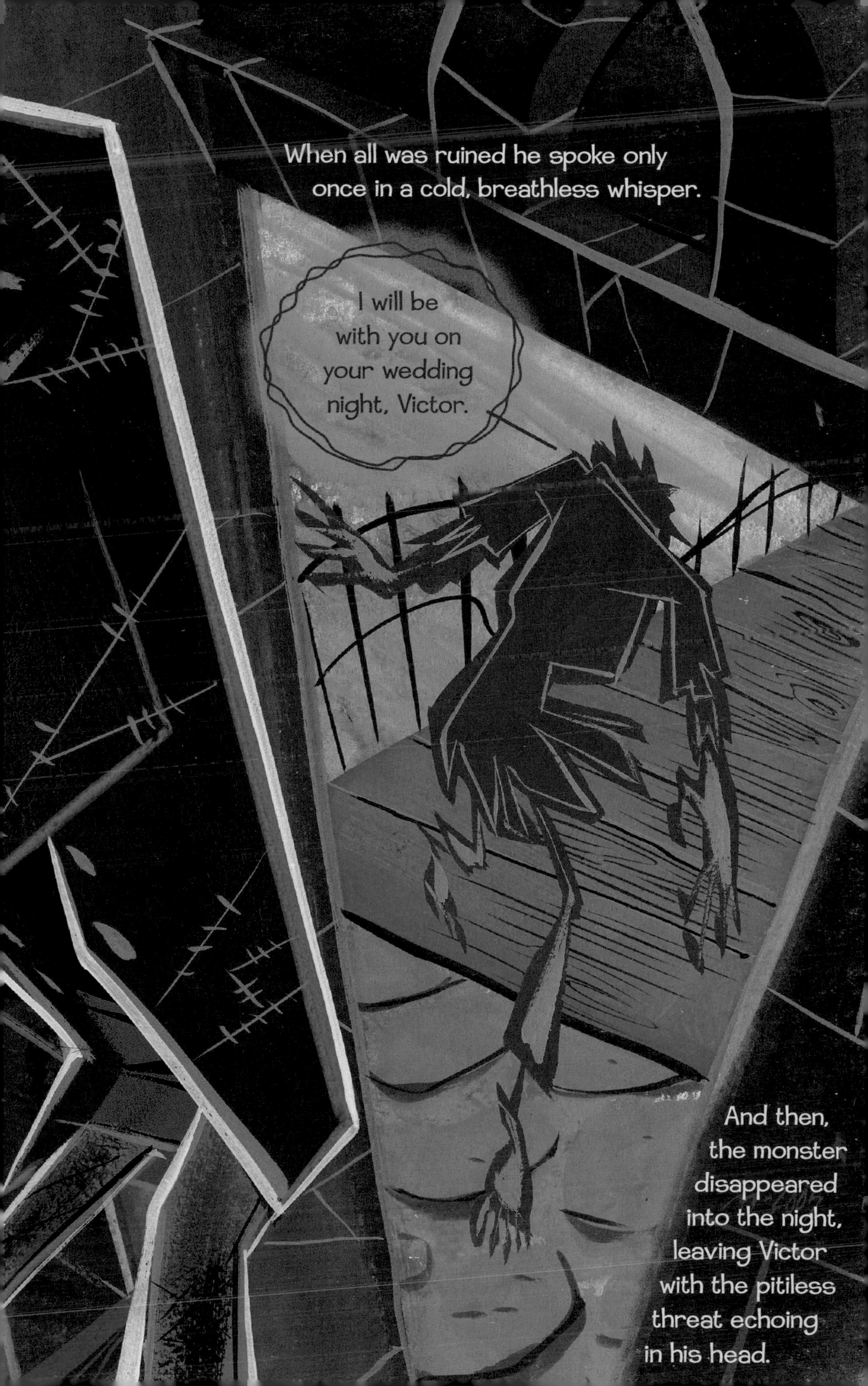
When all was ruined he spoke only once in a cold, breathless whisper.
I will be with you on your wedding night, Victor.
And then, the monster disappeared into the night, leaving Victor with the pitiless threat echoing in his head.

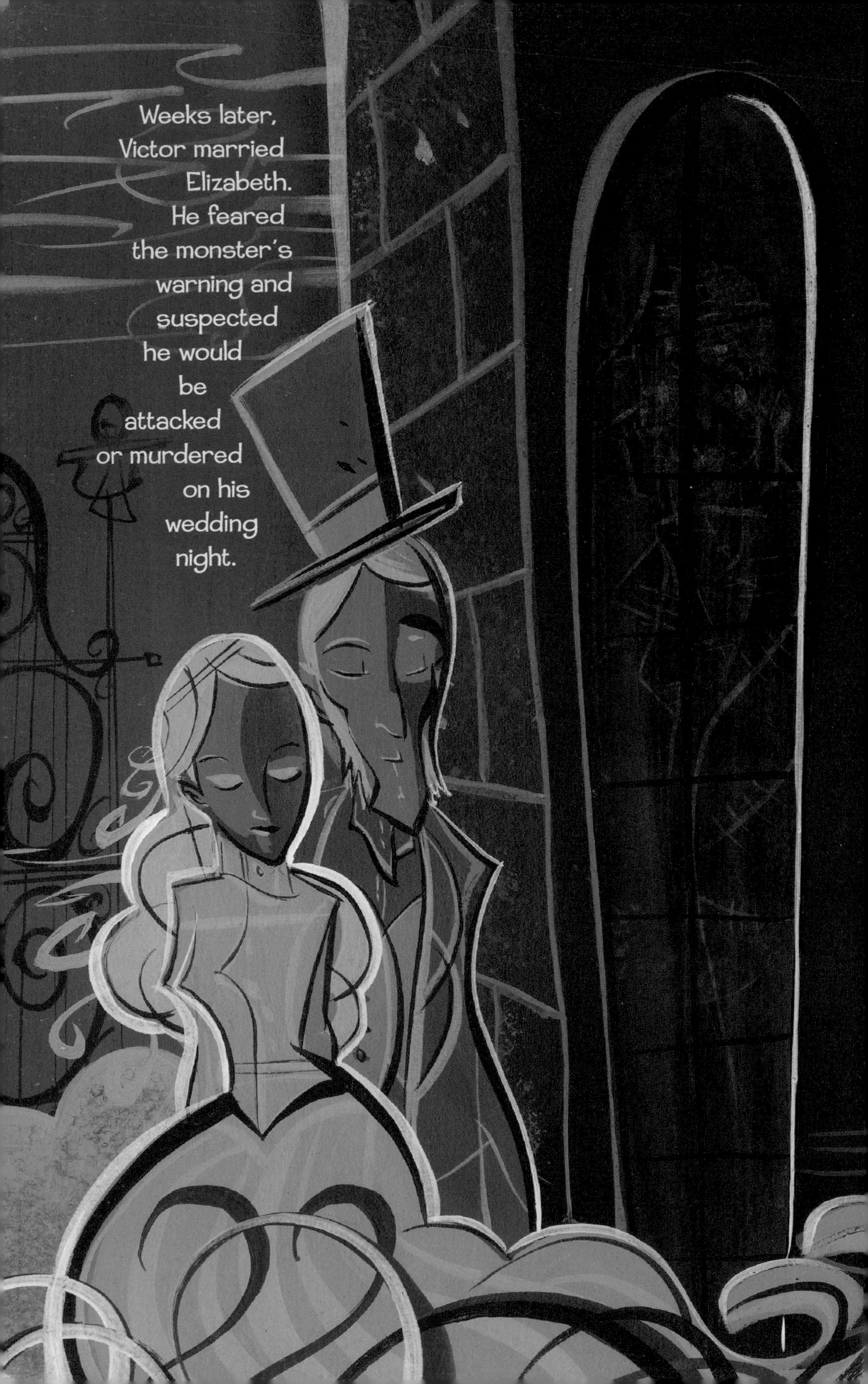
Weeks later, Victor married Elizabeth. He feared the monster's warning and suspected he would be attacked or murdered on his wedding night.

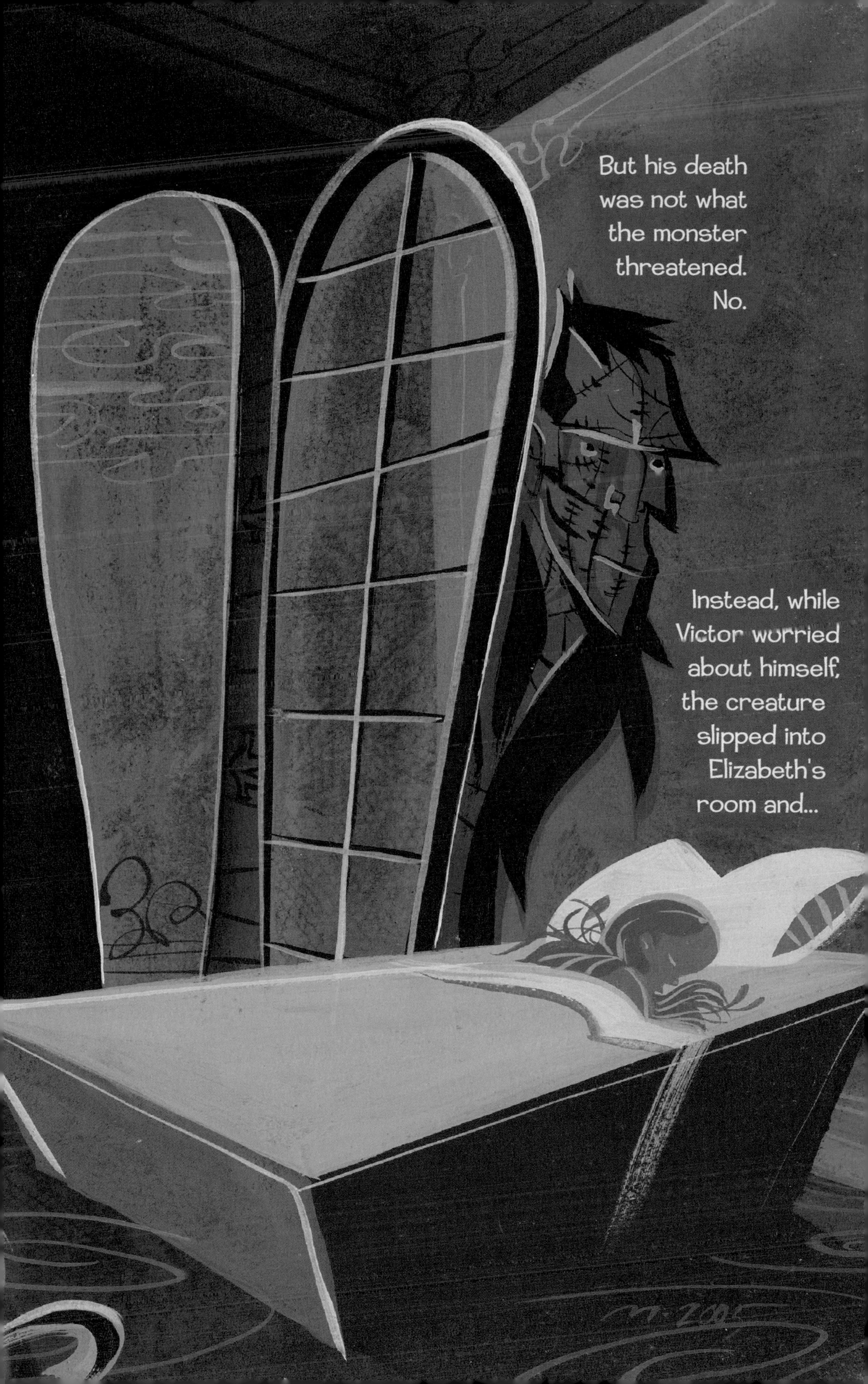
But his death was not what the monster threatened. No.
Instead, while Victor worried about himself, the creature slipped into Elizabeth's room and...

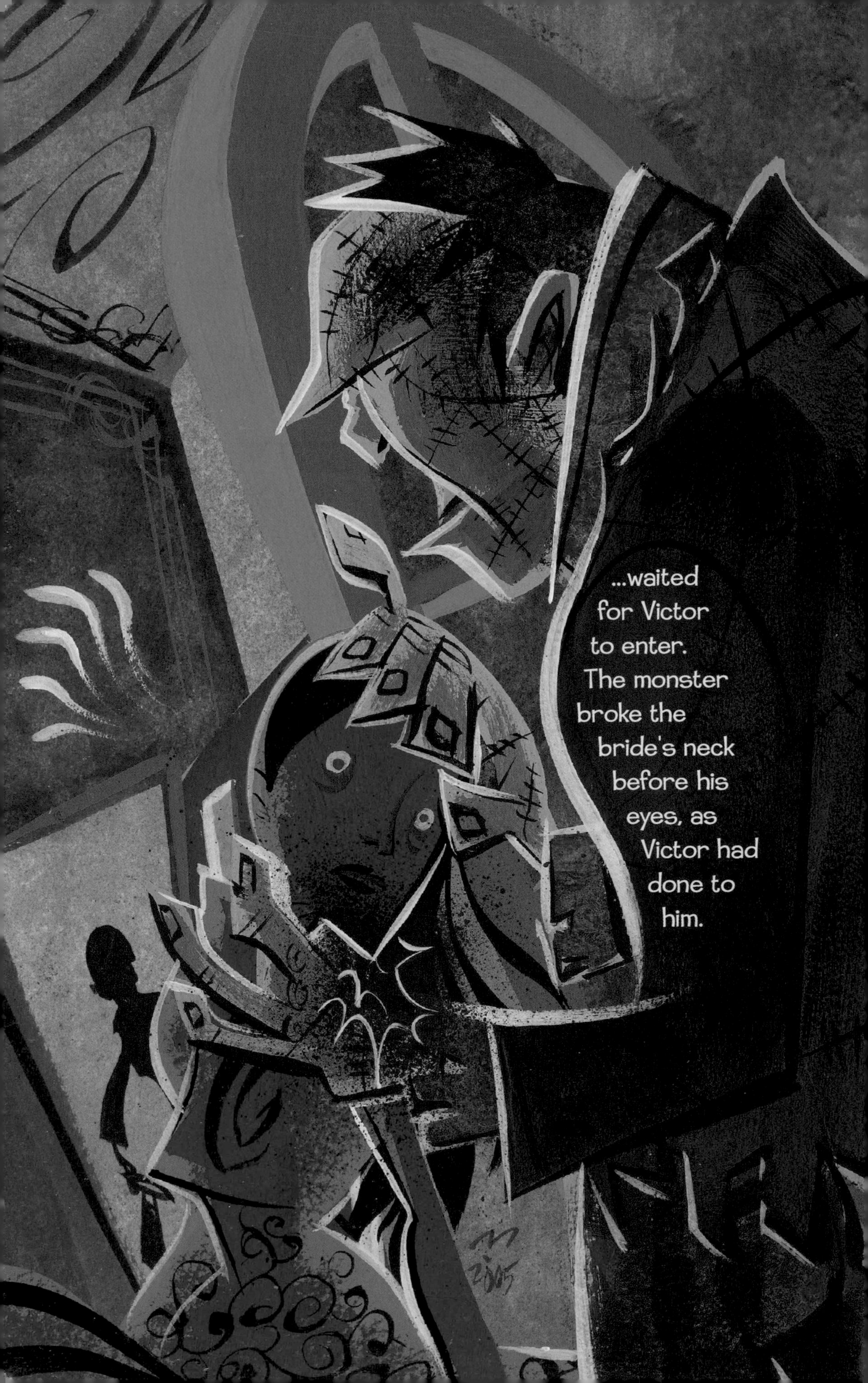
...waited for Victor to enter. The monster broke the bride's neck before his eyes, as Victor had done to him.

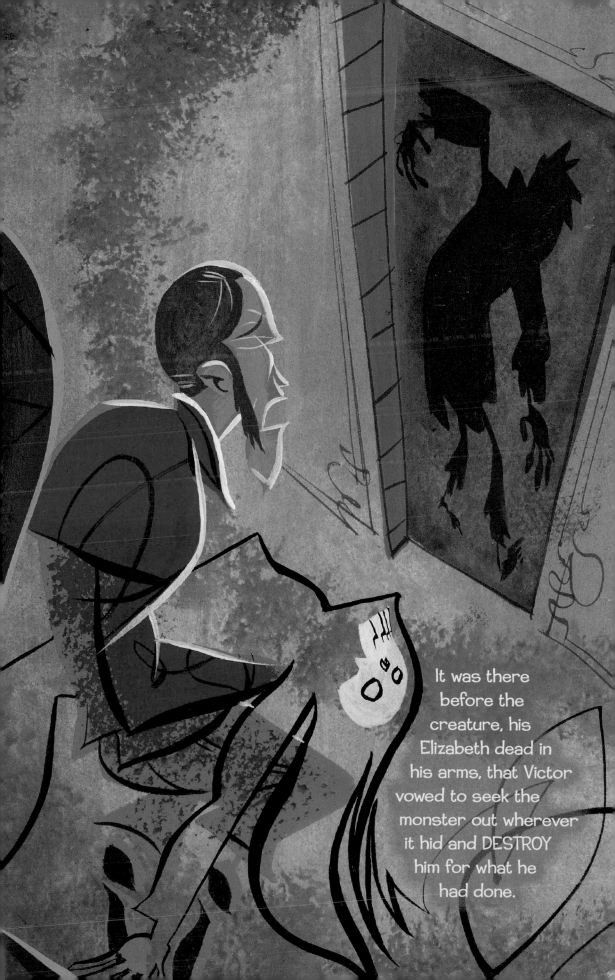

It was there before the creature, his Elizabeth dead in his arms, that Victor vowed to seek the monster out wherever it hid and DESTROY him for what he had done.

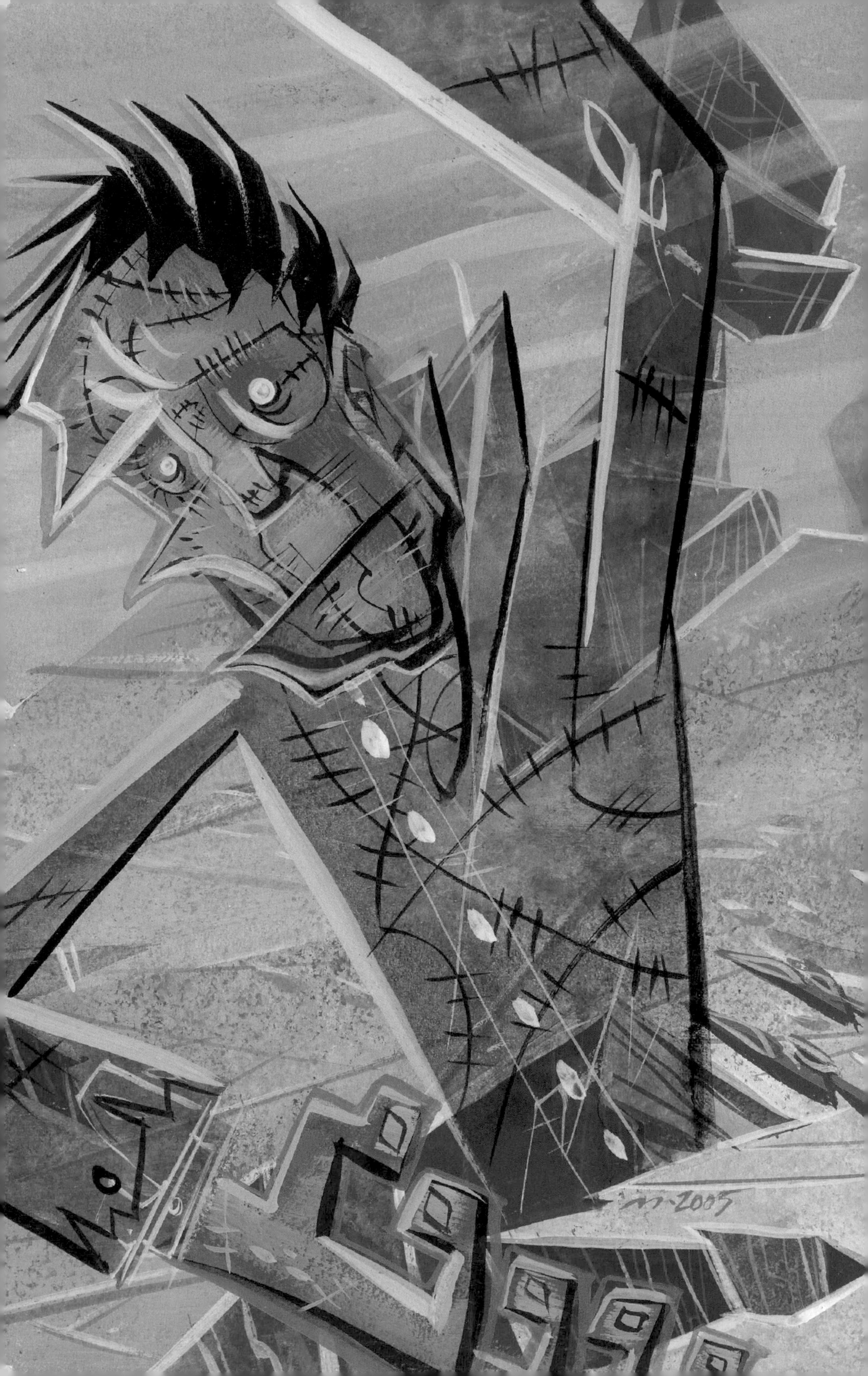

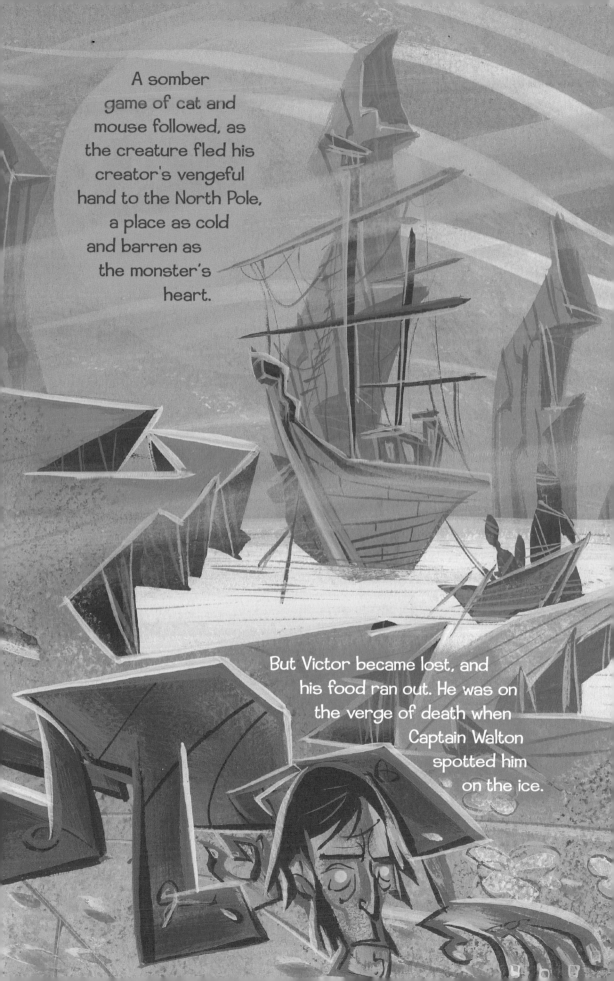

A somber game of cat and mouse followed, as the creature fled his creator's vengeful hand to the North Pole, a place as cold and barren as the monster's heart.

But Victor became lost, and his food ran out. He was on the verge of death when Captain Walton spotted him on the ice.

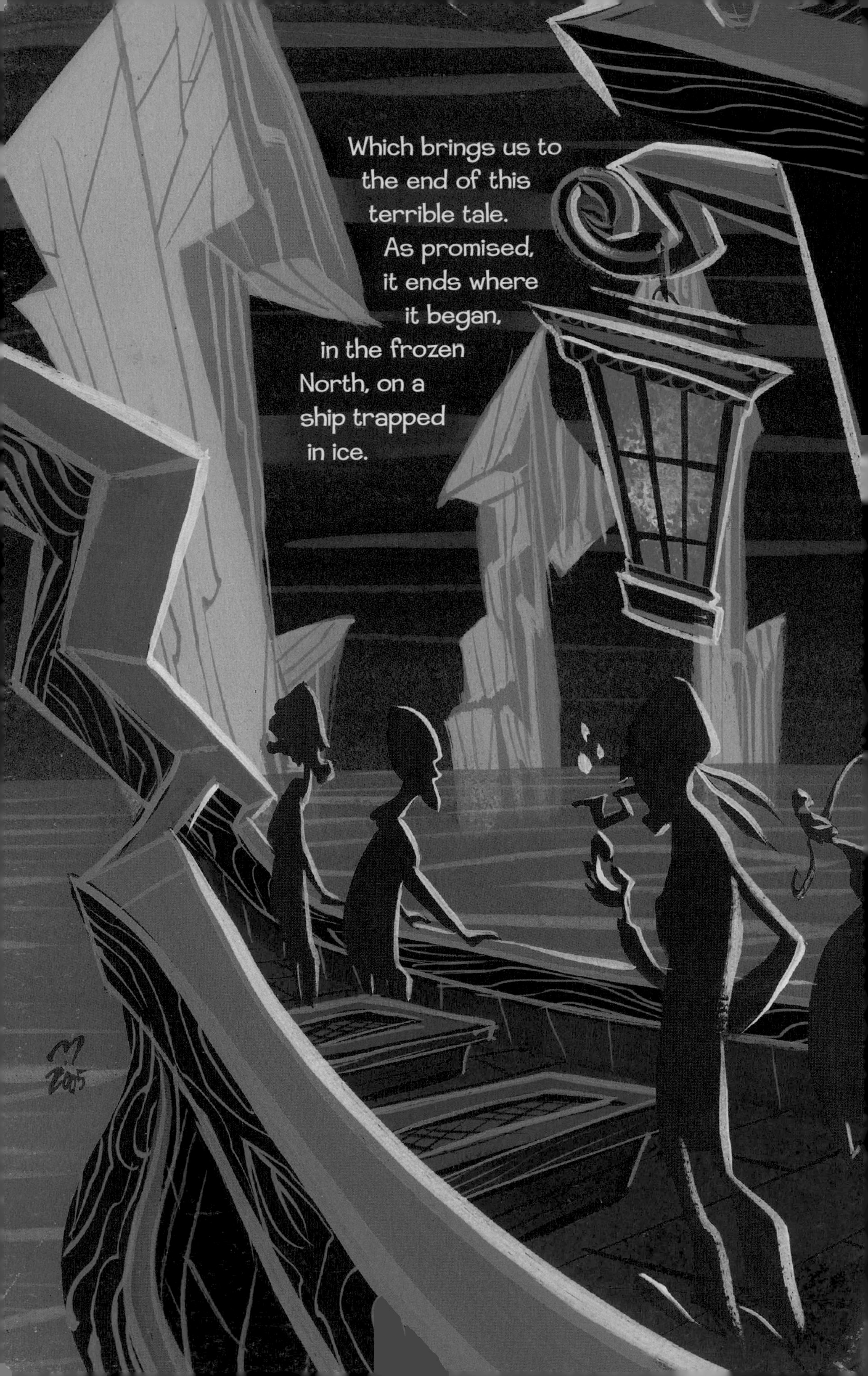
Which brings us to the end of this terrible tale. As promised, it ends where it began, in the frozen North, on a ship trapped in ice.

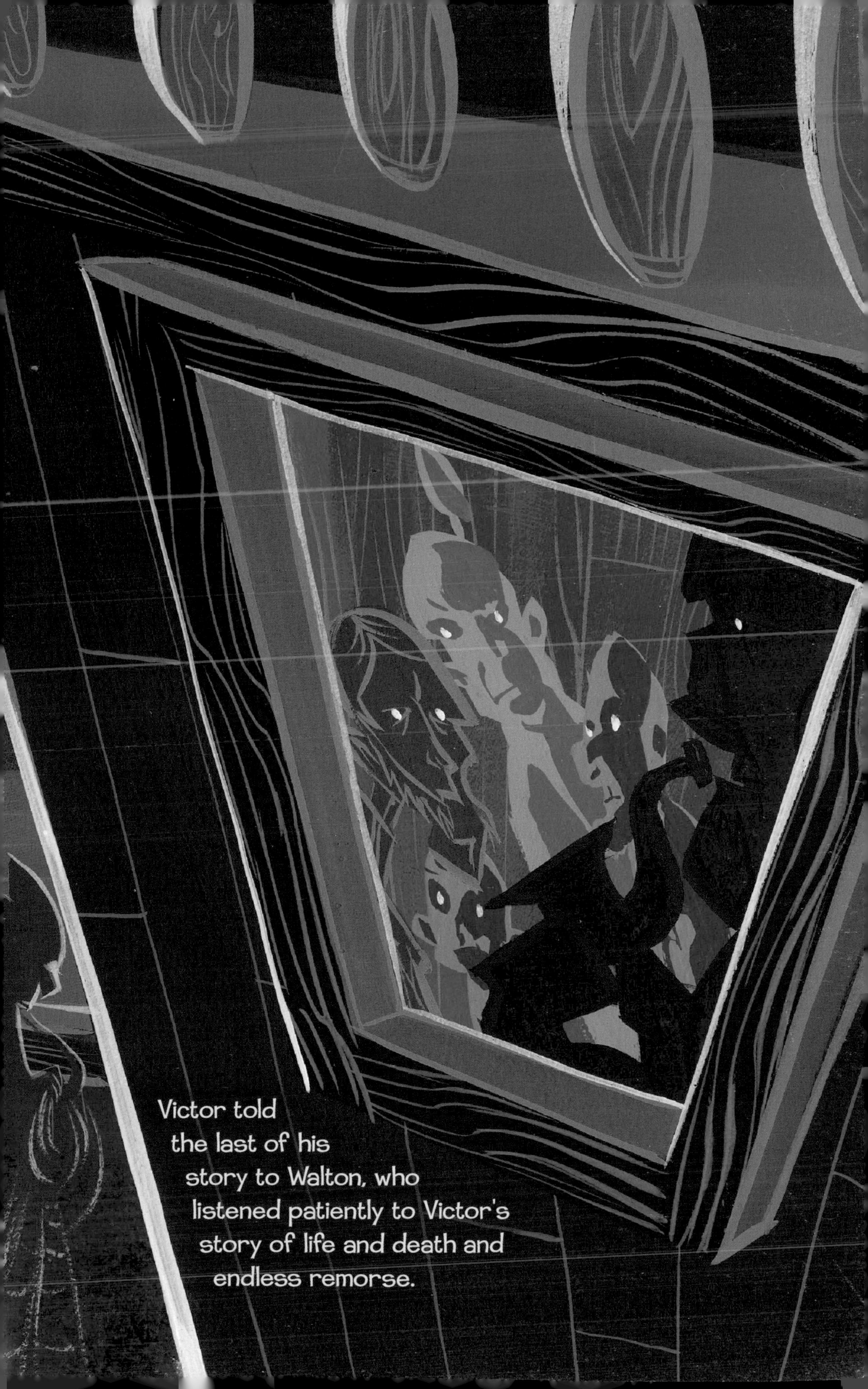
Victor told the last of his story to Walton, who listened patiently to Victor's story of life and death and endless remorse.

And then, as if relieved of the burden of the account, Victor Frankenstein died, leaving Captain Walton to wonder if he had just heard the ranting of a madman. Not a word of what Frankenstein said could possibly be true!

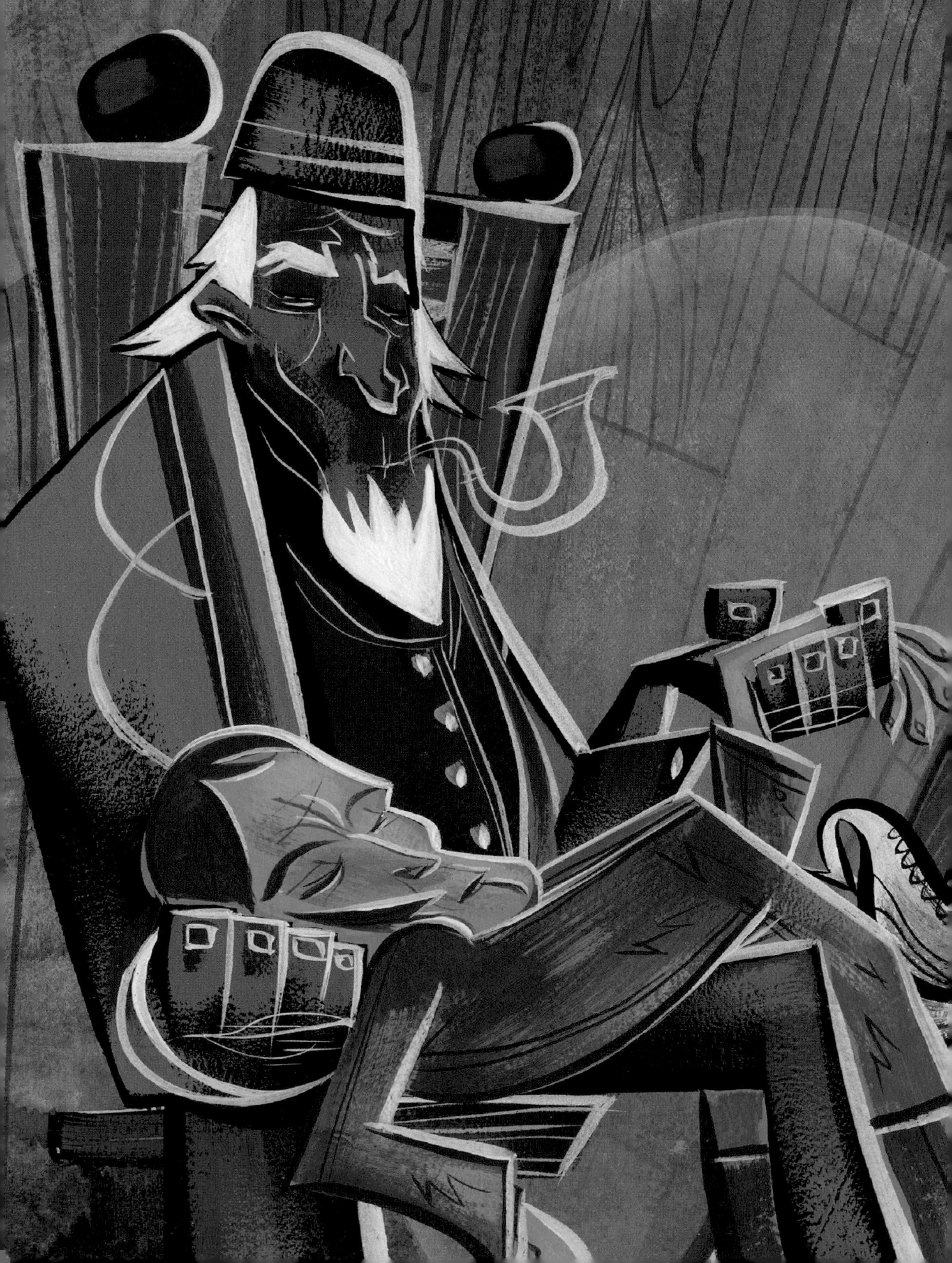

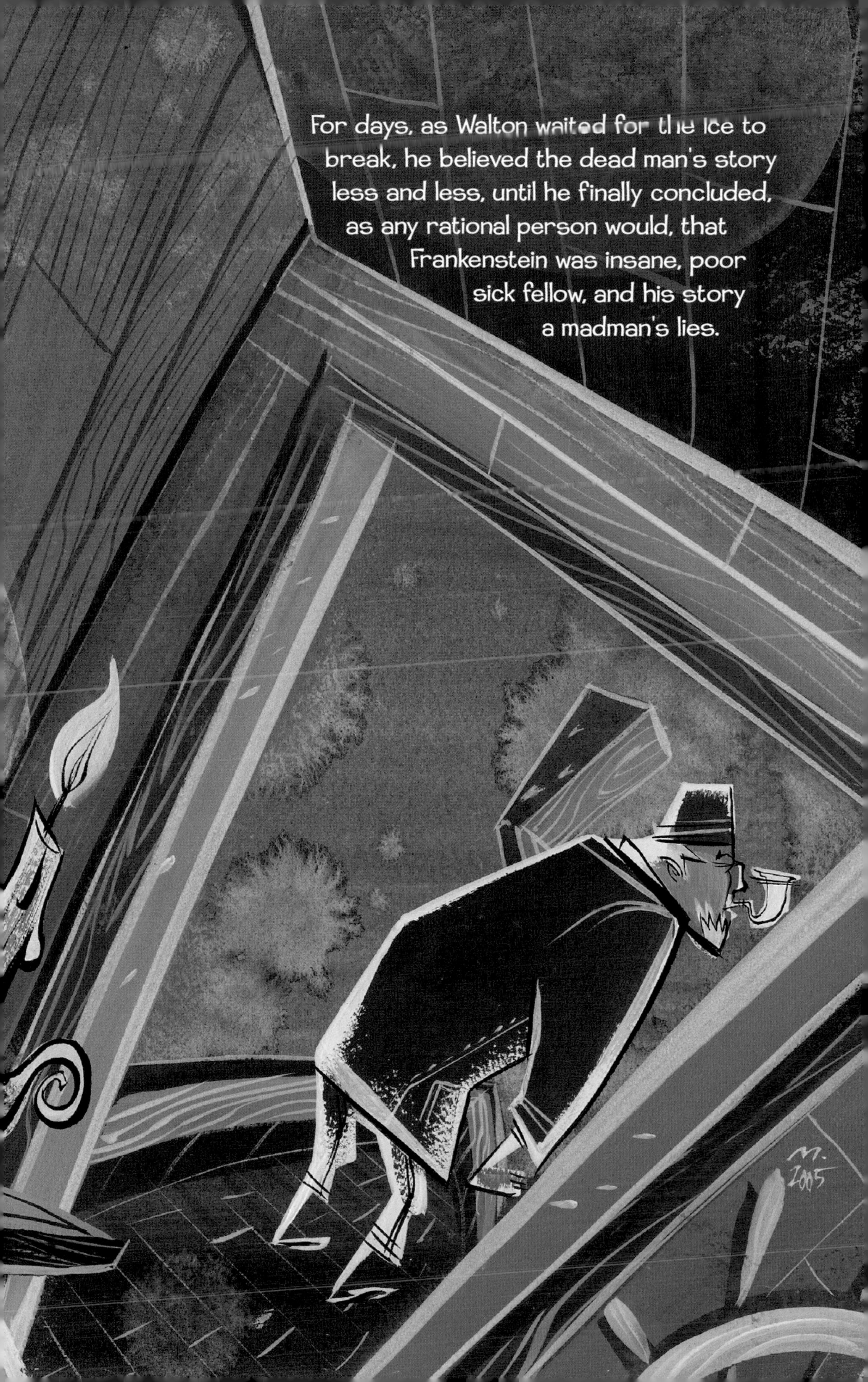
For days, as Walton waited for the ice to break, he believed the dead man's story less and less, until he finally concluded, as any rational person would, that Frankenstein was insane, poor sick fellow, and his story a madman's lies.

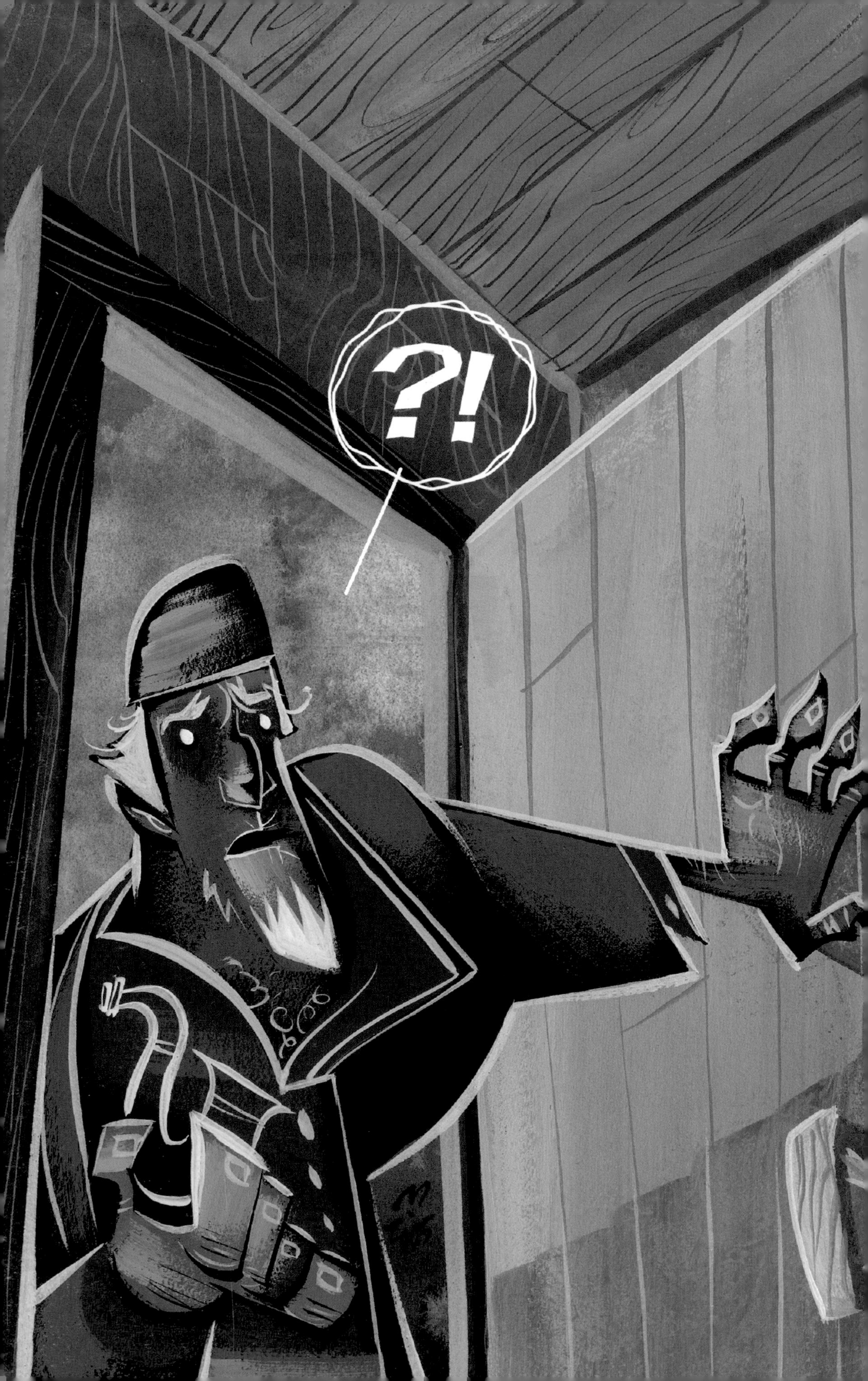
?!

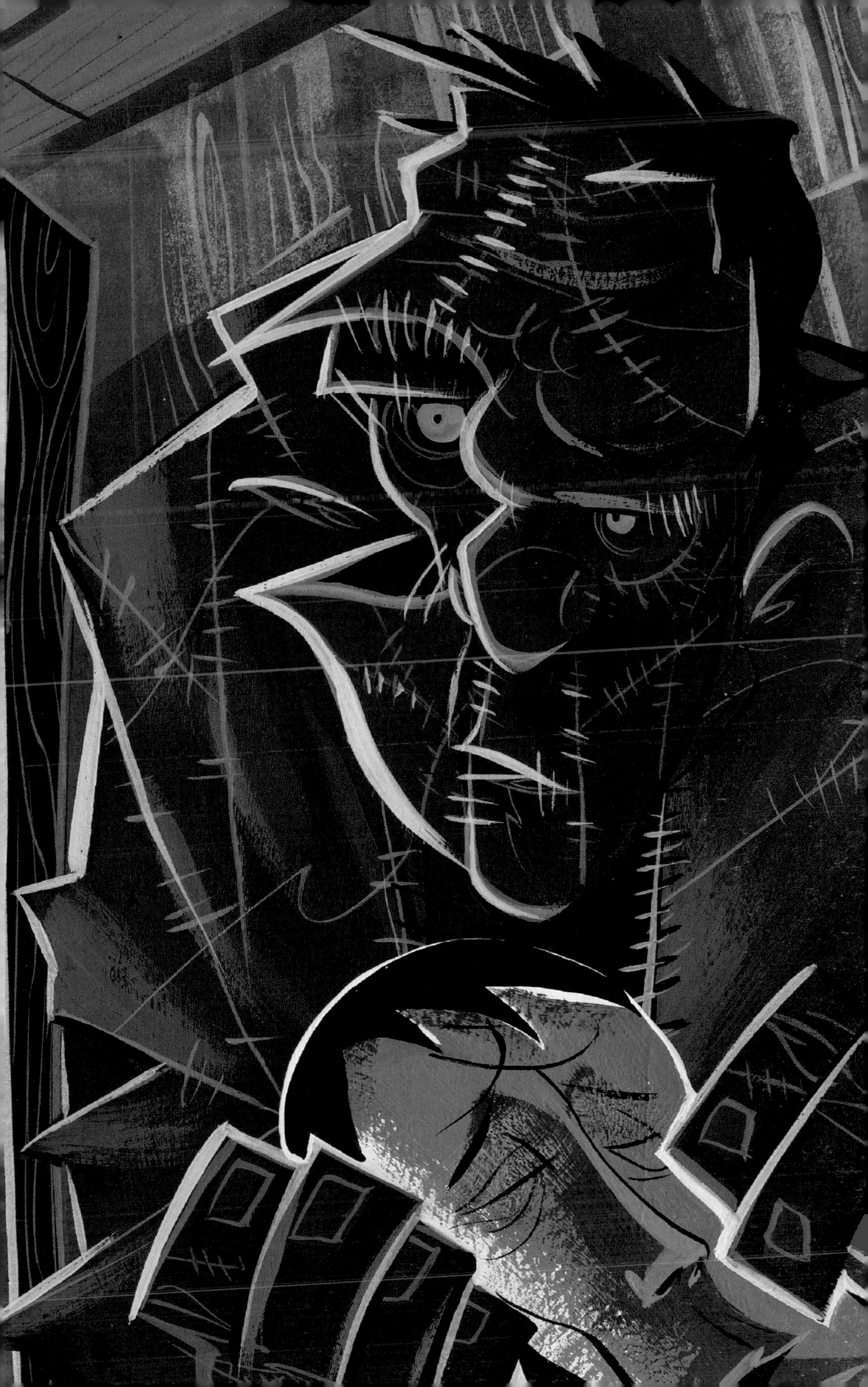

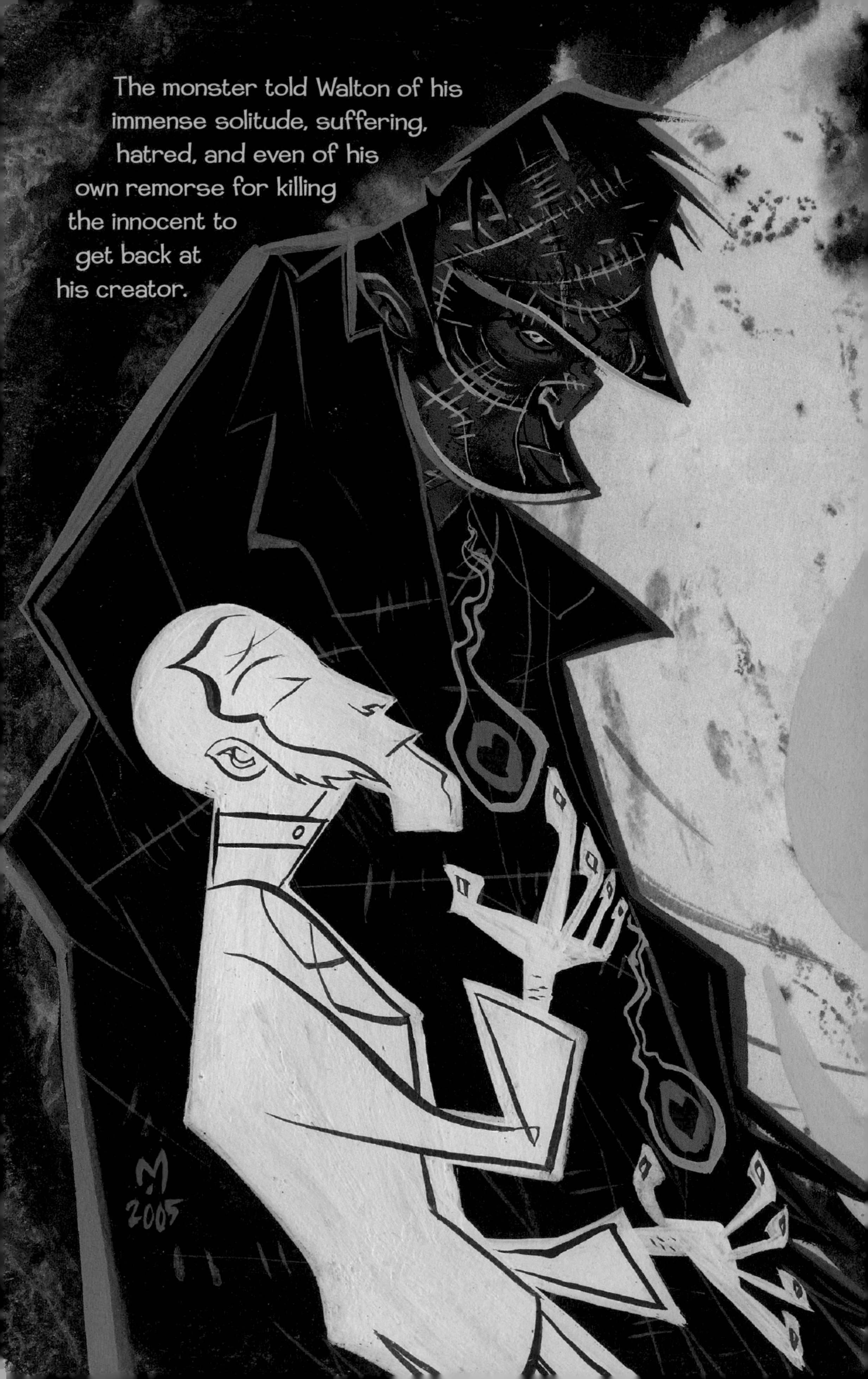
The monster told Walton of his immense solitude, suffering, hatred, and even of his own remorse for killing the innocent to get back at his creator.
2005

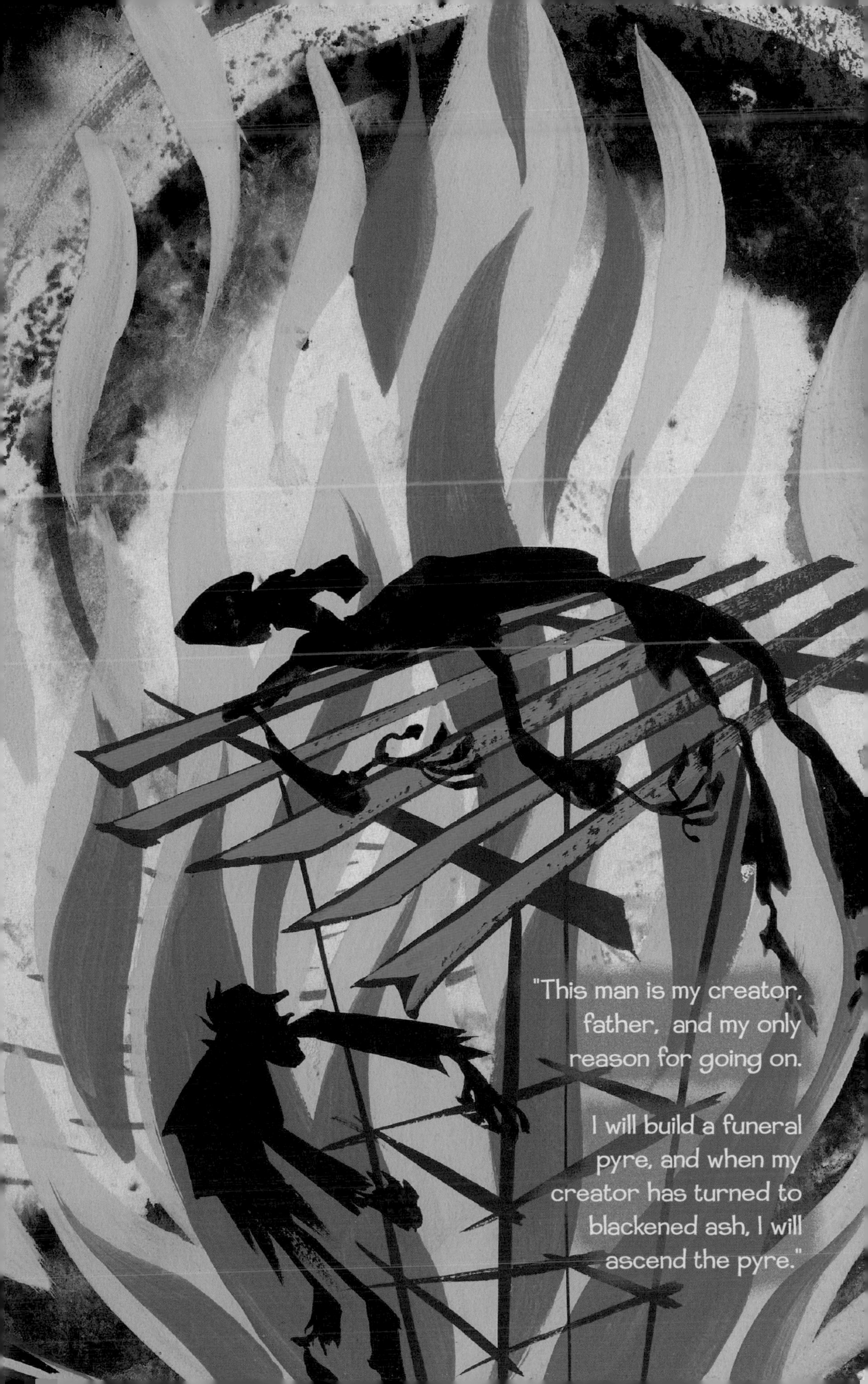
"This man is my creator, father, and my only reason for going on.
I will build a funeral pyre, and when my creator has turned to blackened ash, I will ascend the pyre."

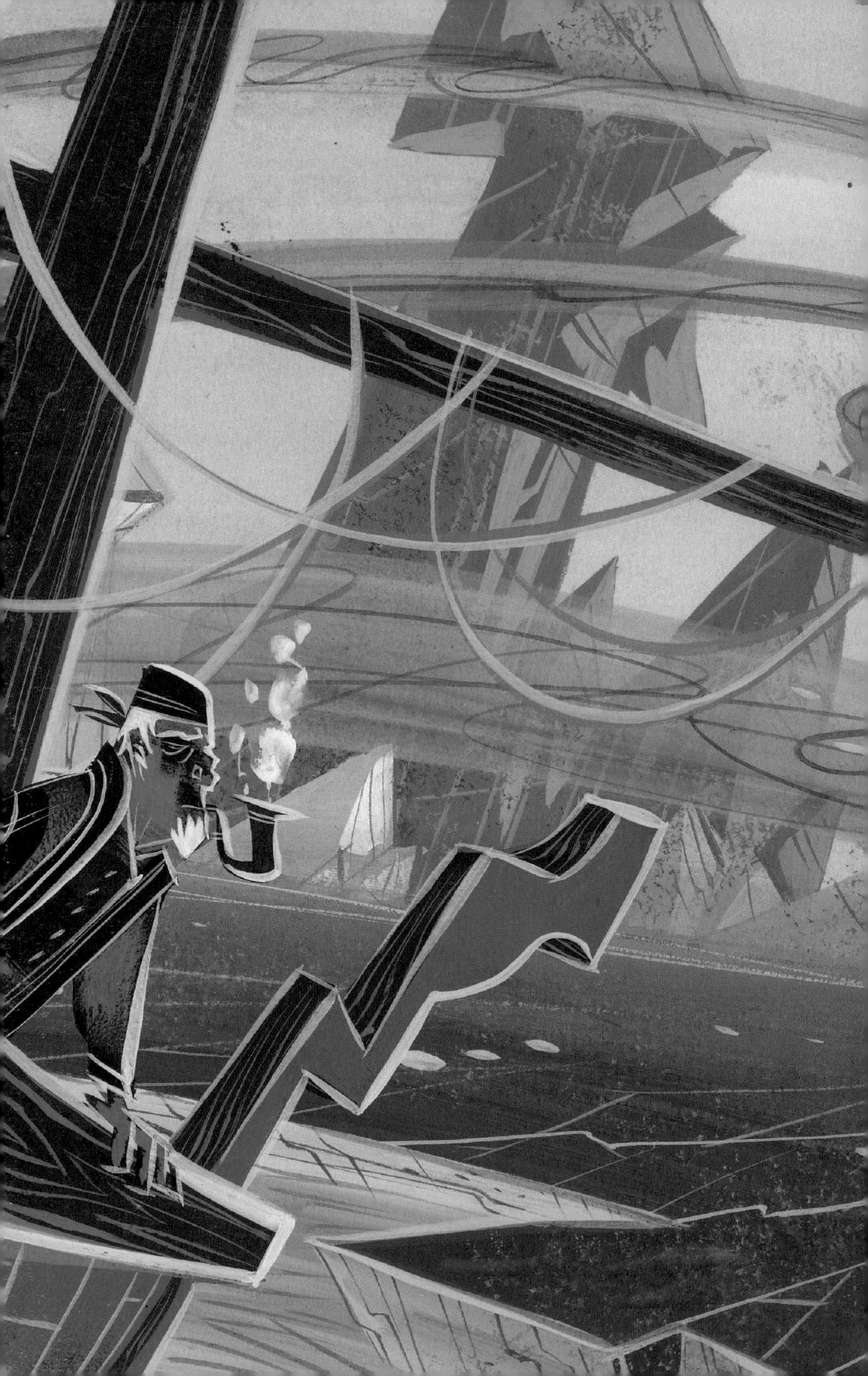

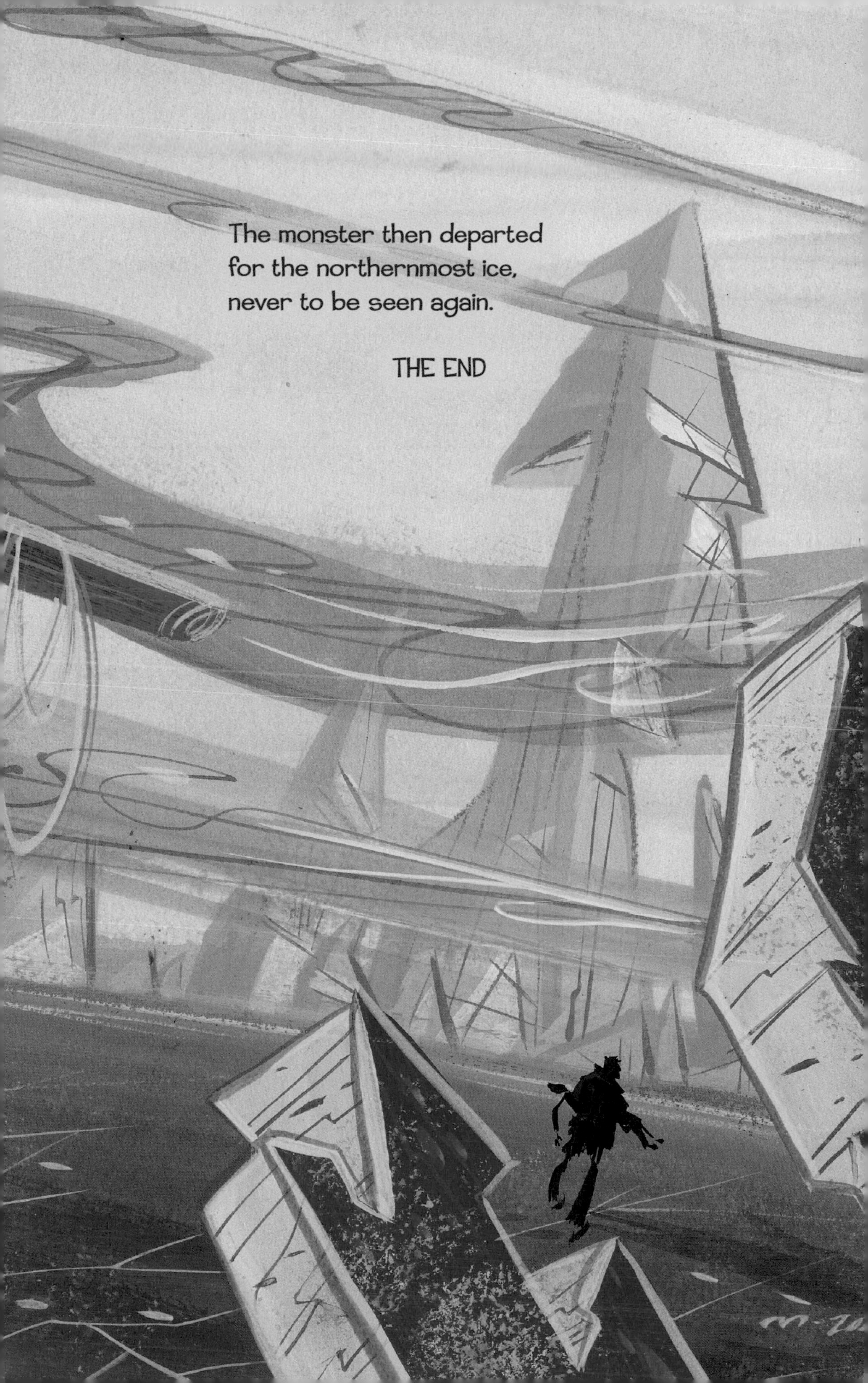

The monster then departed for the northernmost ice, never to be seen again.

THE END

LITTLE BOOK OF HORROR

THE WAR OF THE WORLDS

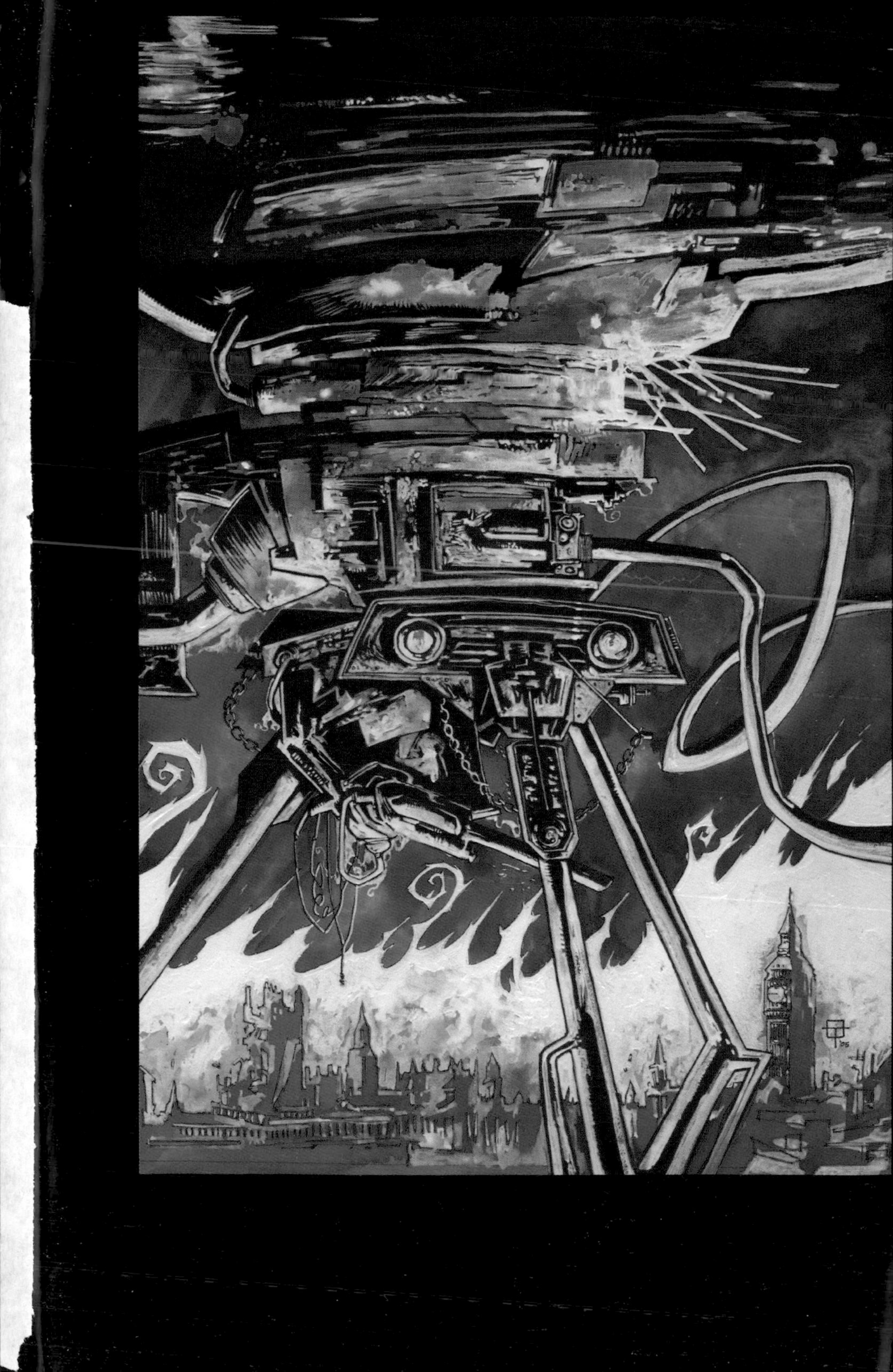

By the end of the nineteenth century, Earth had become a vibrant planet with new technologies and social changes on a global scale. It was the modern age when anything and everything was possible.

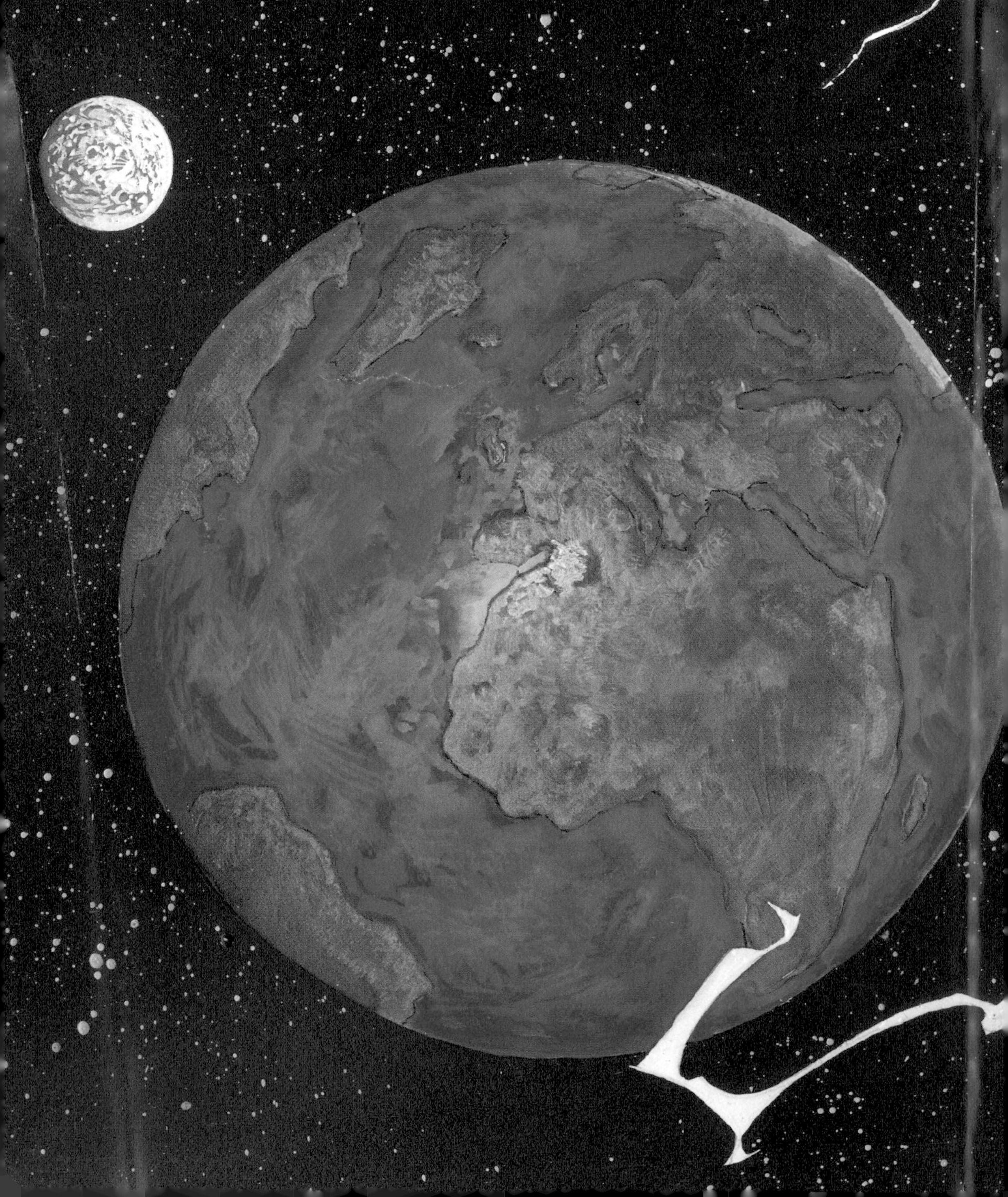

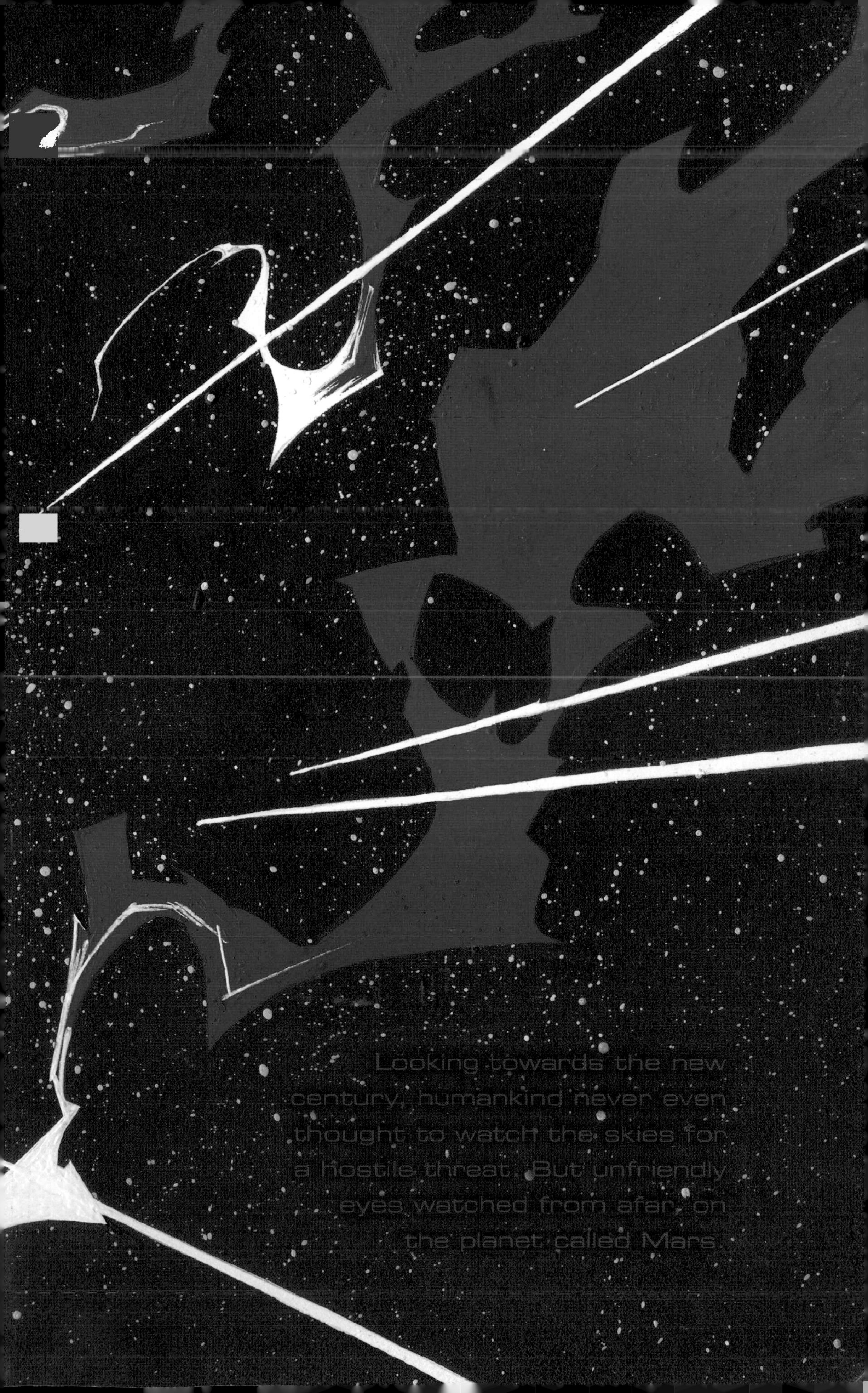
Looking towards the new century, humankind never even thought to watch the skies for a hostile threat. But unfriendly eyes watched from afar, on the planet called Mars.

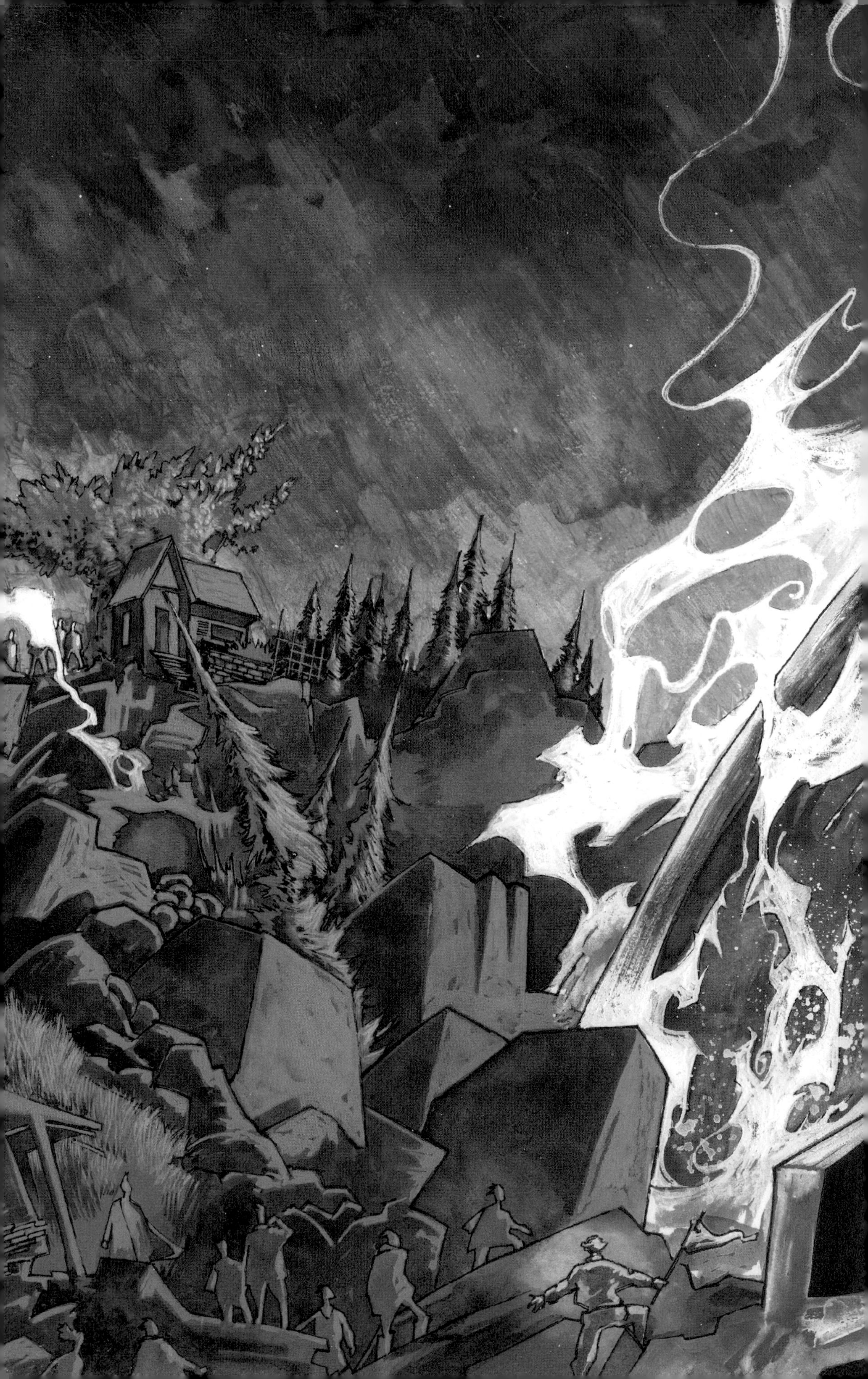

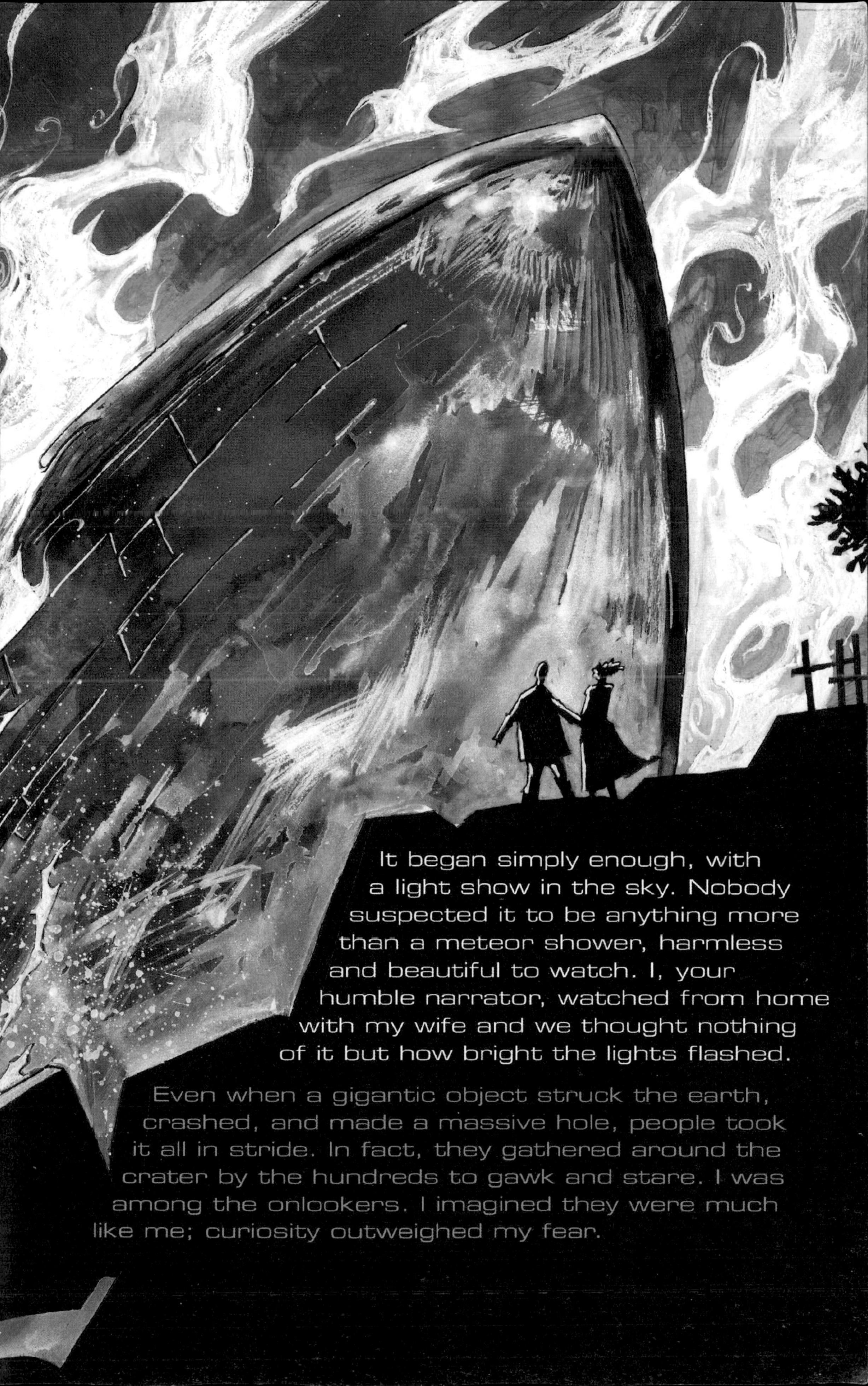

It began simply enough, with a light show in the sky. Nobody suspected it to be anything more than a meteor shower, harmless and beautiful to watch. I, your humble narrator, watched from home with my wife and we thought nothing of it but how bright the lights flashed.

Even when a gigantic object struck the earth, crashed, and made a massive hole, people took it all in stride. In fact, they gathered around the crater by the hundreds to gawk and stare. I was among the onlookers. I imagined they were much like me; curiosity outweighed my fear.

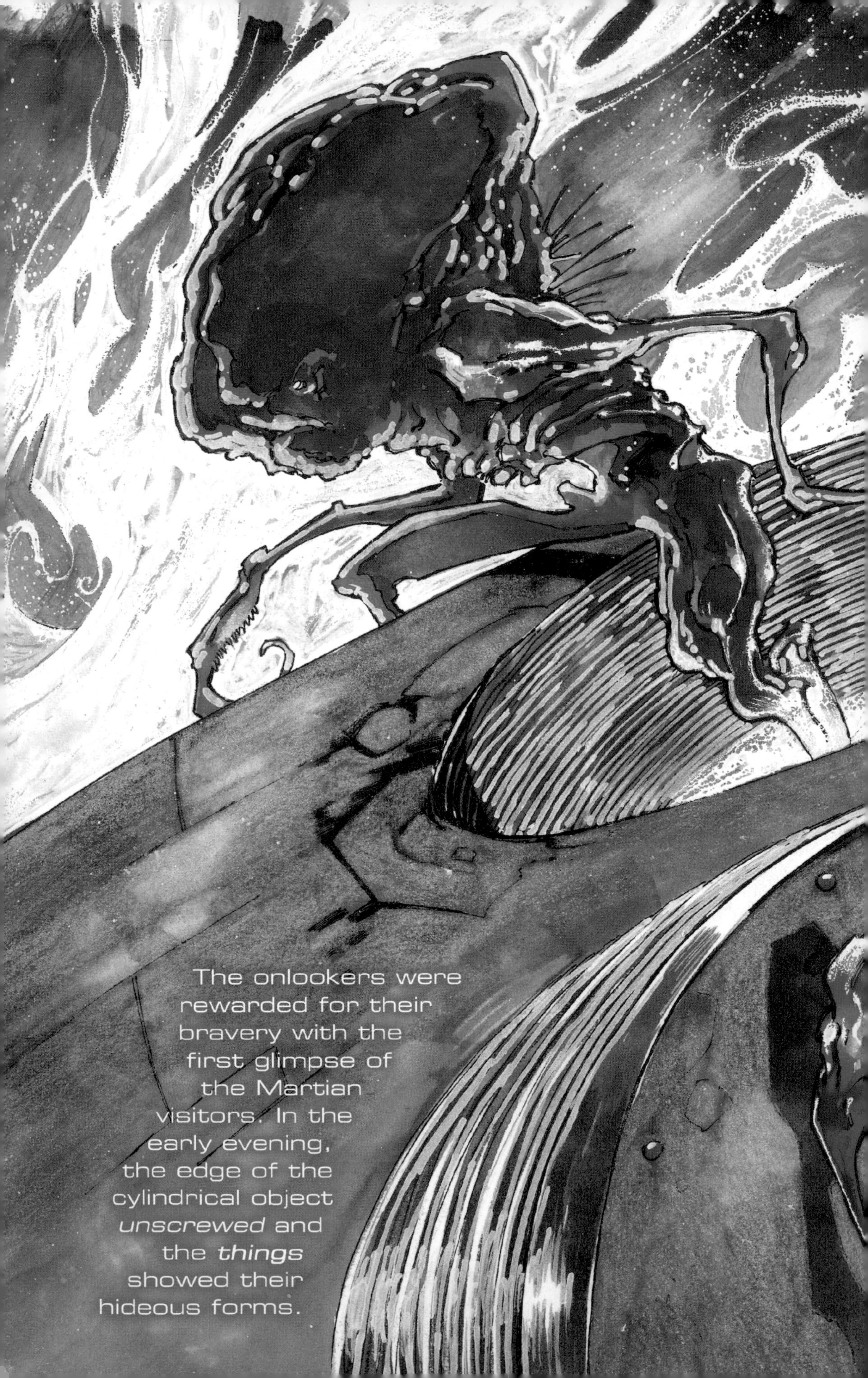
The onlookers were rewarded for their bravery with the first glimpse of the Martian visitors. In the early evening, the edge of the cylindrical object *unscrewed* and the *things* showed their hideous forms.

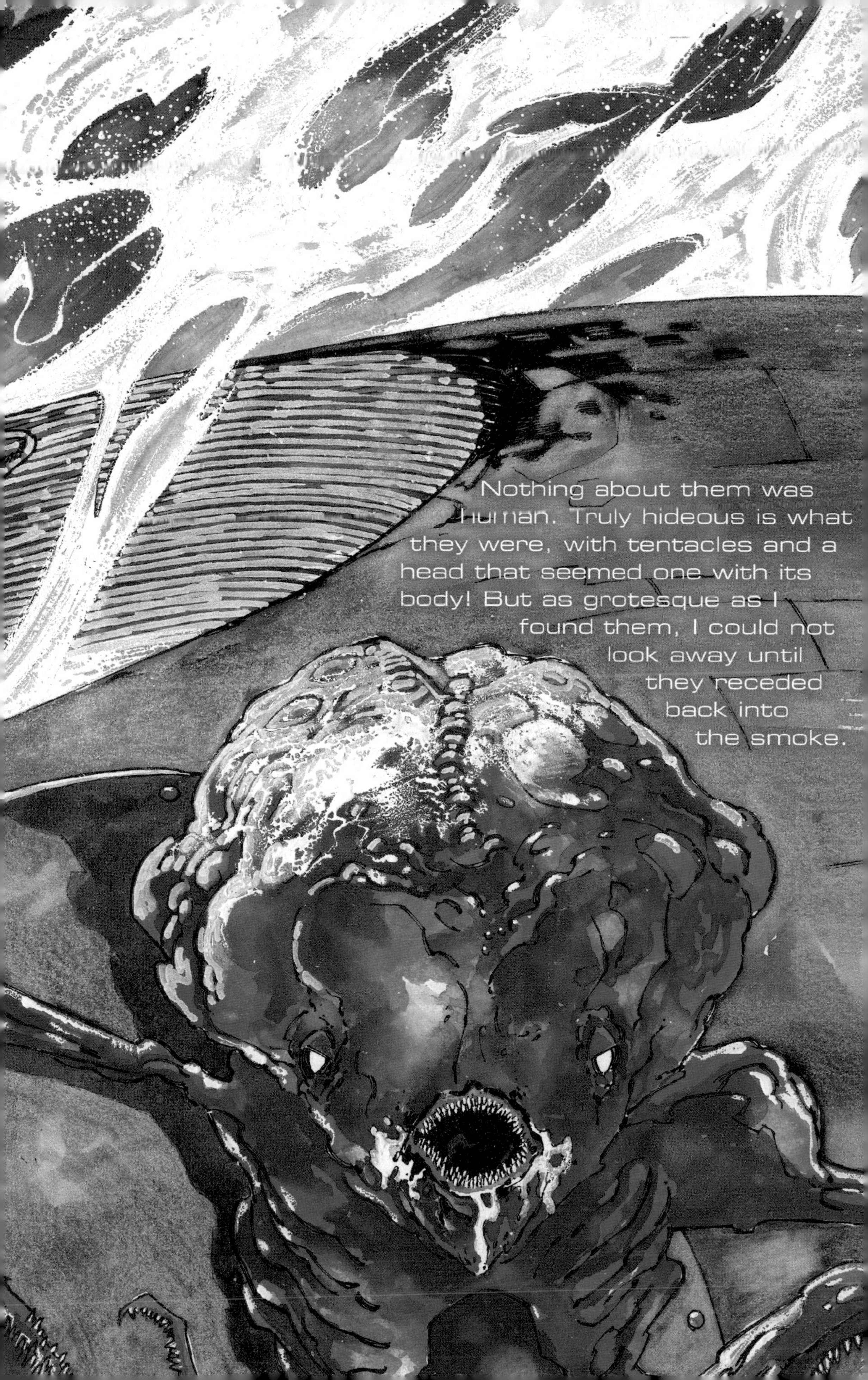
Nothing about them was human. Truly hideous is what they were, with tentacles and a head that seemed one with its body! But as grotesque as I found them, I could not look away until they receded back into the smoke.

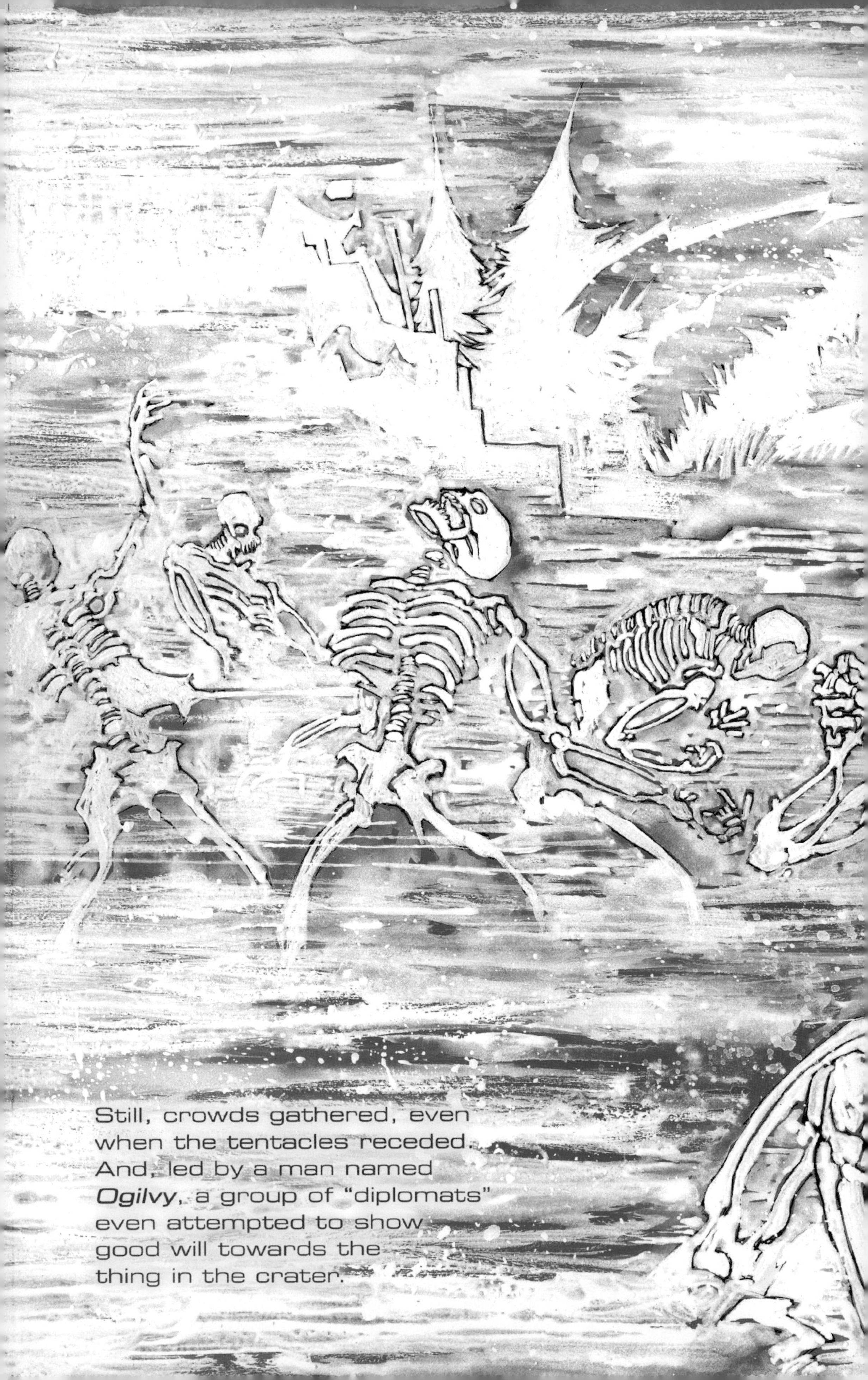
Still, crowds gathered, even when the tentacles receded. And, led by a man named *Ogilvy*, a group of "diplomats" even attempted to show good will towards the thing in the crater.

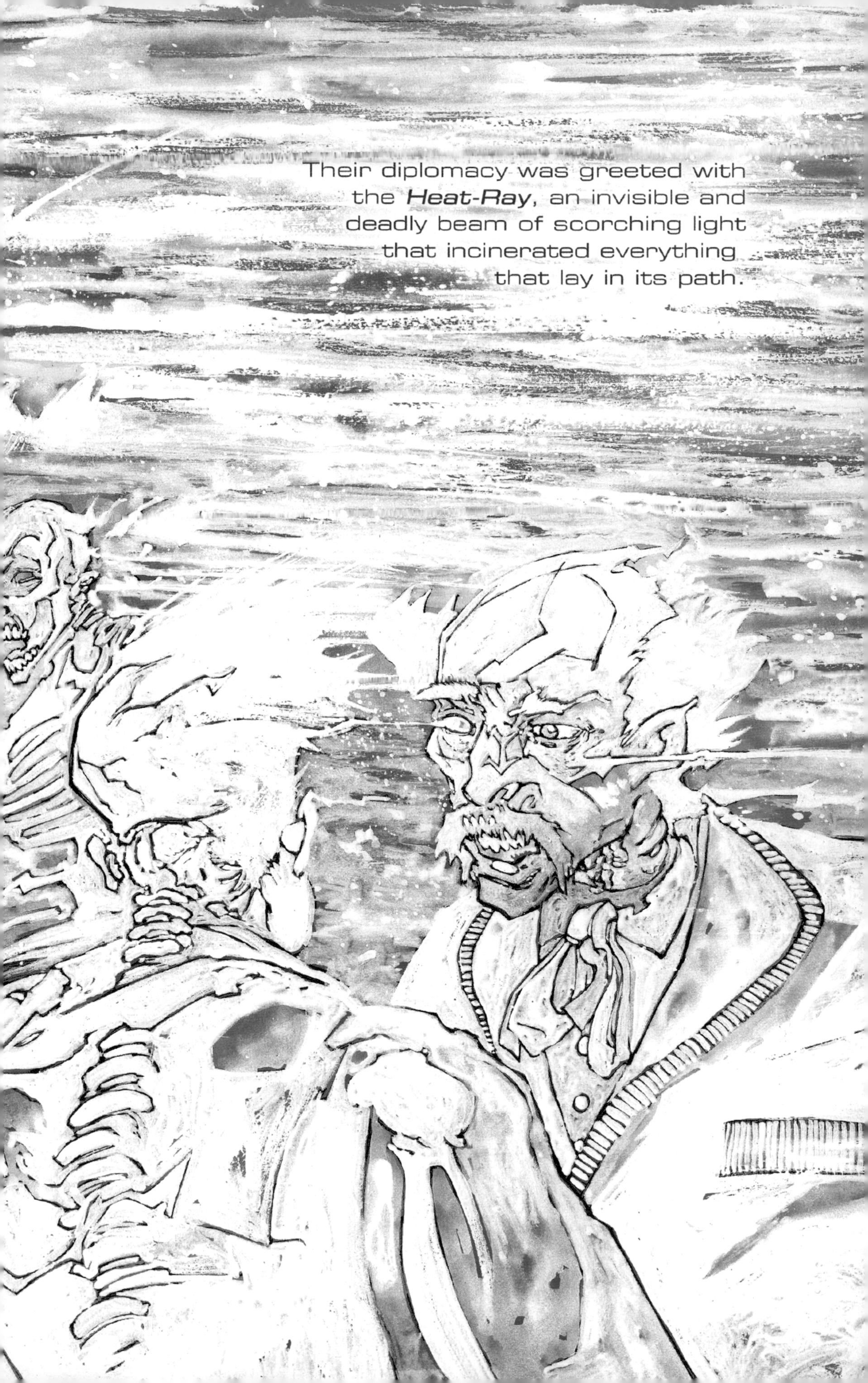
Their diplomacy was greeted with the *Heat-Ray*, an invisible and deadly beam of scorching light that incinerated everything that lay in its path.

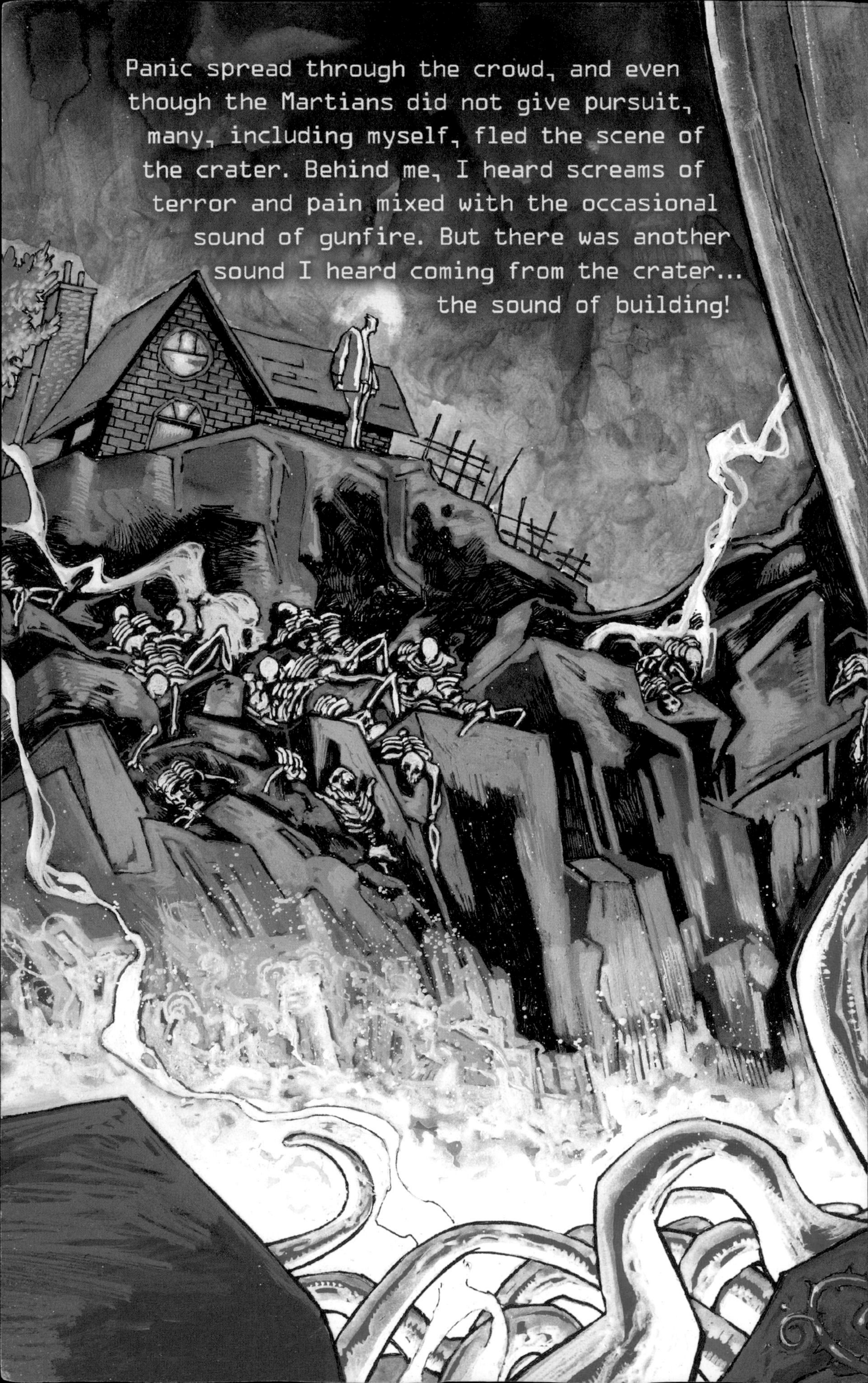
Panic spread through the crowd, and even though the Martians did not give pursuit, many, including myself, fled the scene of the crater. Behind me, I heard screams of terror and pain mixed with the occasional sound of gunfire. But there was another sound I heard coming from the crater... the sound of building!

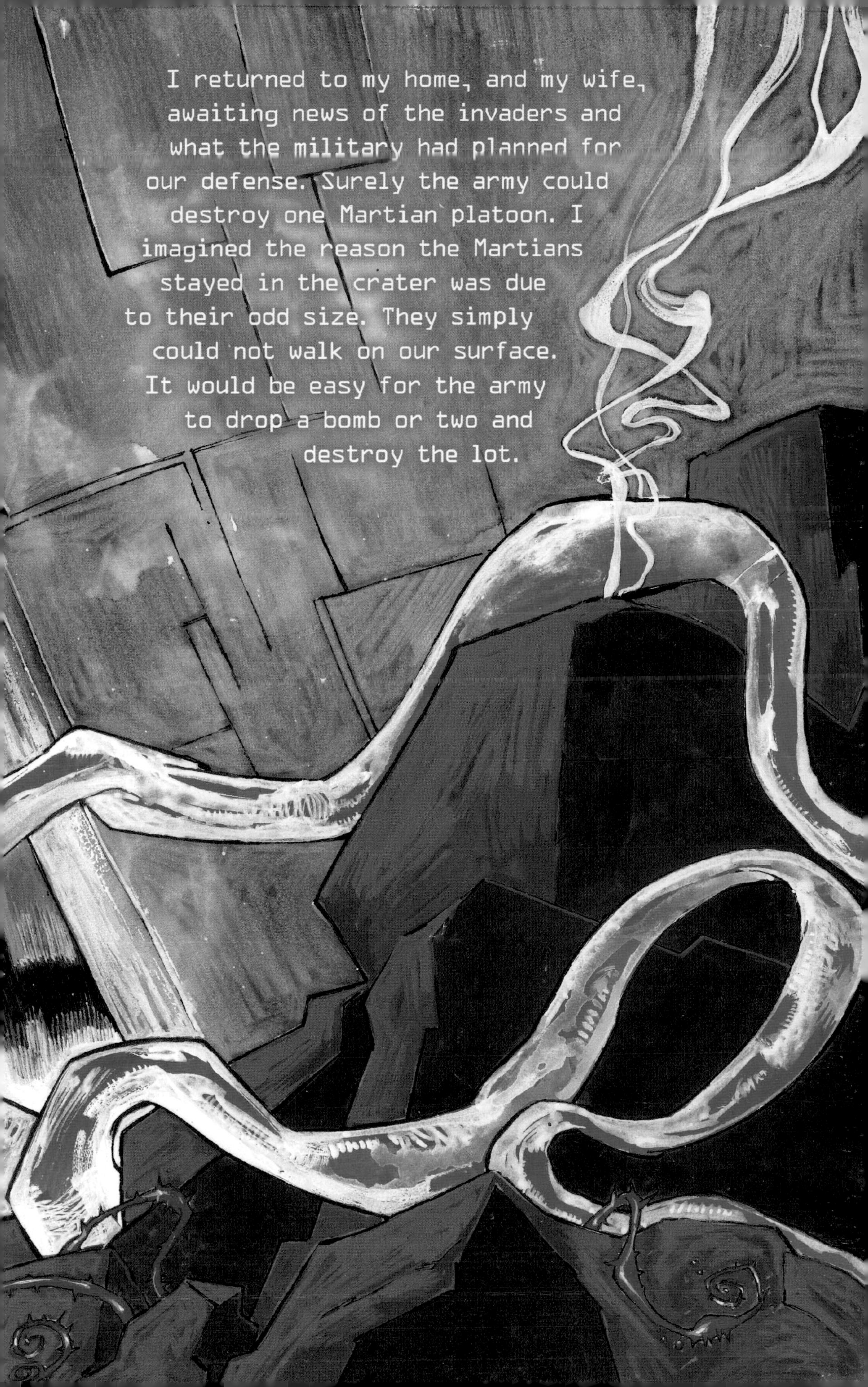
I returned to my home, and my wife, awaiting news of the invaders and what the military had planned for our defense. Surely the army could destroy one Martian platoon. I imagined the reason the Martians stayed in the crater was due to their odd size. They simply could not walk on our surface. It would be easy for the army to drop a bomb or two and destroy the lot.

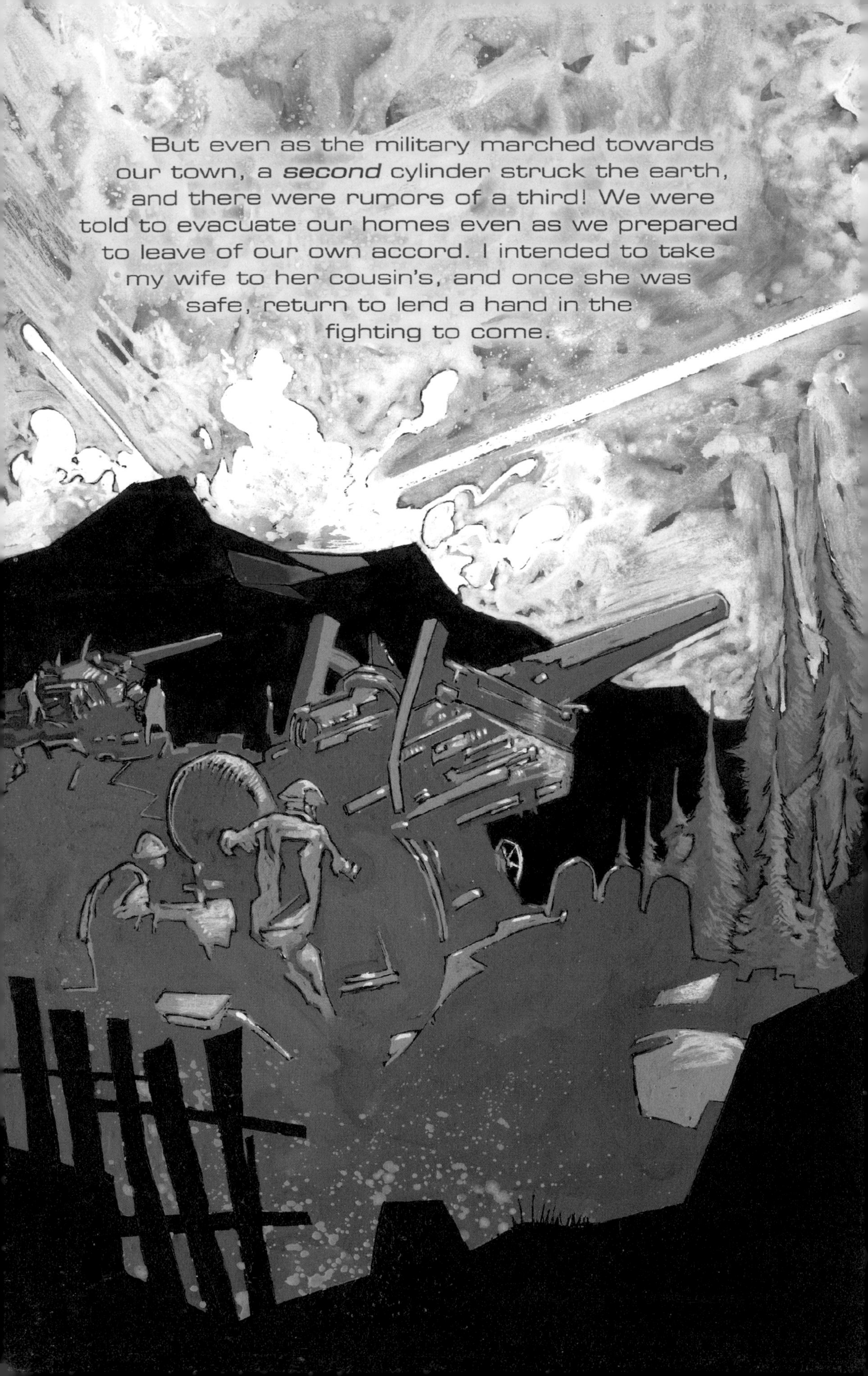
`But even as the military marched towards our town, a *second* cylinder struck the earth, and there were rumors of a third! We were told to evacuate our homes even as we prepared to leave of our own accord. I intended to take my wife to her cousin's, and once she was safe, return to lend a hand in the fighting to come.

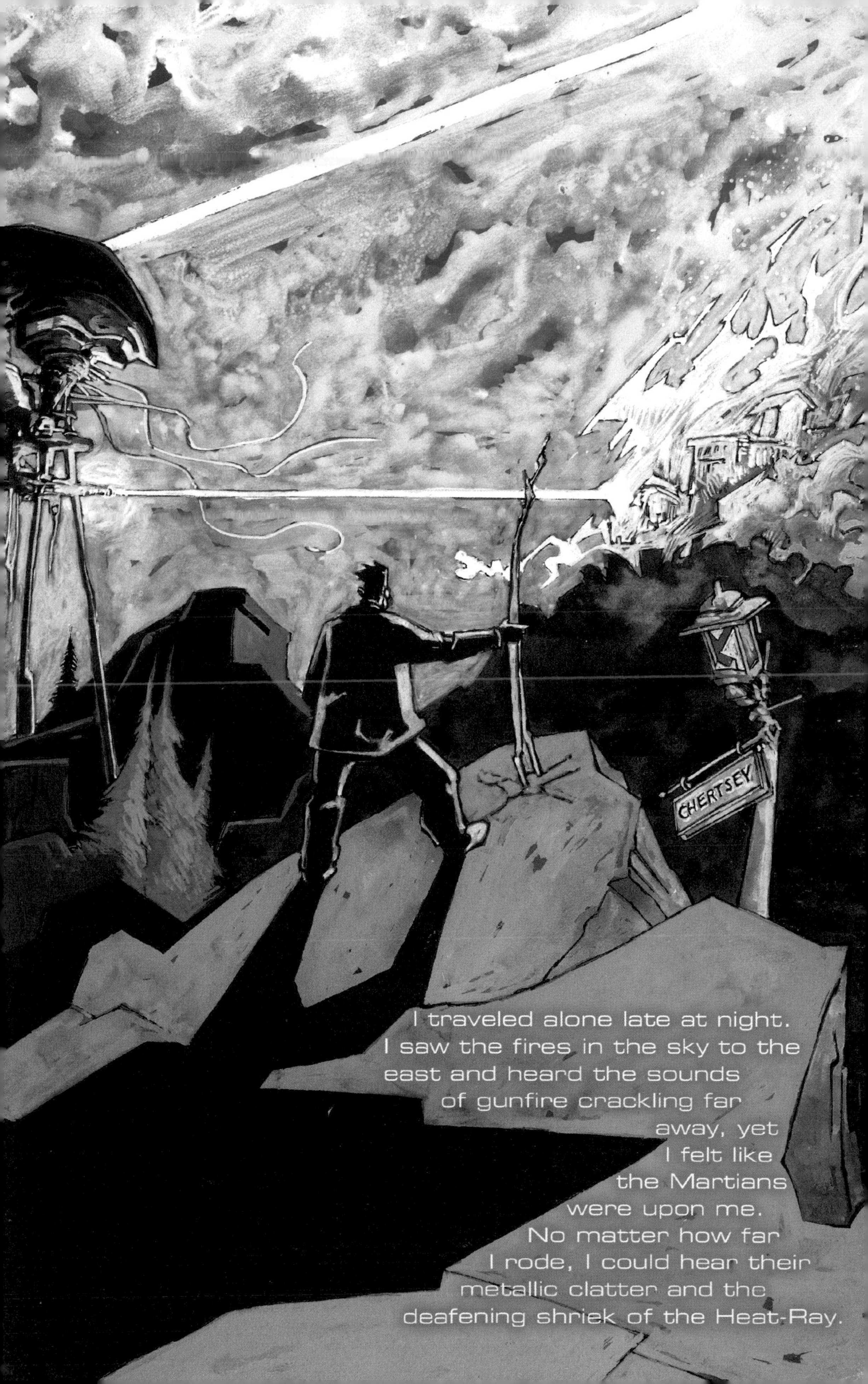
CHERTSEY
I traveled alone late at night.
I saw the fires in the sky to the
east and heard the sounds
of gunfire crackling far
away, yet
I felt like
the Martians
were upon me.
No matter how far
I rode, I could hear their
metallic clatter and the
deafening shriek of the Heat-Ray.

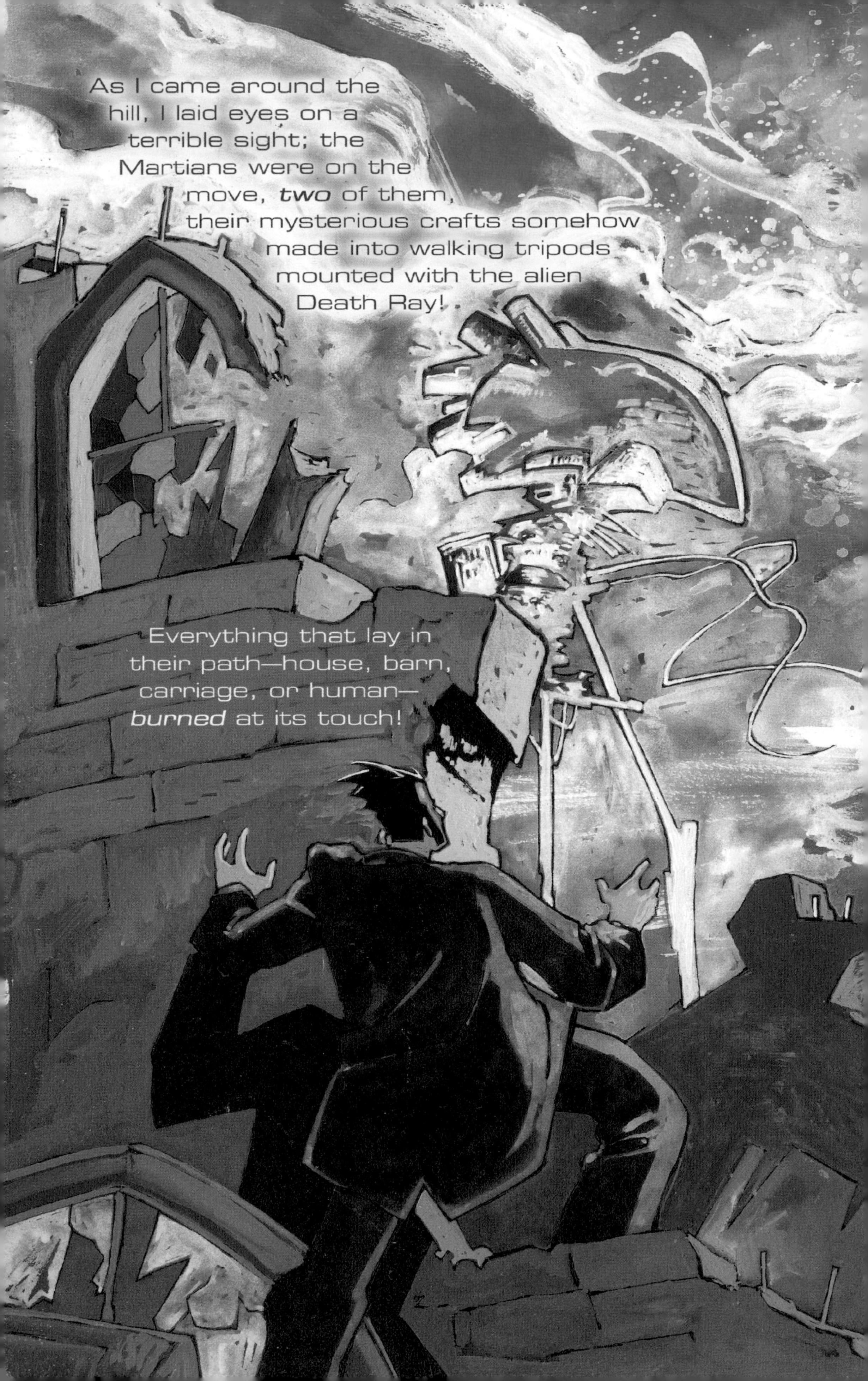
As I came around the hill, I laid eyes on a terrible sight; the Martians were on the move, *two* of them, their mysterious crafts somehow made into walking tripods mounted with the alien Death Ray!
Everything that lay in their path—house, barn, carriage, or human—*burned* at its touch!

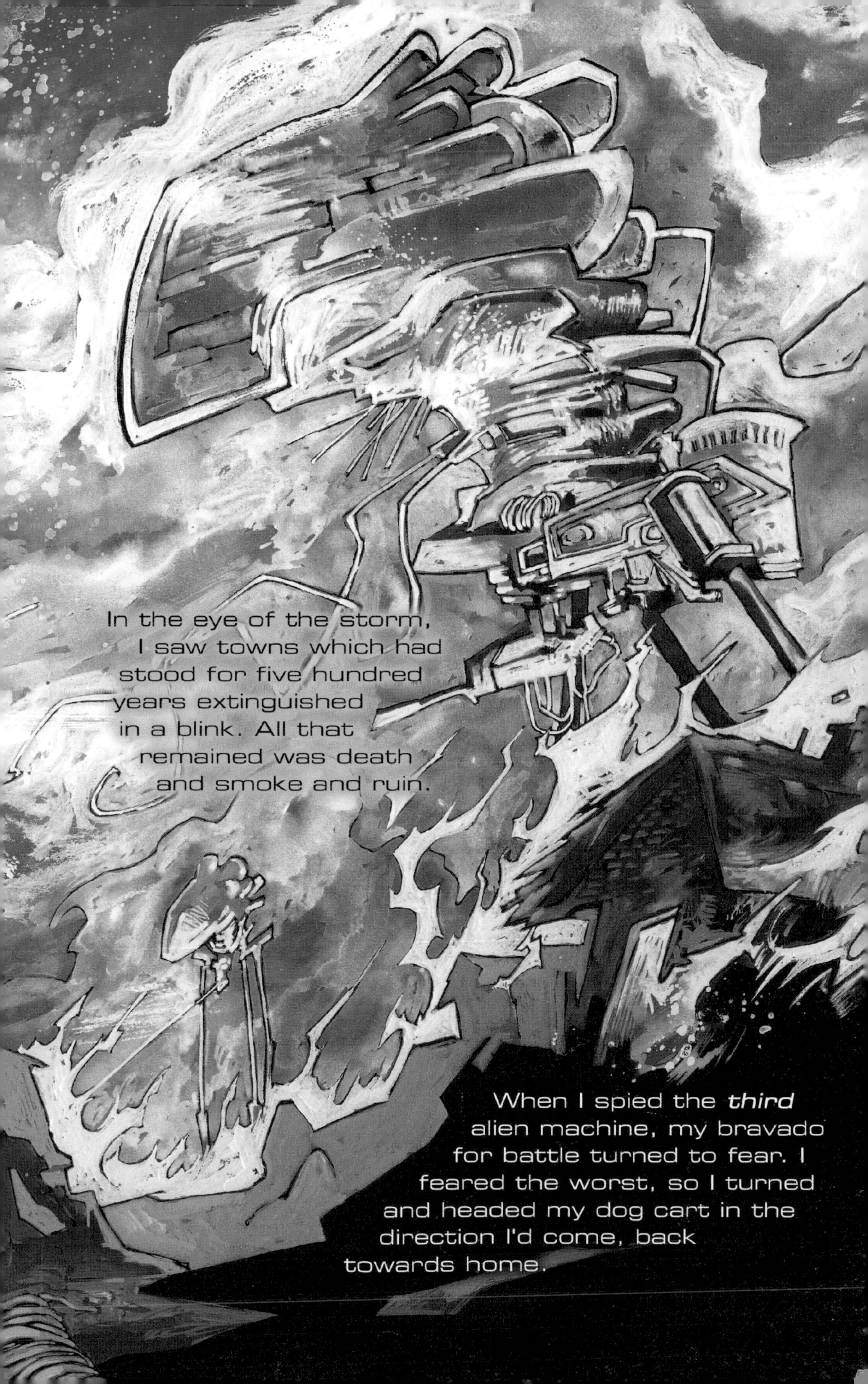
In the eye of the storm, I saw towns which had stood for five hundred years extinguished in a blink. All that remained was death and smoke and ruin.
When I spied the *third* alien machine, my bravado for battle turned to fear. I feared the worst, so I turned and headed my dog cart in the direction I'd come, back towards home.

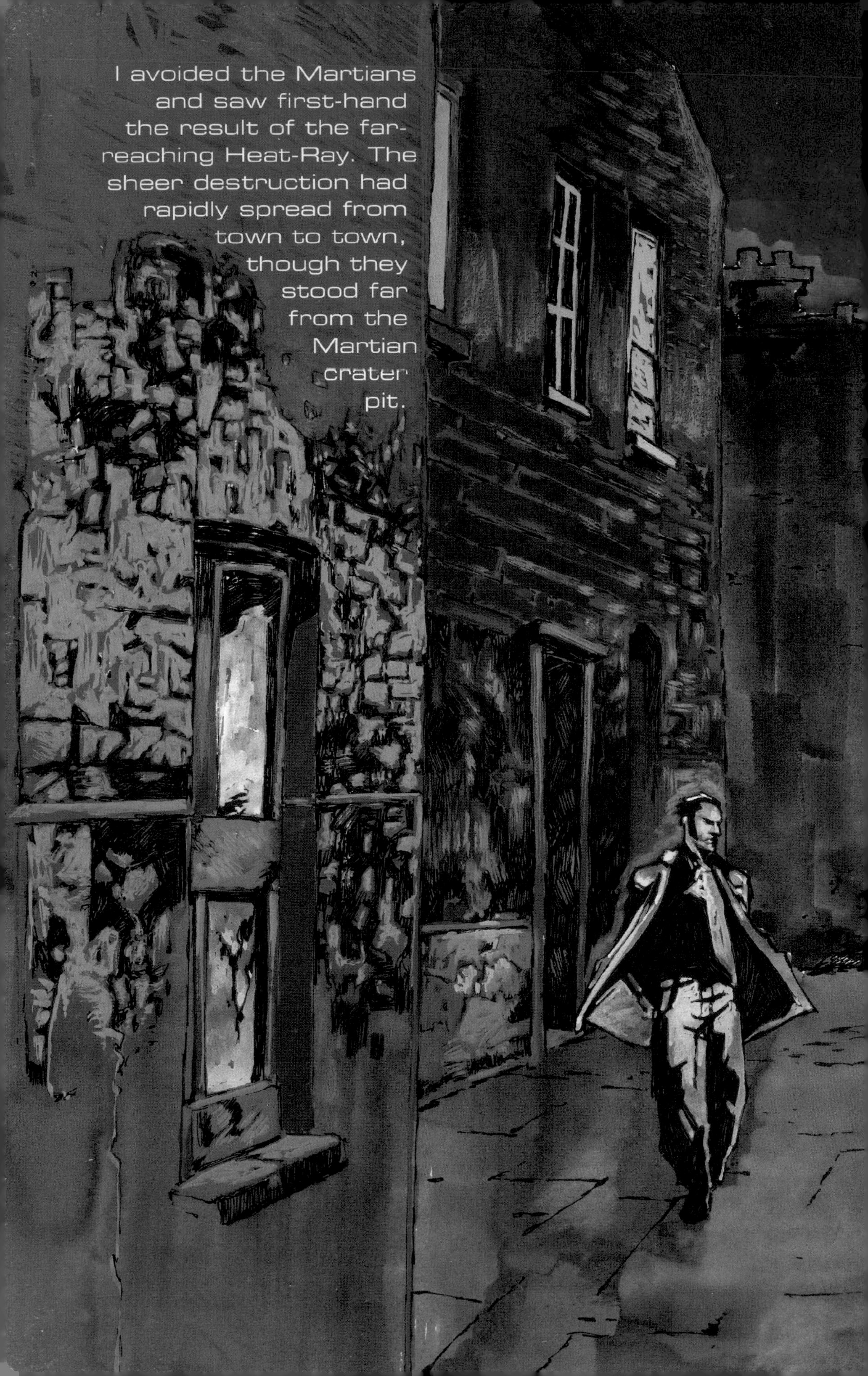
I avoided the Martians and saw first-hand the result of the far-reaching Heat-Ray. The sheer destruction had rapidly spread from town to town, though they stood far from the Martian crater pit.

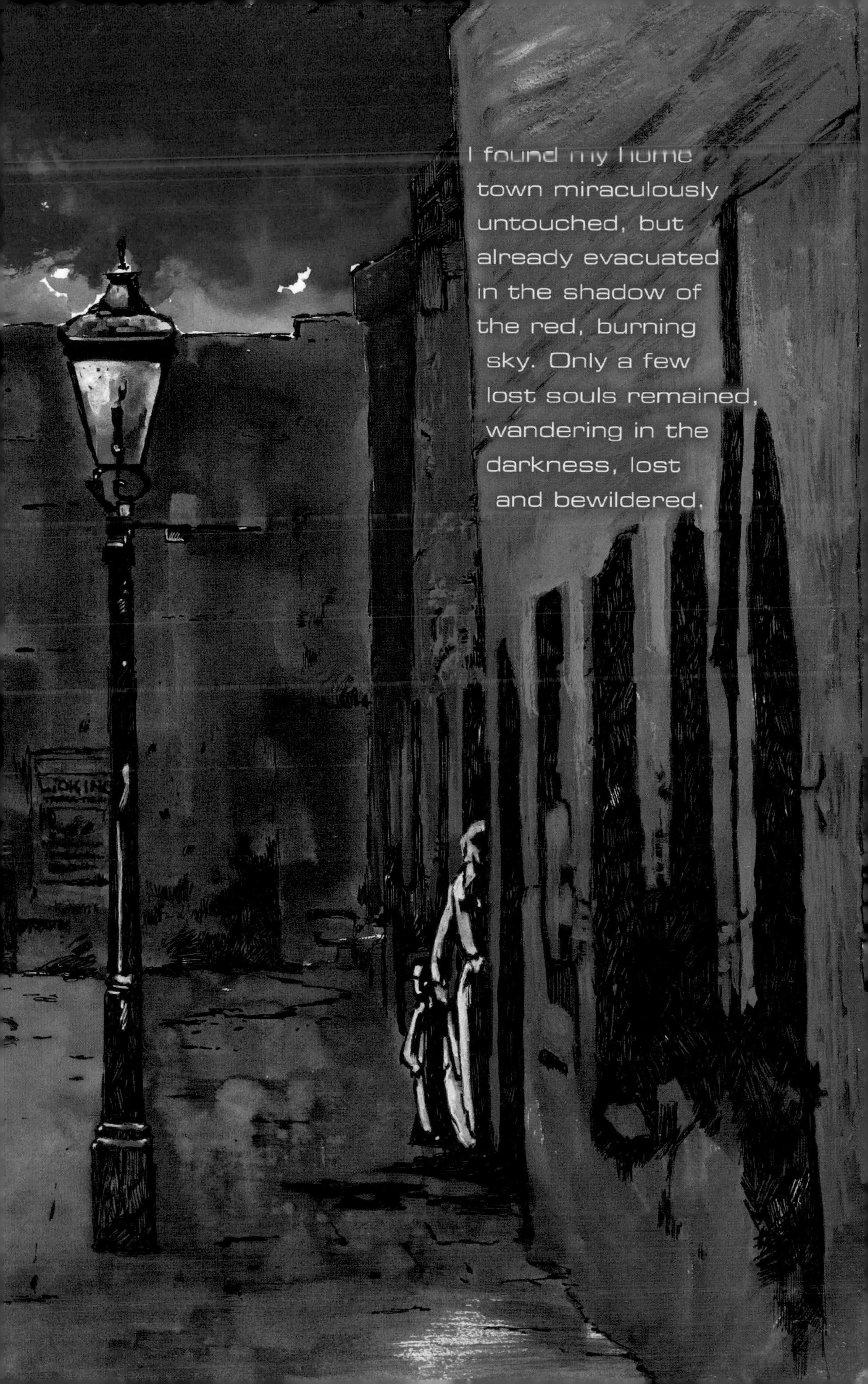
I found my home town miraculously untouched, but already evacuated in the shadow of the red, burning sky. Only a few lost souls remained, wandering in the darkness, lost and bewildered.

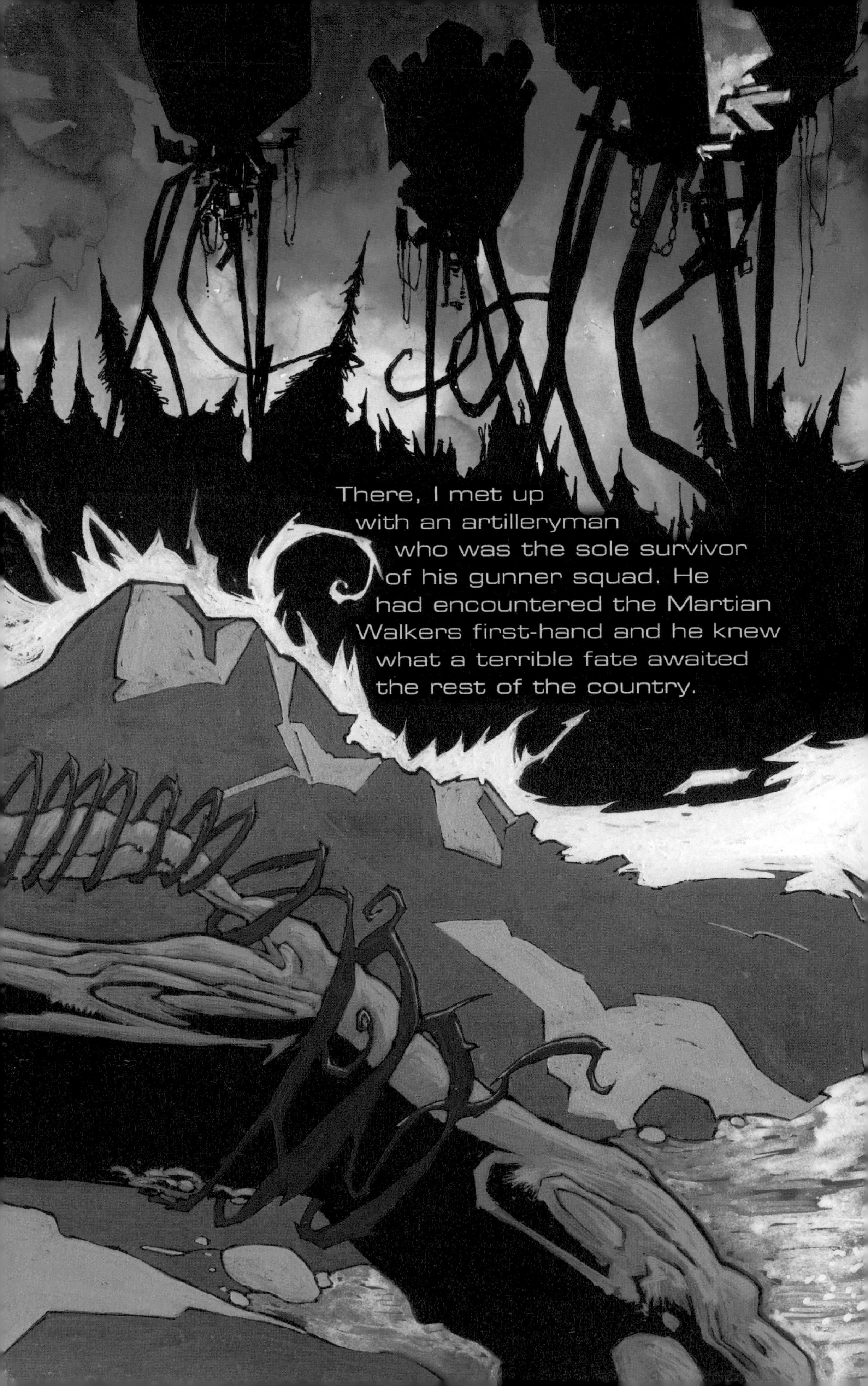
There, I met up with an artilleryman who was the sole survivor of his gunner squad. He had encountered the Martian Walkers first-hand and he knew what a terrible fate awaited the rest of the country.

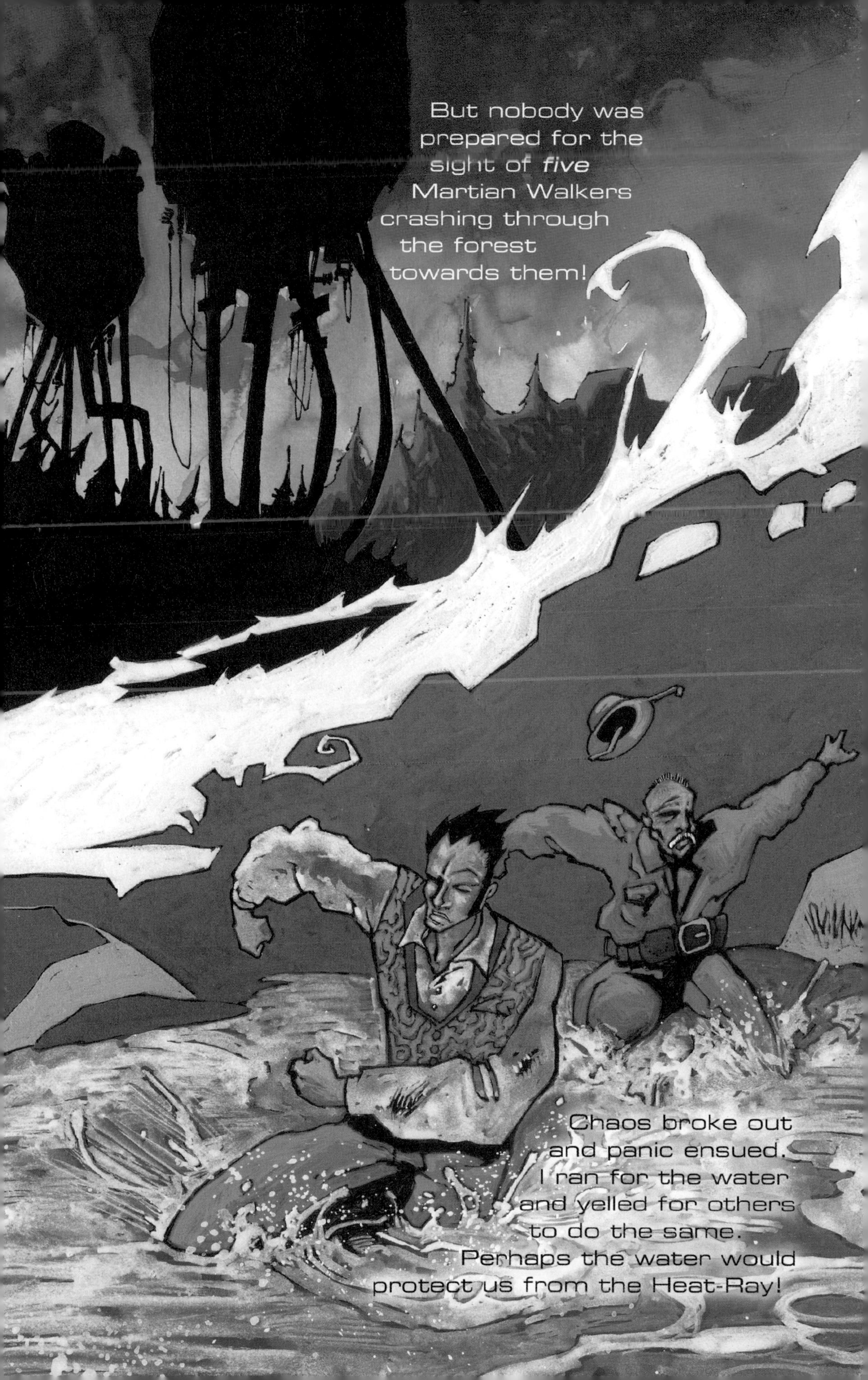

But nobody was prepared for the sight of *five* Martian Walkers crashing through the forest towards them!
Chaos broke out and panic ensued. I ran for the water and yelled for others to do the same. Perhaps the water would protect us from the Heat-Ray!

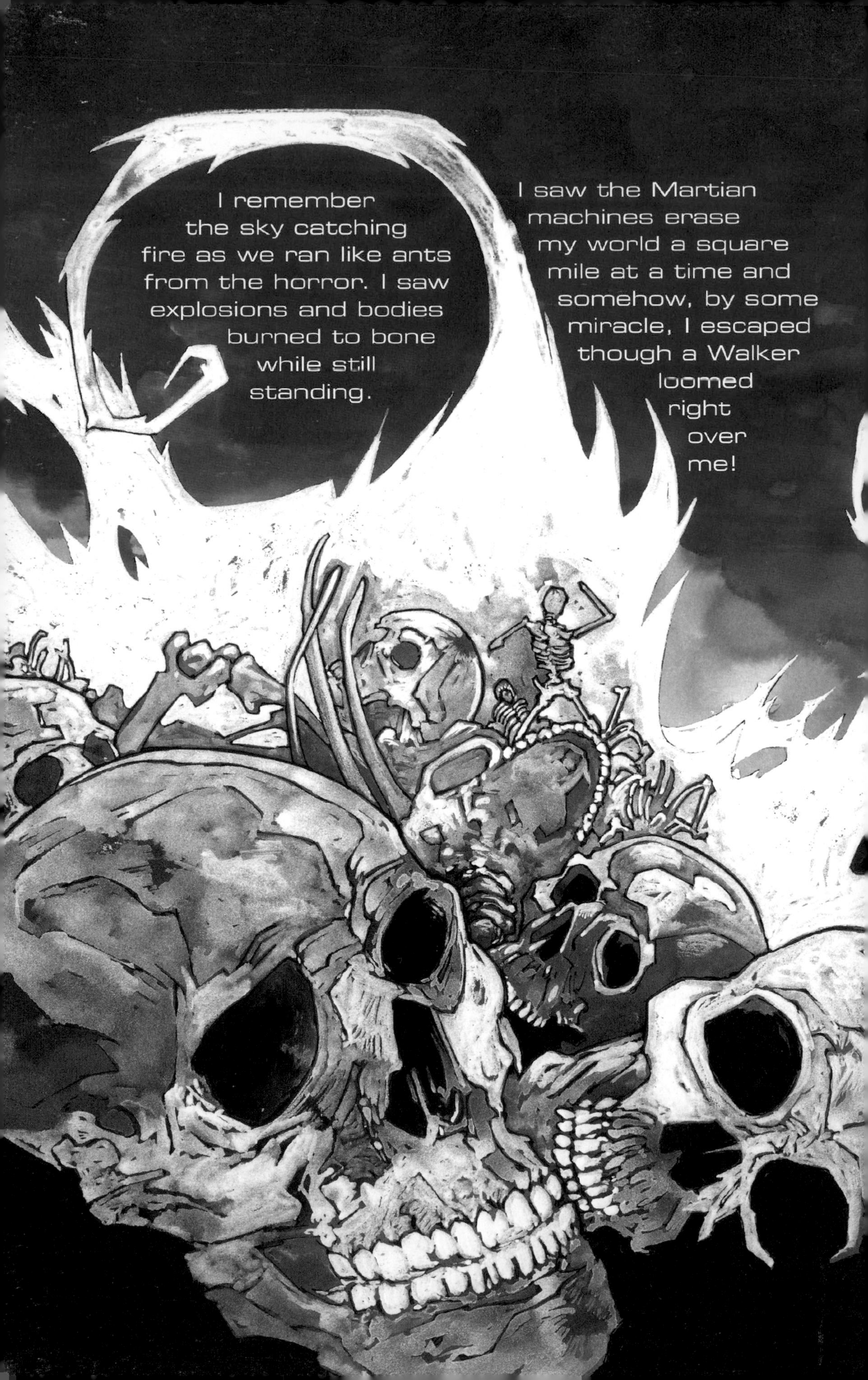
I remember the sky catching fire as we ran like ants from the horror. I saw explosions and bodies burned to bone while still standing.
I saw the Martian machines erase my world a square mile at a time and somehow, by some miracle, I escaped though a Walker loomed right over me!

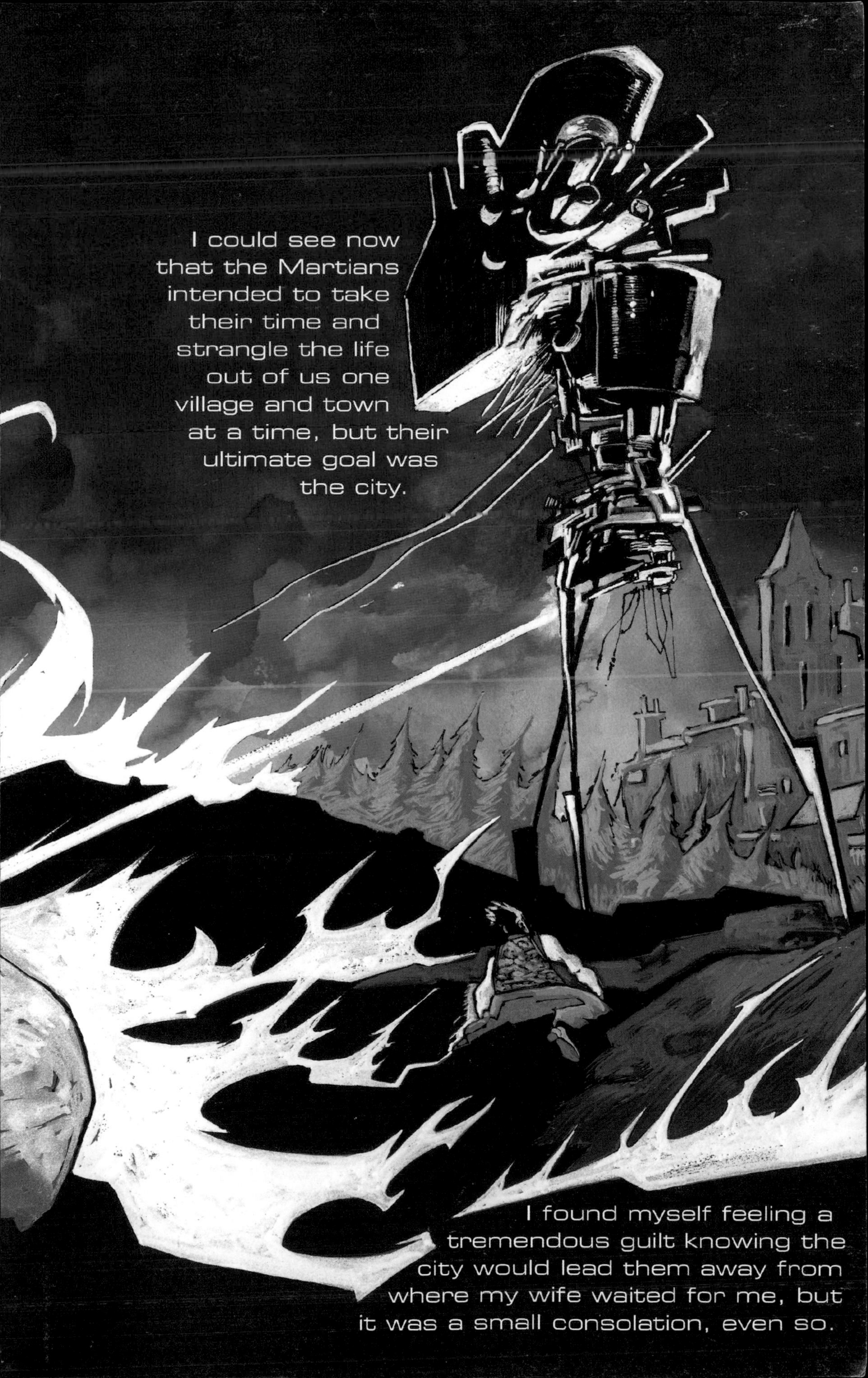
I could see now that the Martians intended to take their time and strangle the life out of us one village and town at a time, but their ultimate goal was the city.
I found myself feeling a tremendous guilt knowing the city would lead them away from where my wife waited for me, but it was a small consolation, even so.

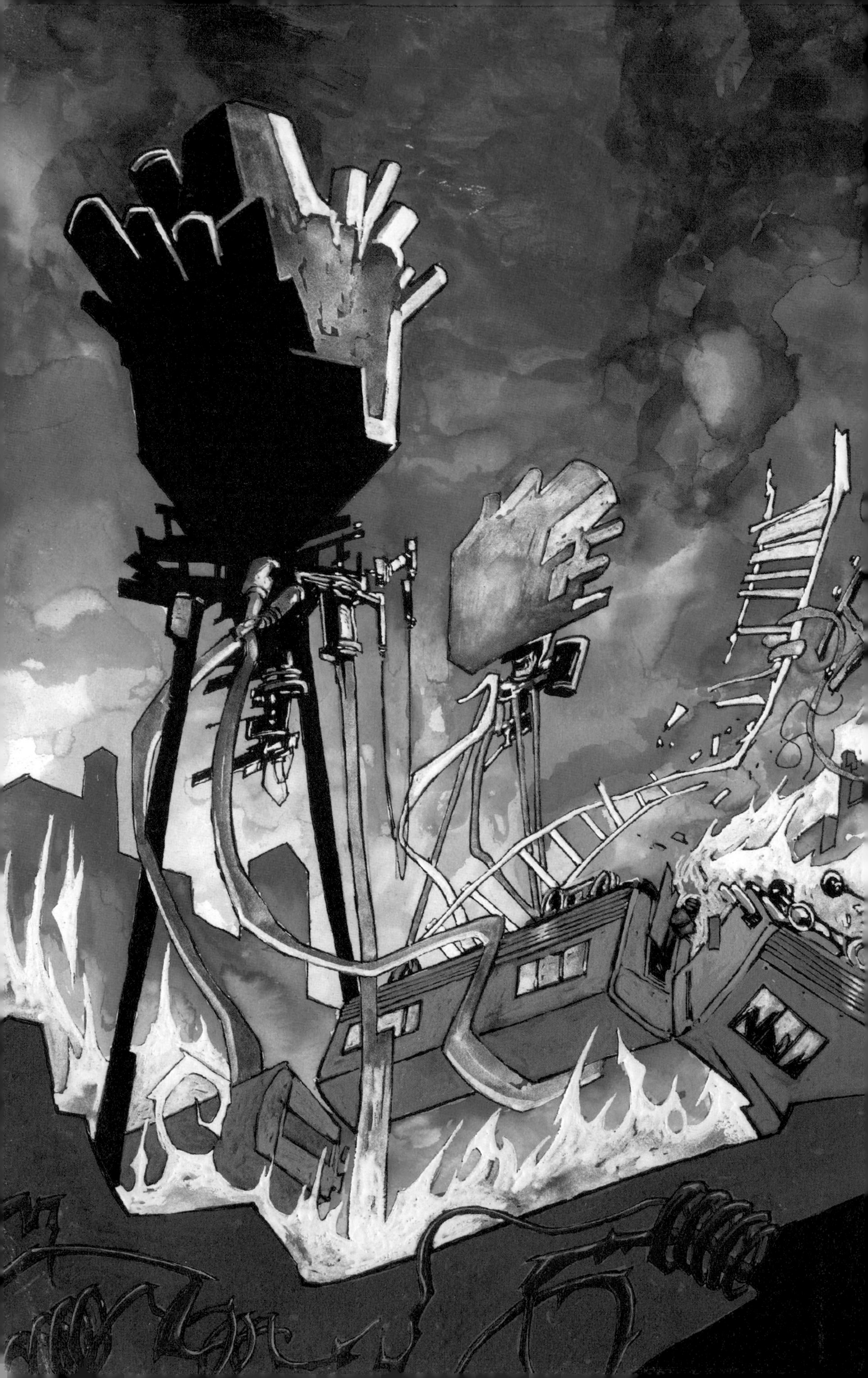

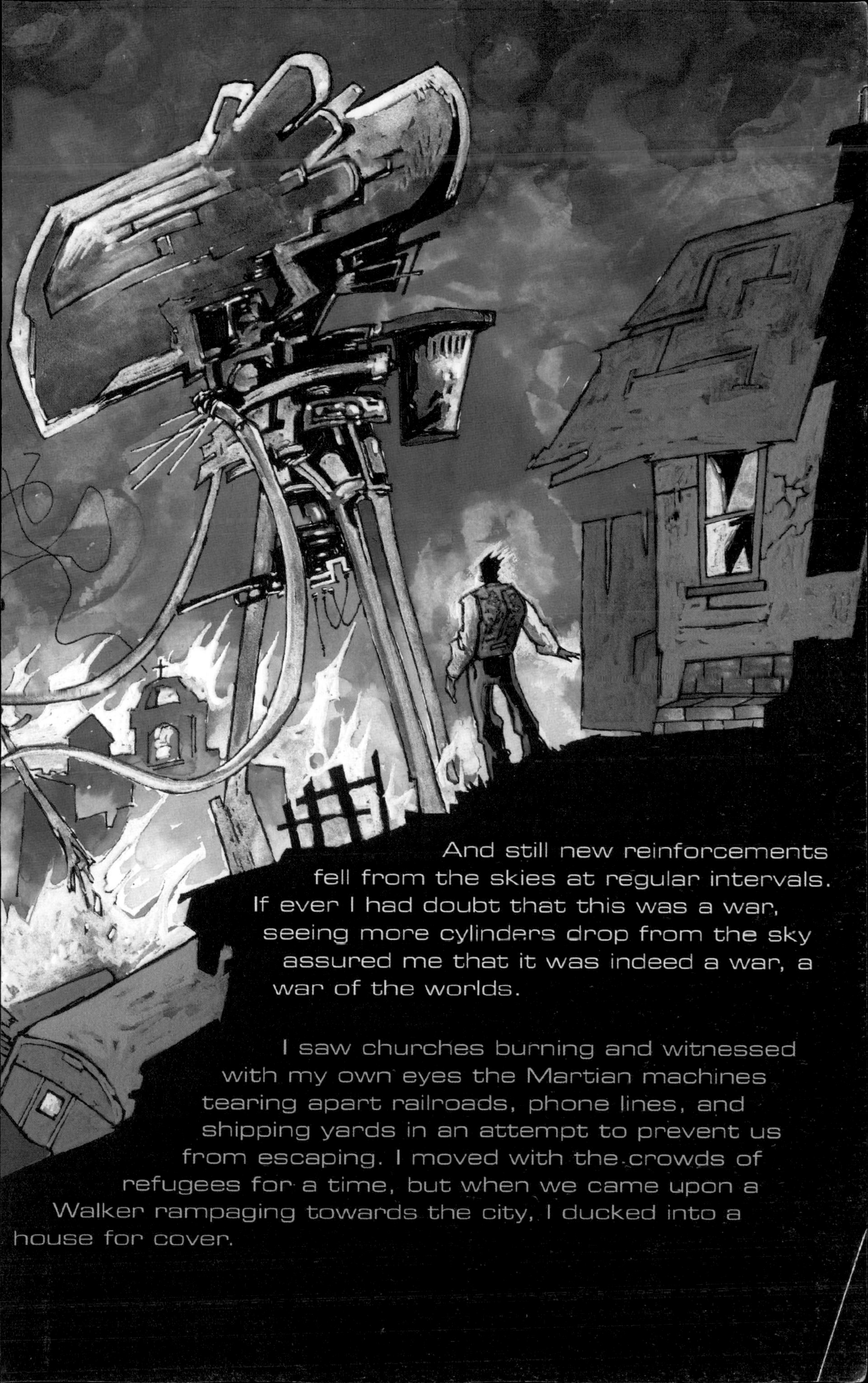

And still new reinforcements fell from the skies at regular intervals. If ever I had doubt that this was a war, seeing more cylinders drop from the sky assured me that it was indeed a war, a war of the worlds.

I saw churches burning and witnessed with my own eyes the Martian machines tearing apart railroads, phone lines, and shipping yards in an attempt to prevent us from escaping. I moved with the crowds of refugees for a time, but when we came upon a Walker rampaging towards the city, I ducked into a house for cover.

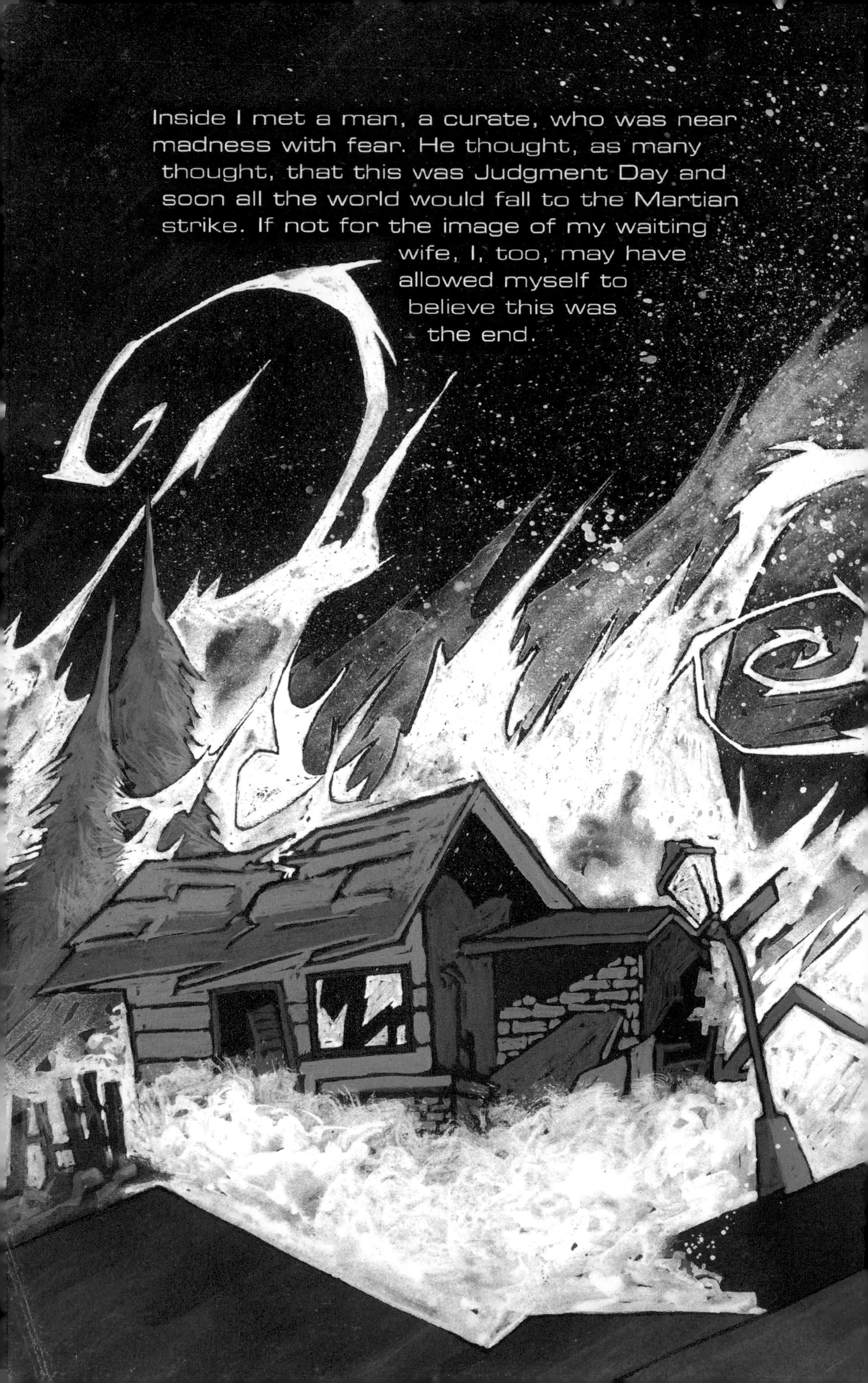
Inside I met a man, a curate, who was near madness with fear. He thought, as many thought, that this was Judgment Day and soon all the world would fall to the Martian strike. If not for the image of my waiting wife, I, too, may have allowed myself to believe this was the end.

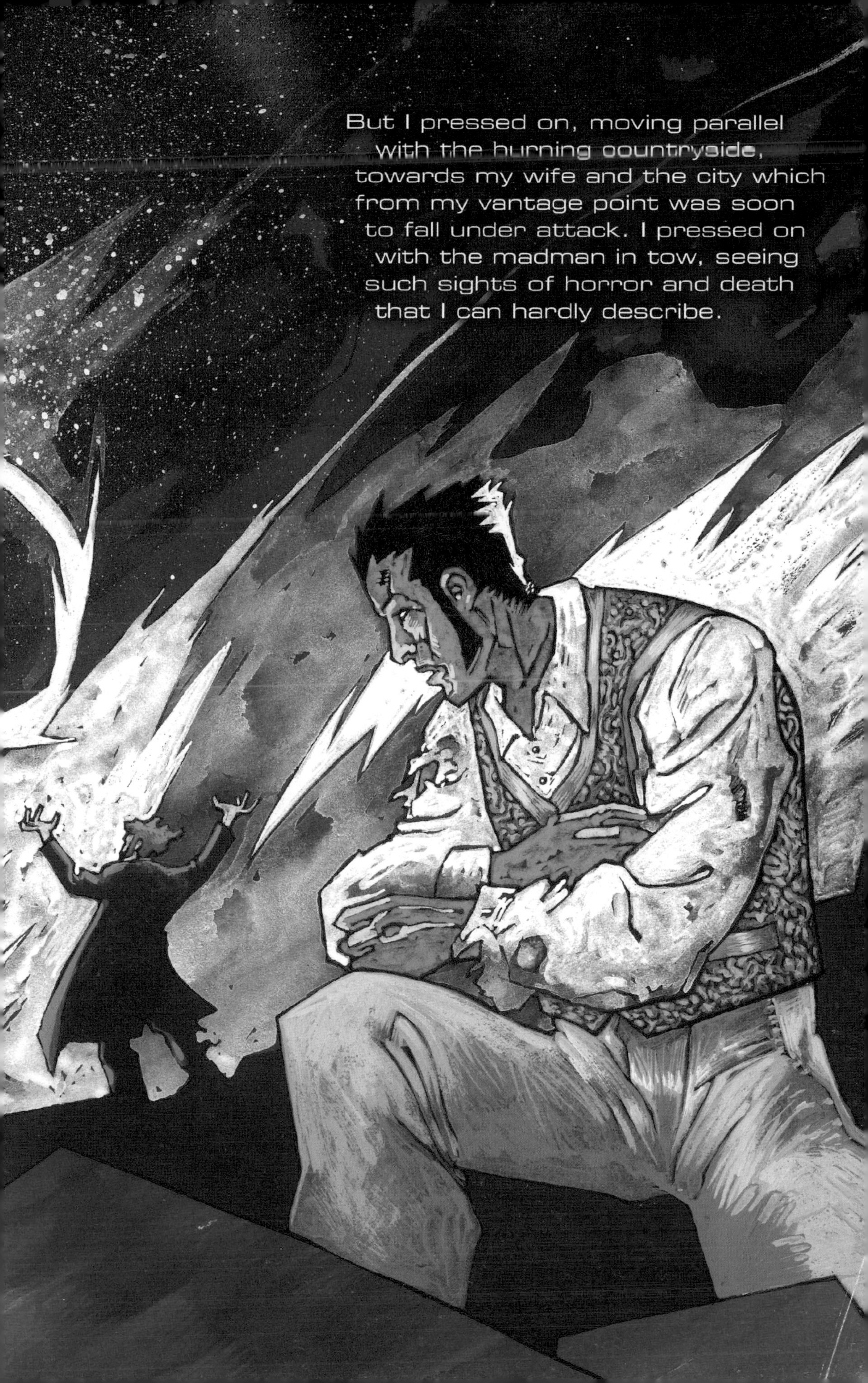
But I pressed on, moving parallel with the burning countryside, towards my wife and the city which from my vantage point was soon to fall under attack. I pressed on with the madman in tow, seeing such sights of horror and death that I can hardly describe.

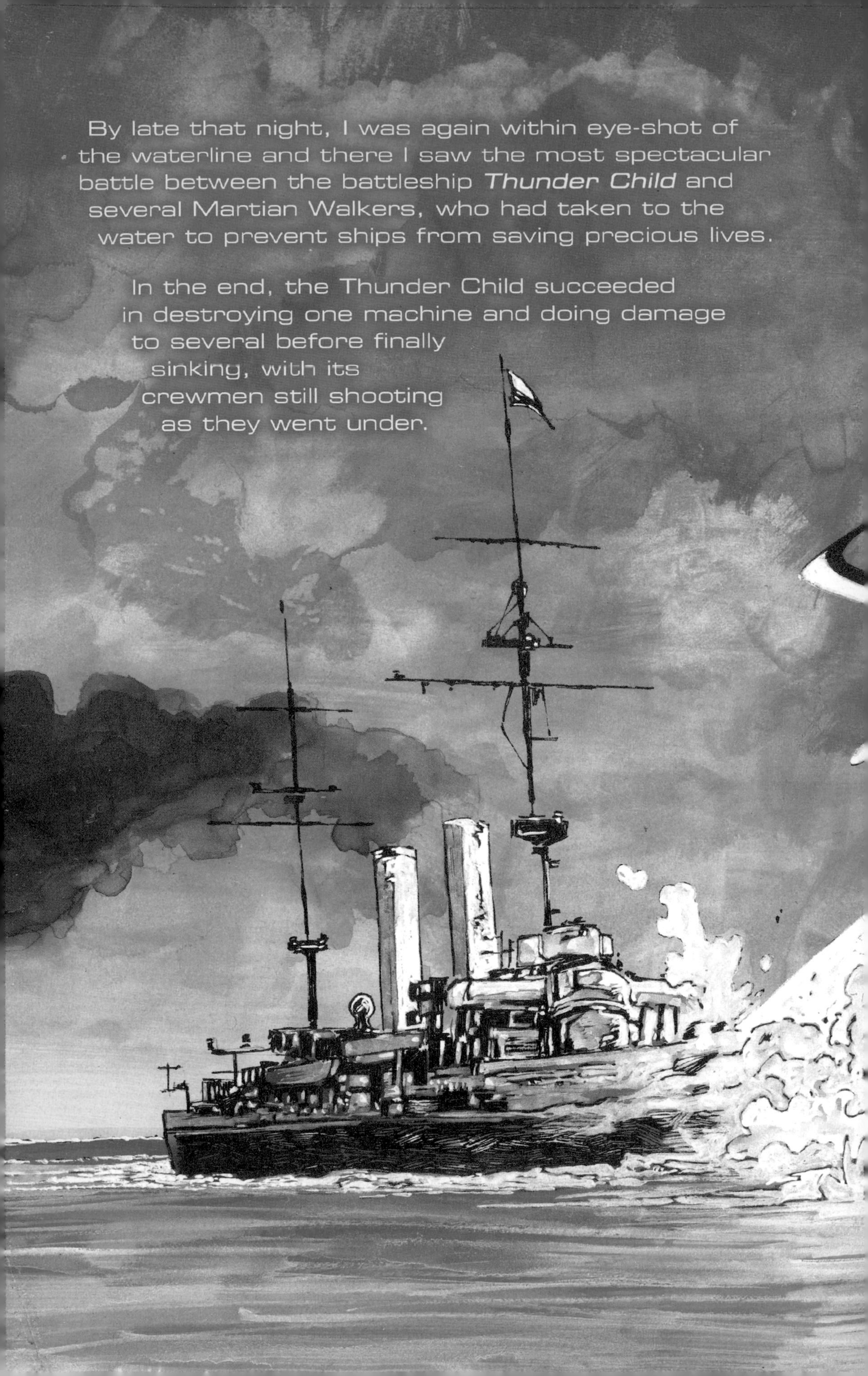
By late that night, I was again within eye-shot of the waterline and there I saw the most spectacular battle between the battleship *Thunder Child* and several Martian Walkers, who had taken to the water to prevent ships from saving precious lives.
In the end, the Thunder Child succeeded in destroying one machine and doing damage to several before finally sinking, with its crewmen still shooting as they went under.

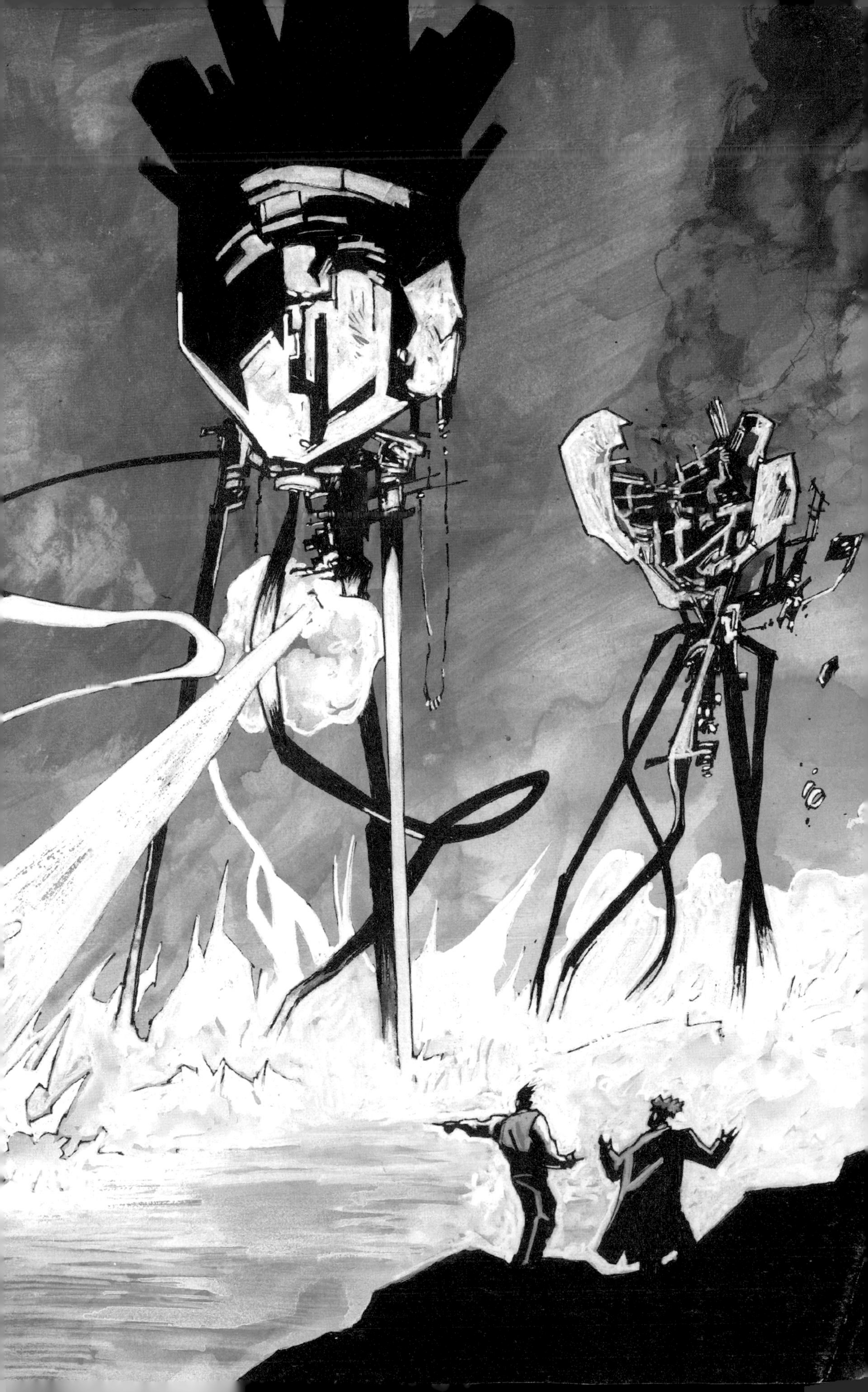

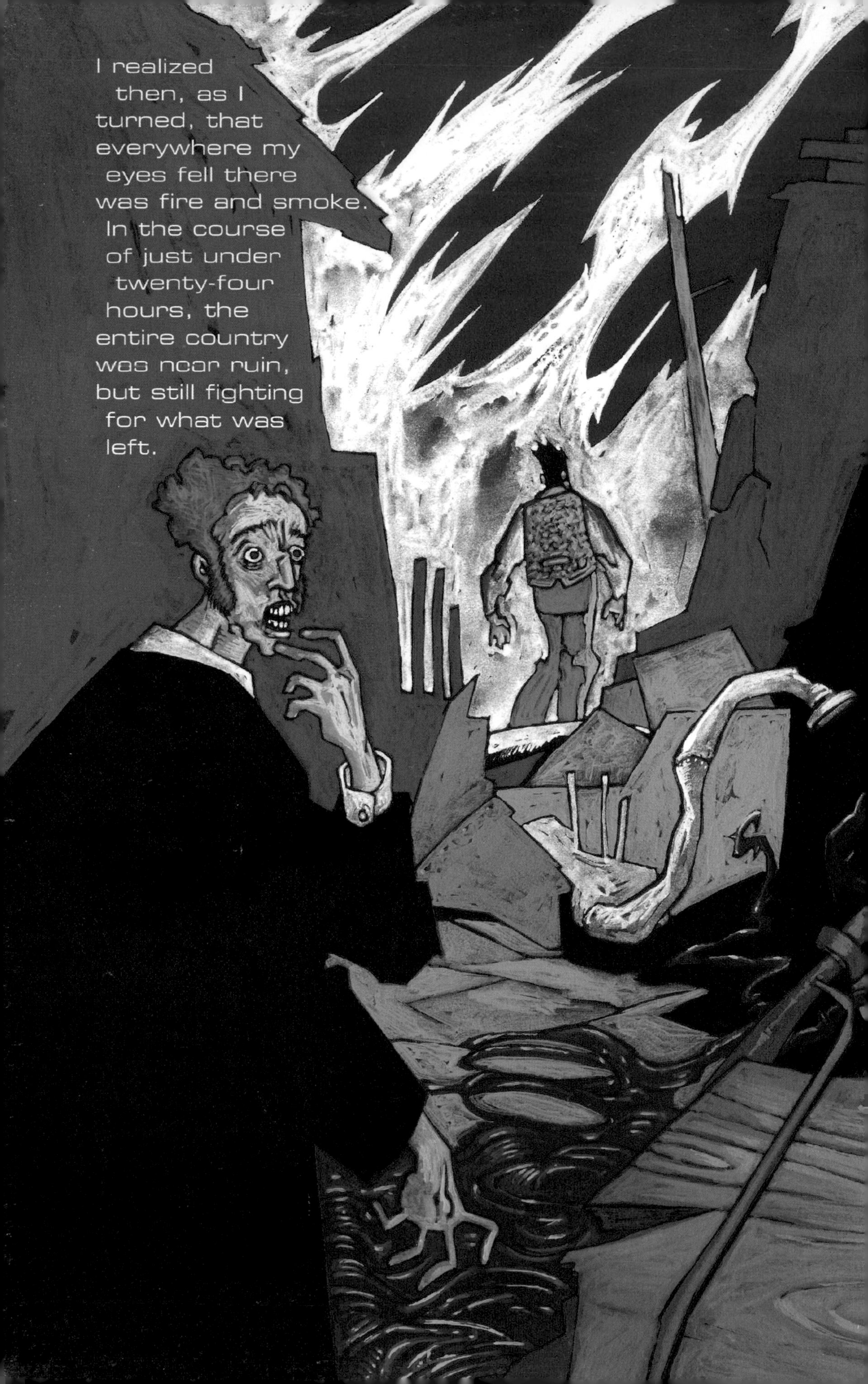
I realized then, as I turned, that everywhere my eyes fell there was fire and smoke. In the course of just under twenty-four hours, the entire country was near ruin, but still fighting for what was left.

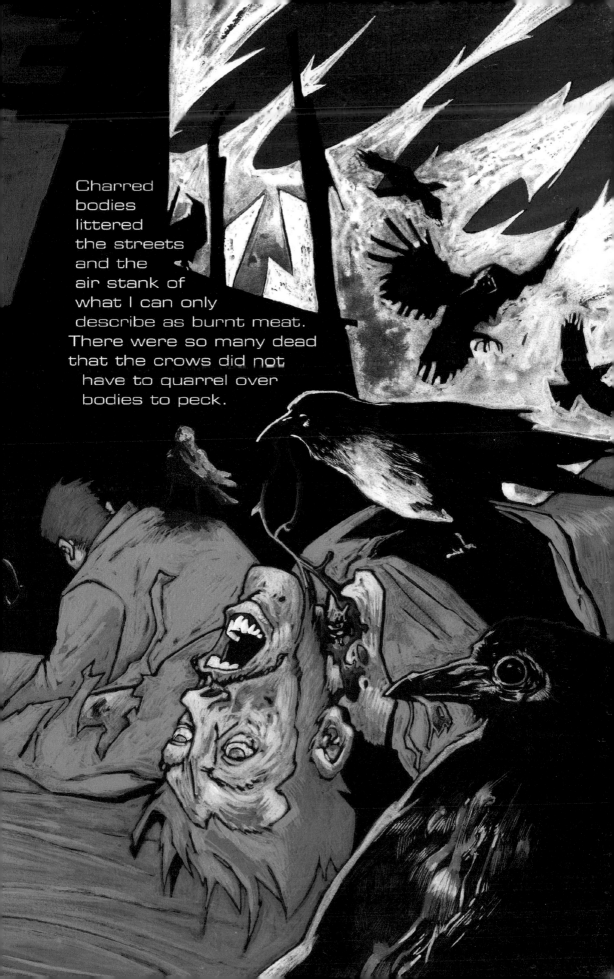

Charred bodies littered the streets and the air stank of what I can only describe as burnt meat. There were so many dead that the crows did not have to quarrel over bodies to peck.

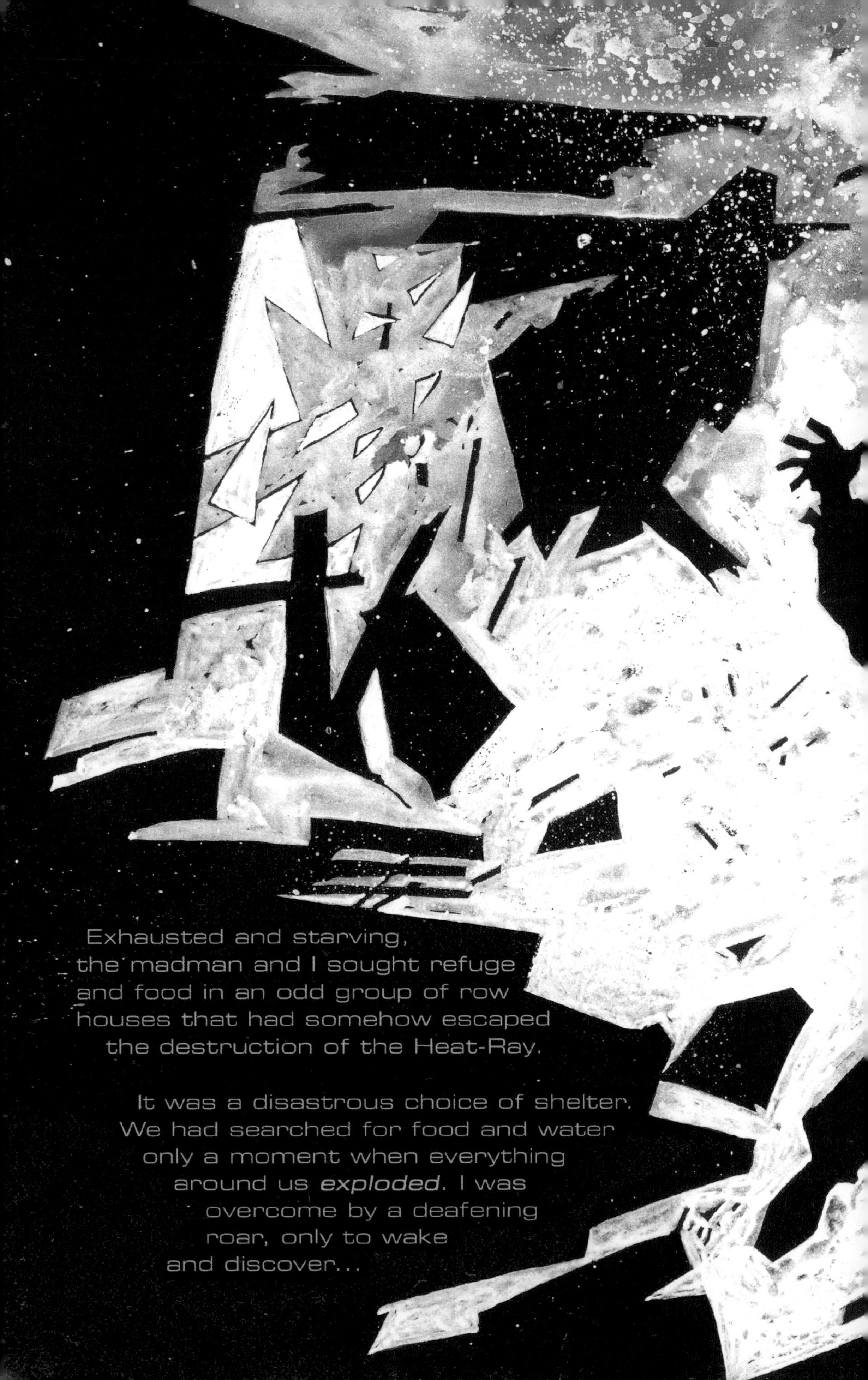
Exhausted and starving, the madman and I sought refuge and food in an odd group of row houses that had somehow escaped the destruction of the Heat-Ray.
It was a disastrous choice of shelter. We had searched for food and water only a moment when everything around us *exploded*. I was overcome by a deafening roar, only to wake and discover...

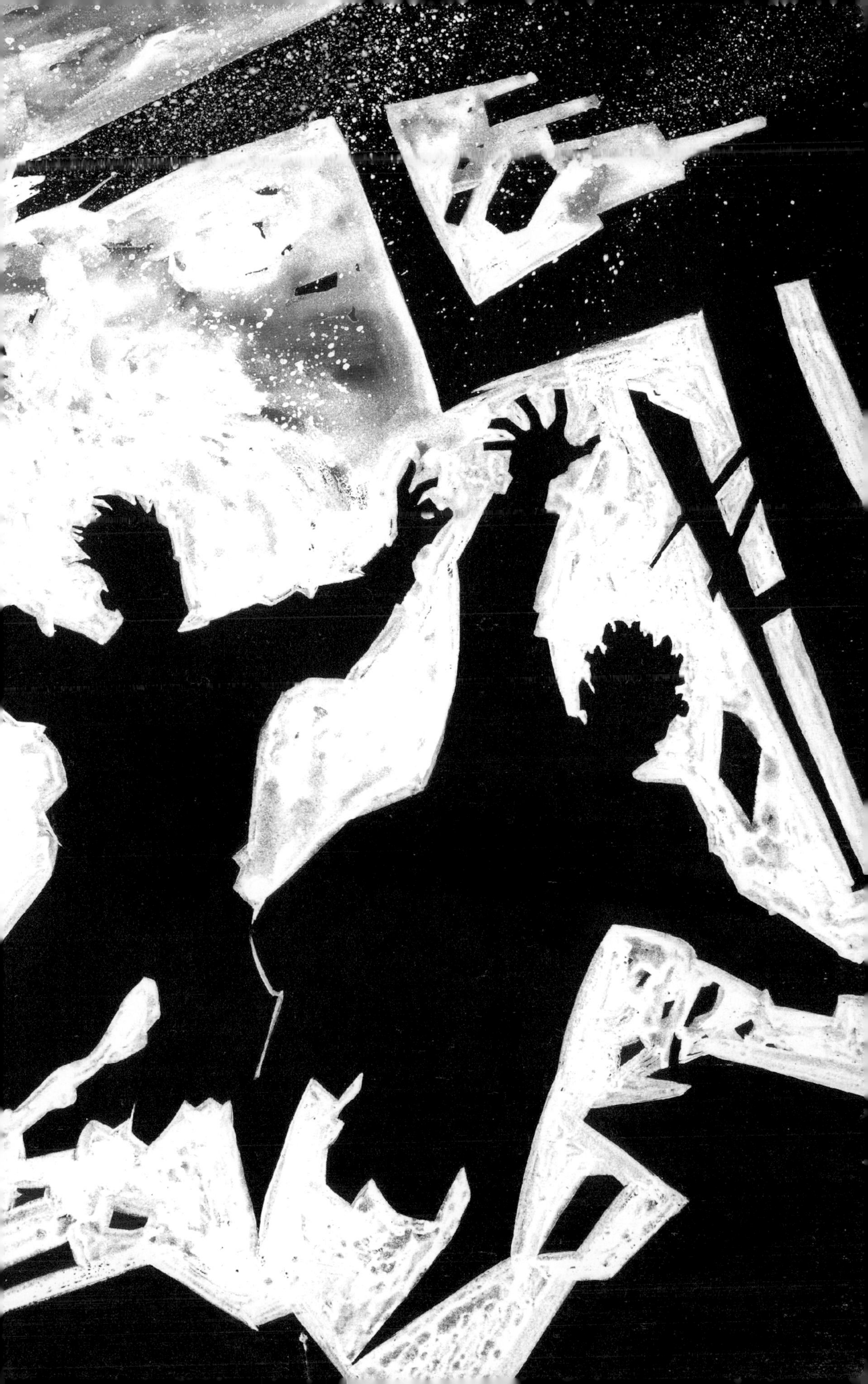

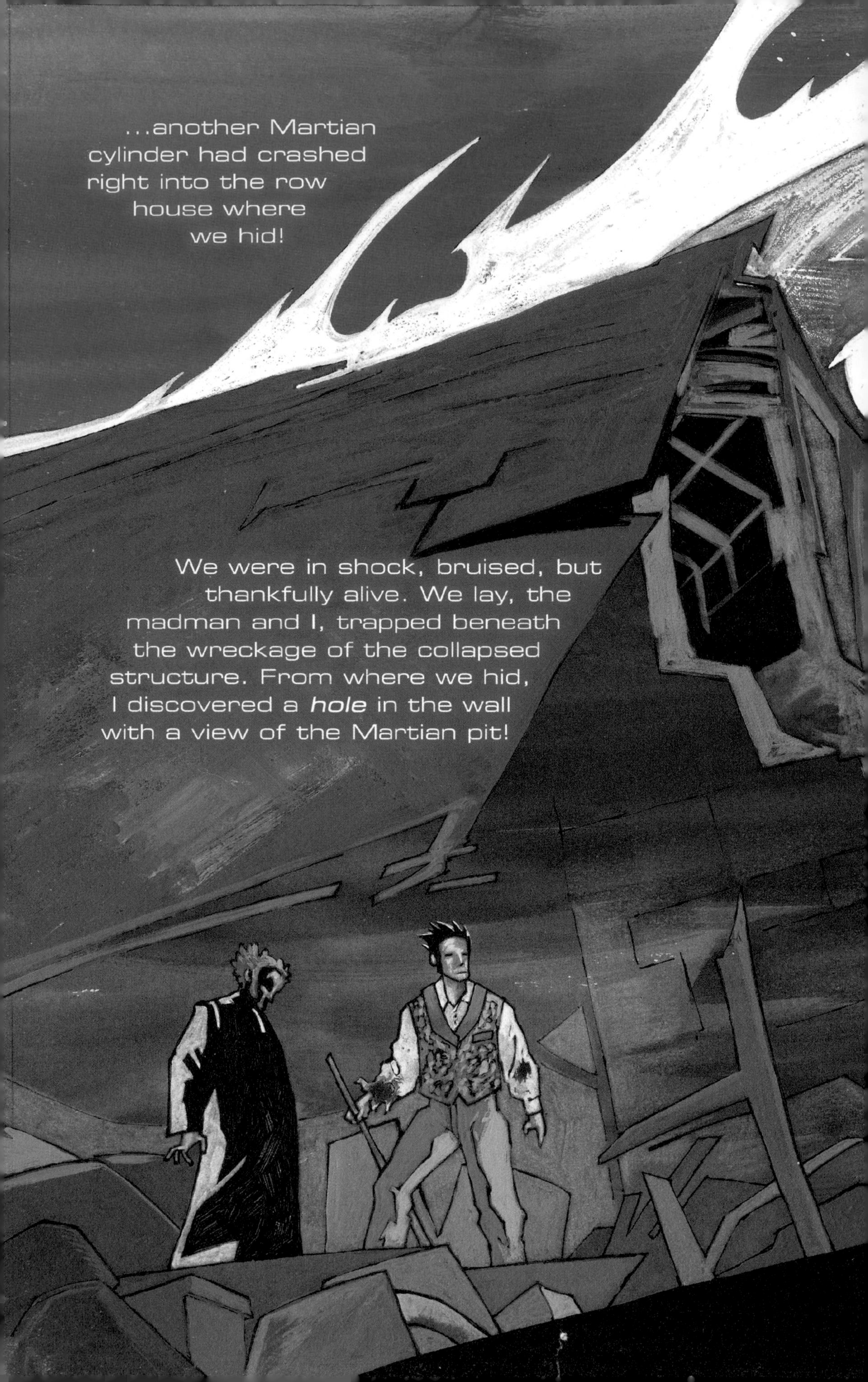
...another Martian cylinder had crashed right into the row house where we hid!
We were in shock, bruised, but thankfully alive. We lay, the madman and I, trapped beneath the wreckage of the collapsed structure. From where we hid, I discovered a *hole* in the wall with a view of the Martian pit!

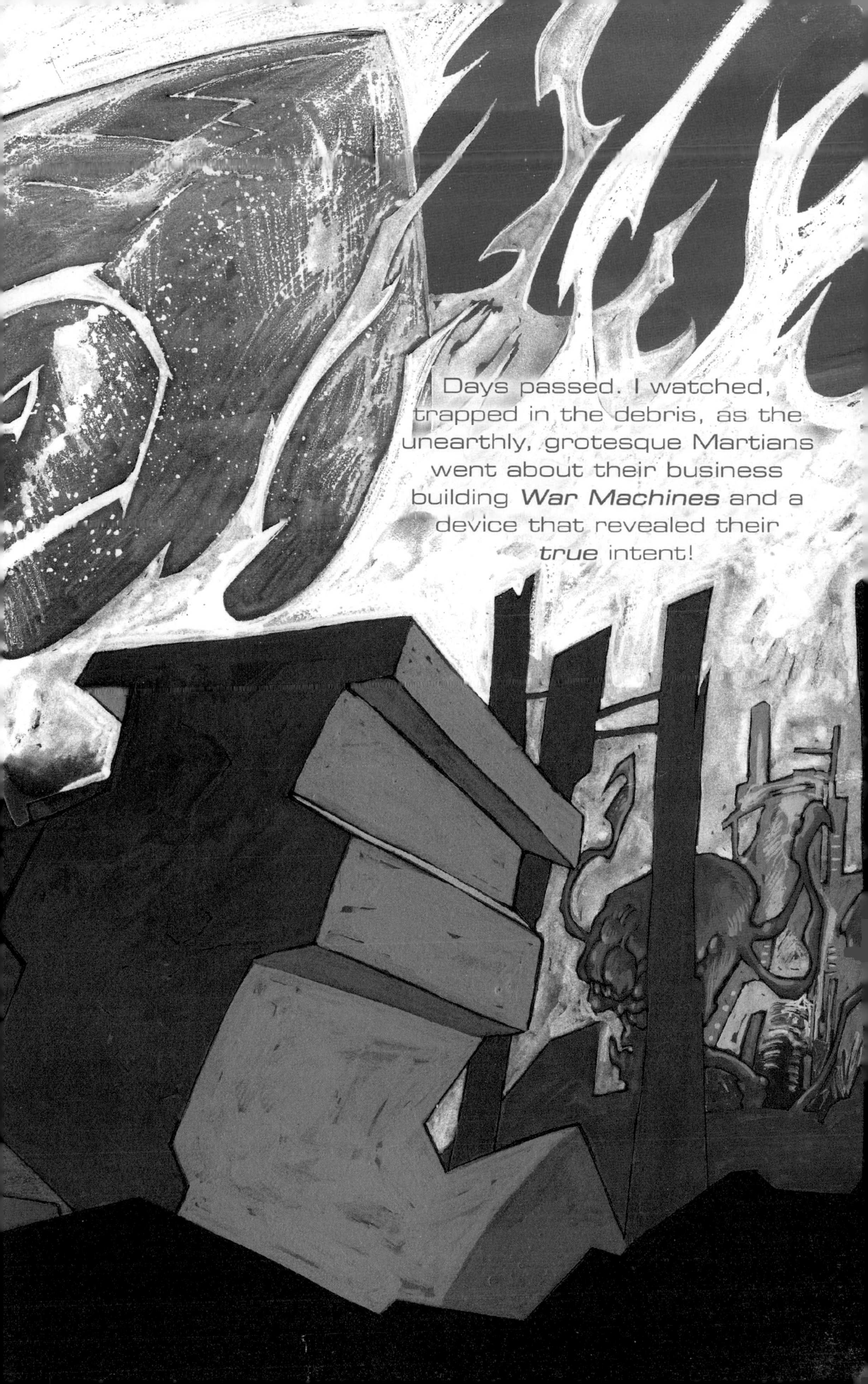
Days passed. I watched, trapped in the debris, as the unearthly, grotesque Martians went about their business building *War Machines* and a device that revealed their *true* intent!

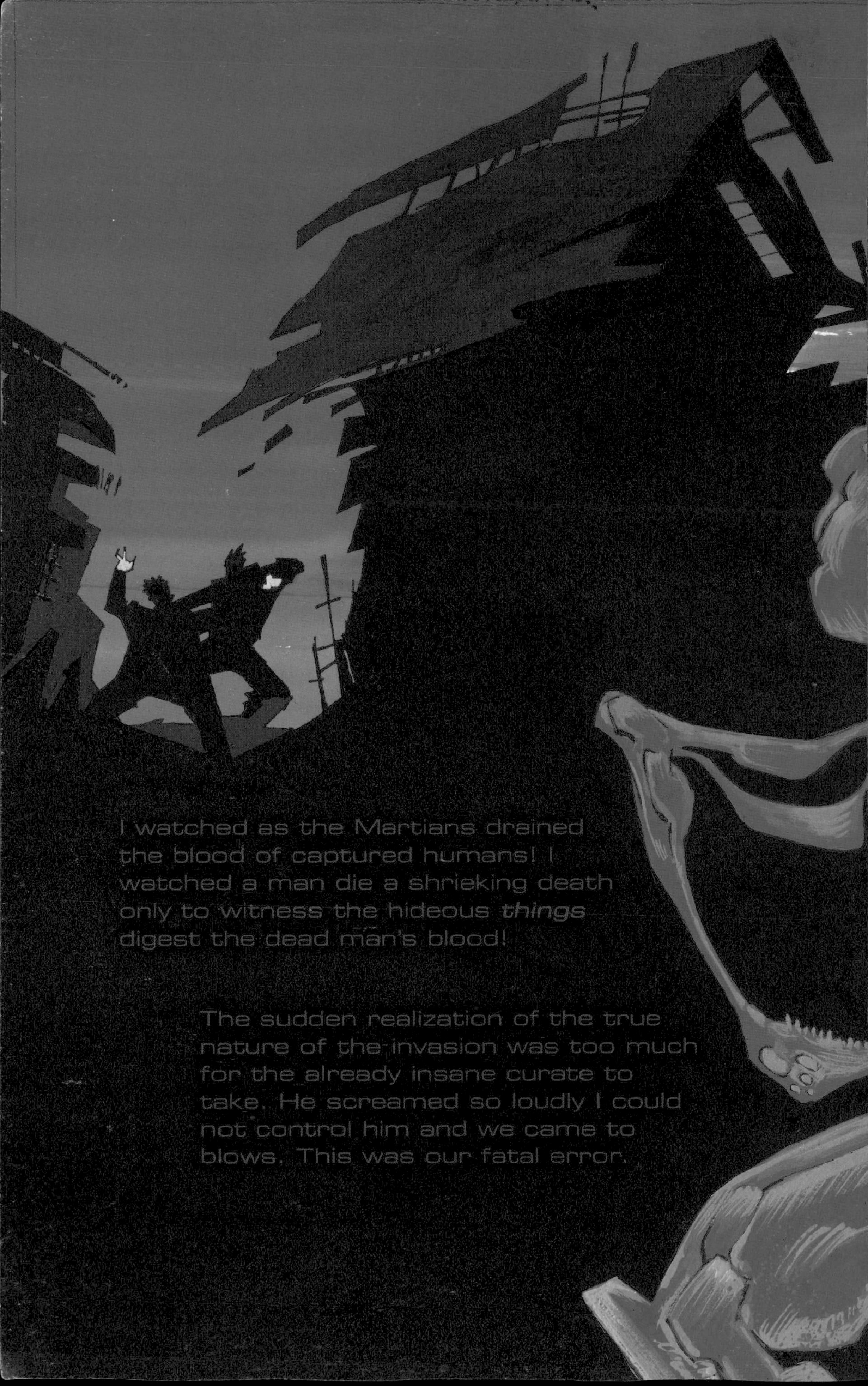
I watched as the Martians drained the blood of captured humans! I watched a man die a shrieking death only to witness the hideous *things* digest the dead man's blood!
The sudden realization of the true nature of the invasion was too much for the already insane curate to take. He screamed so loudly I could not control him and we came to blows. This was our fatal error.

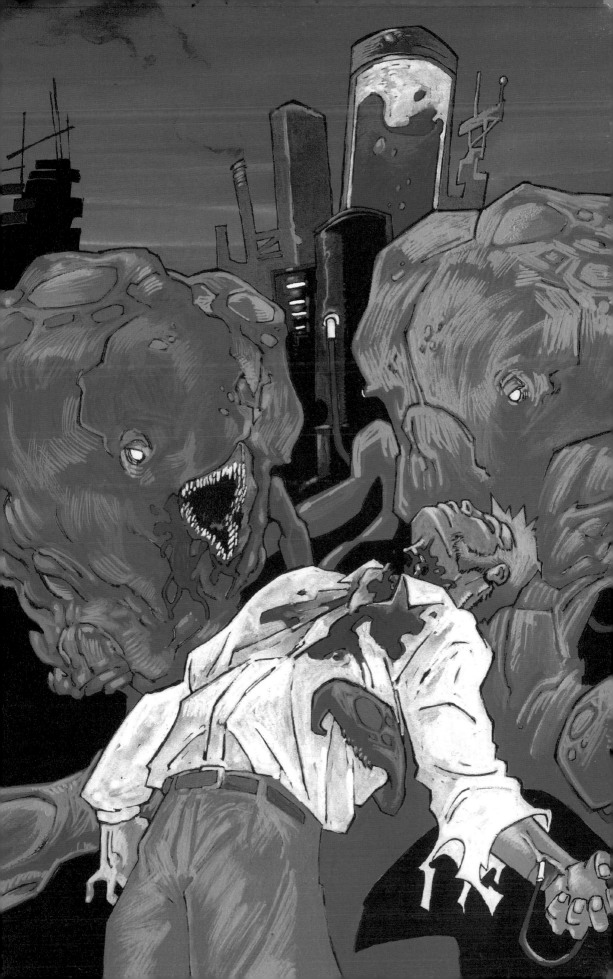

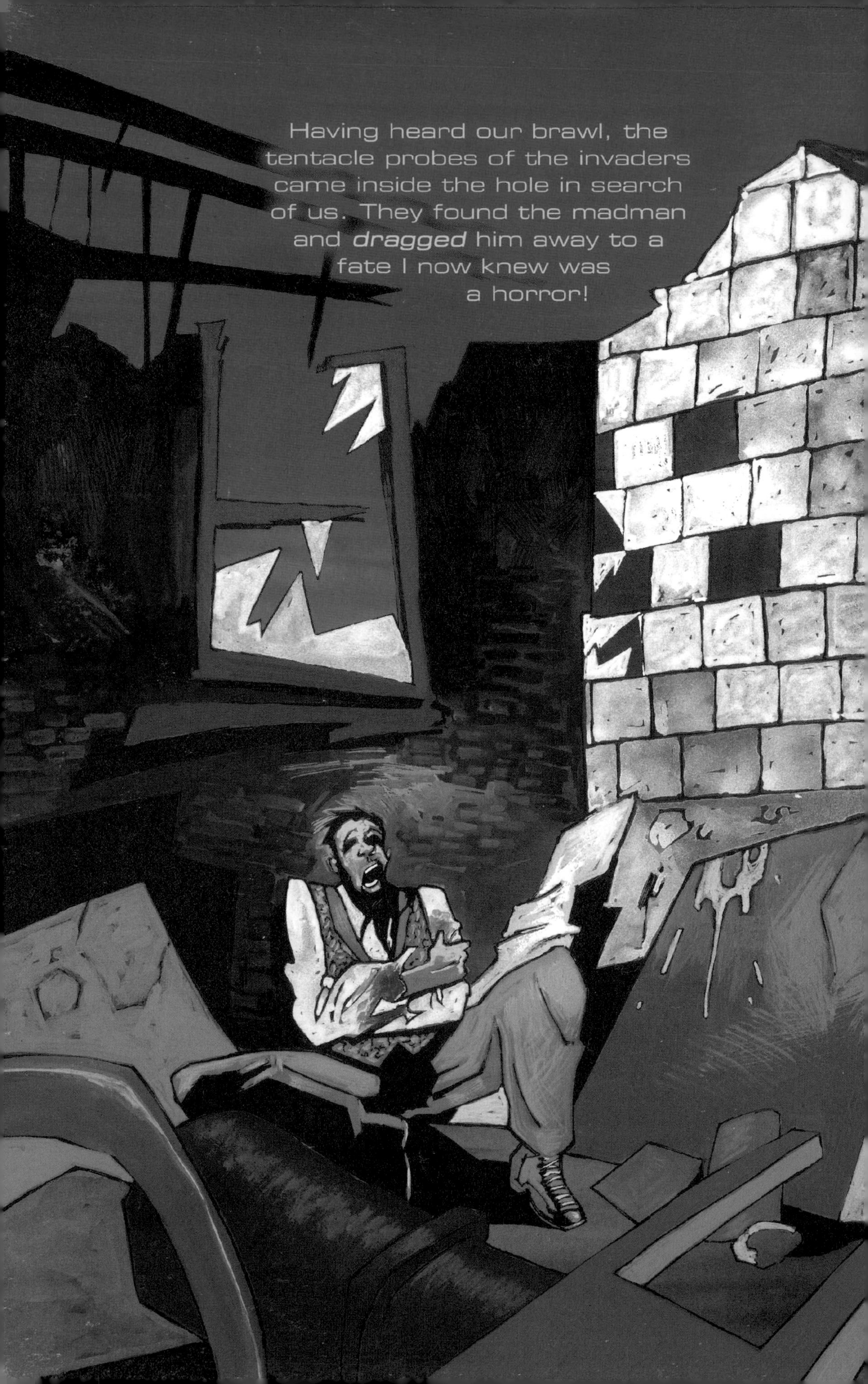
Having heard our brawl, the tentacle probes of the invaders came inside the hole in search of us. They found the madman and *dragged* him away to a fate I now knew was a horror!

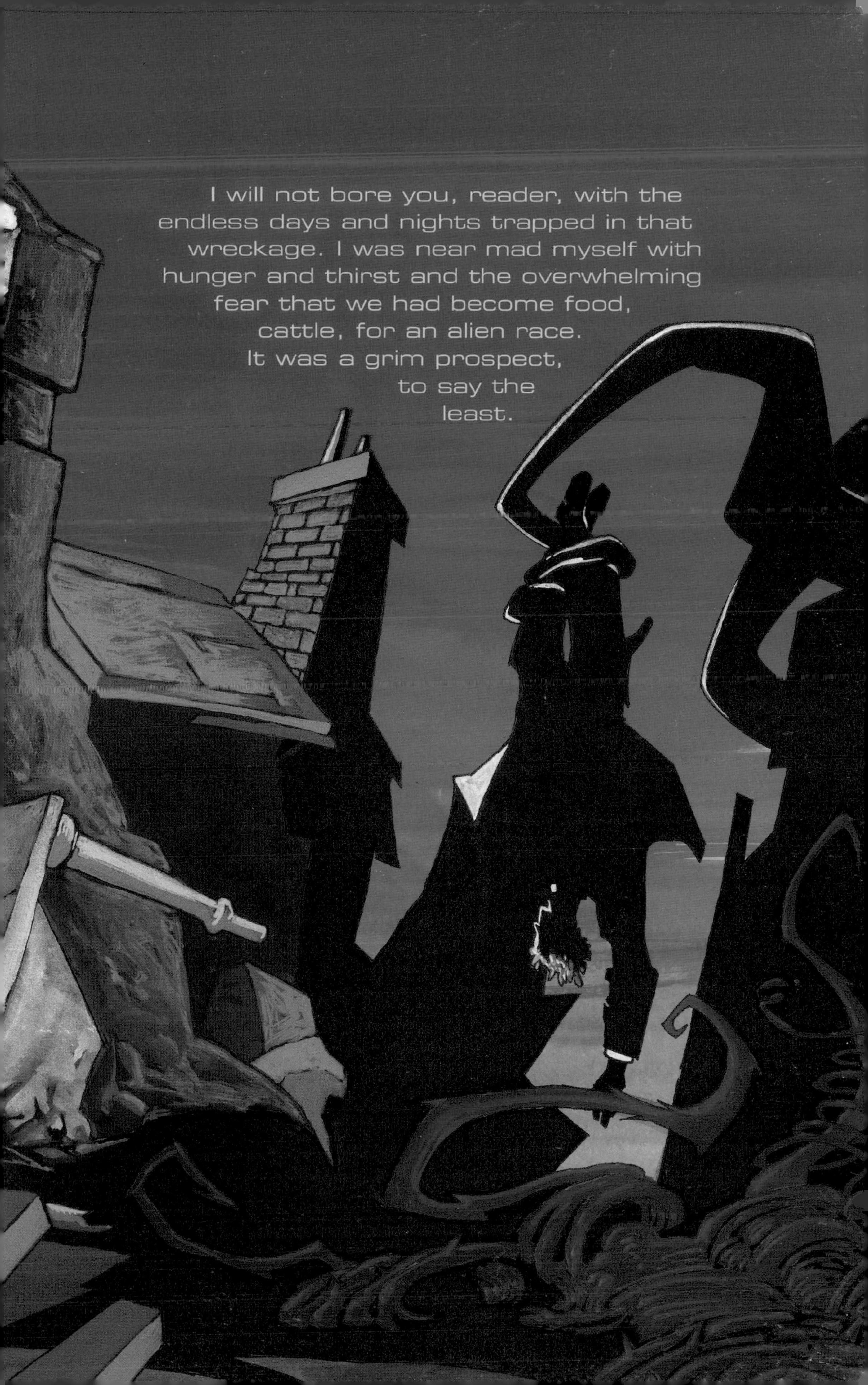
I will not bore you, reader, with the endless days and nights trapped in that wreckage. I was near mad myself with hunger and thirst and the overwhelming fear that we had become food, cattle, for an alien race. It was a grim prospect, to say the least.

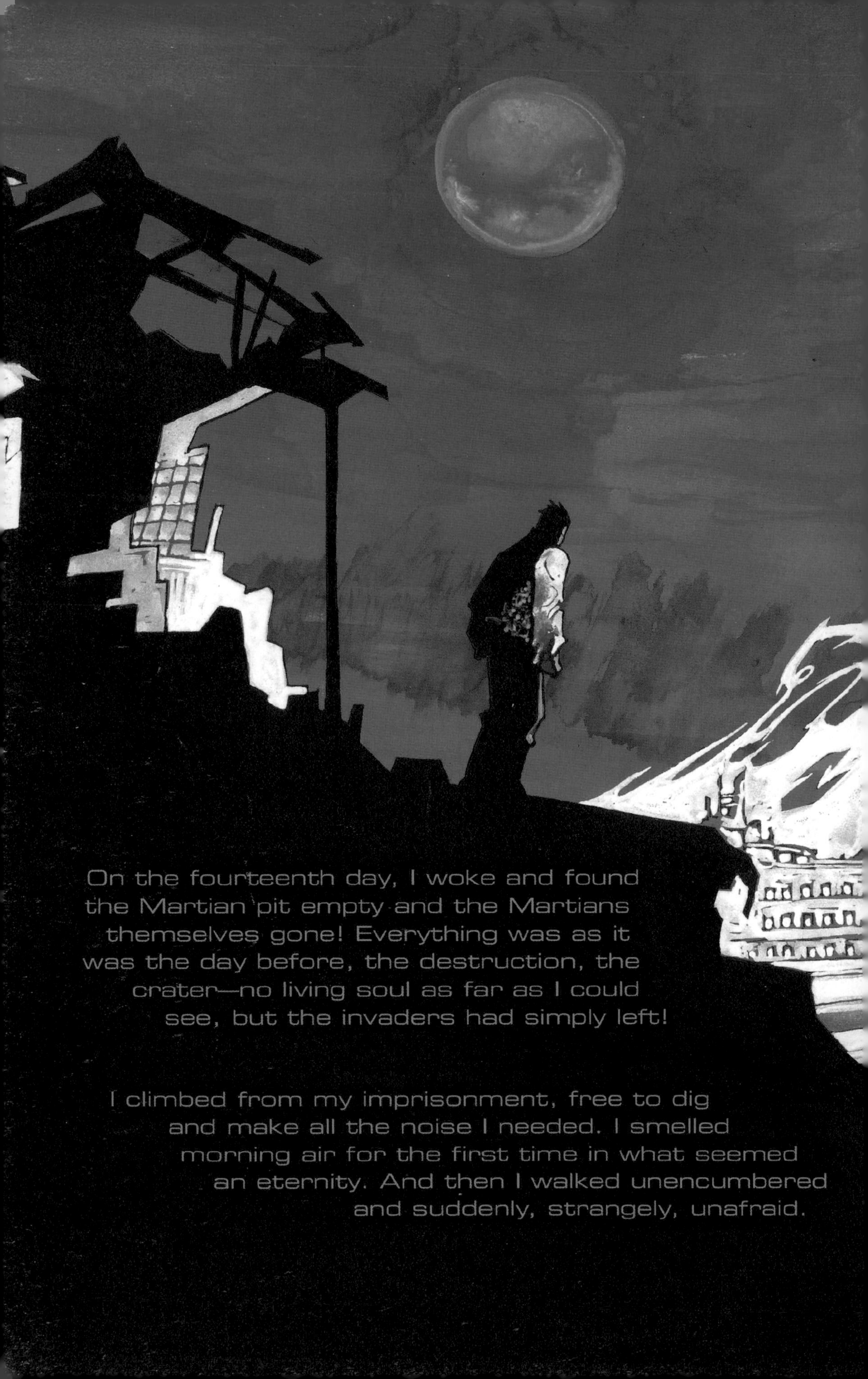
On the fourteenth day, I woke and found the Martian pit empty and the Martians themselves gone! Everything was as it was the day before, the destruction, the crater—no living soul as far as I could see, but the invaders had simply left!
I climbed from my imprisonment, free to dig and make all the noise I needed. I smelled morning air for the first time in what seemed an eternity. And then I walked unencumbered and suddenly, strangely, unafraid.

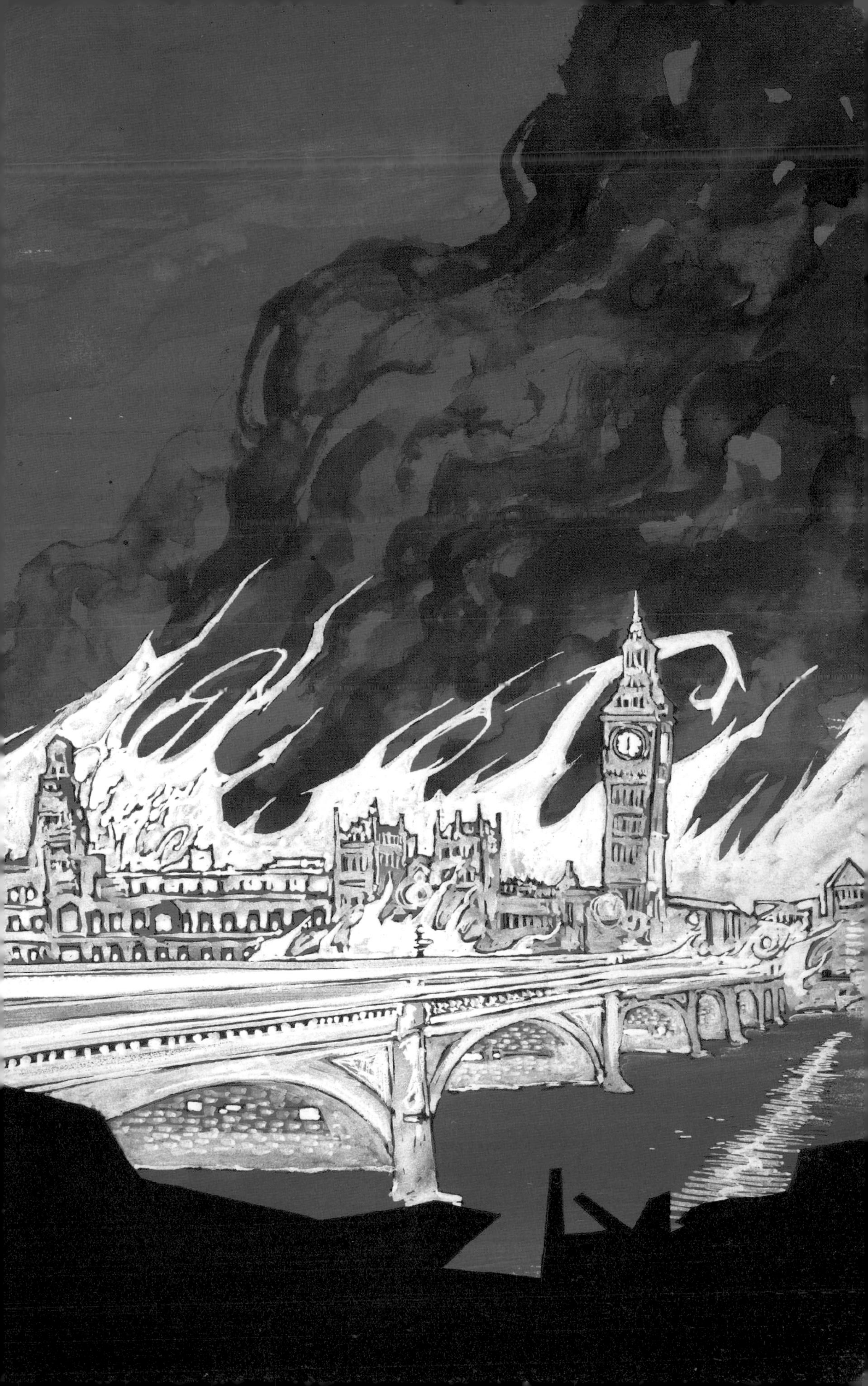

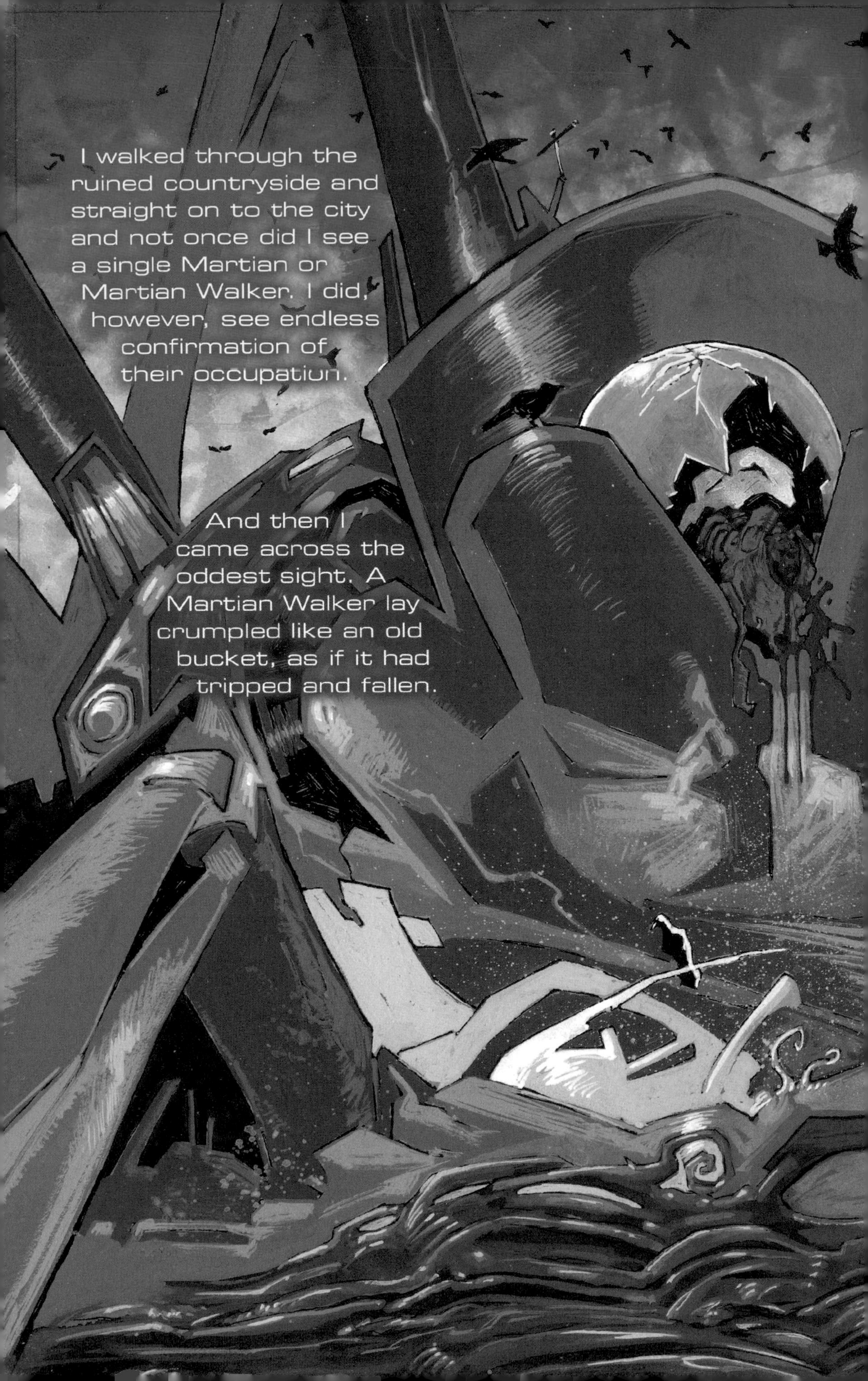
I walked through the ruined countryside and straight on to the city and not once did I see a single Martian or Martian Walker. I did, however, see endless confirmation of their occupation.
And then I came across the oddest sight. A Martian Walker lay crumpled like an old bucket, as if it had tripped and fallen.

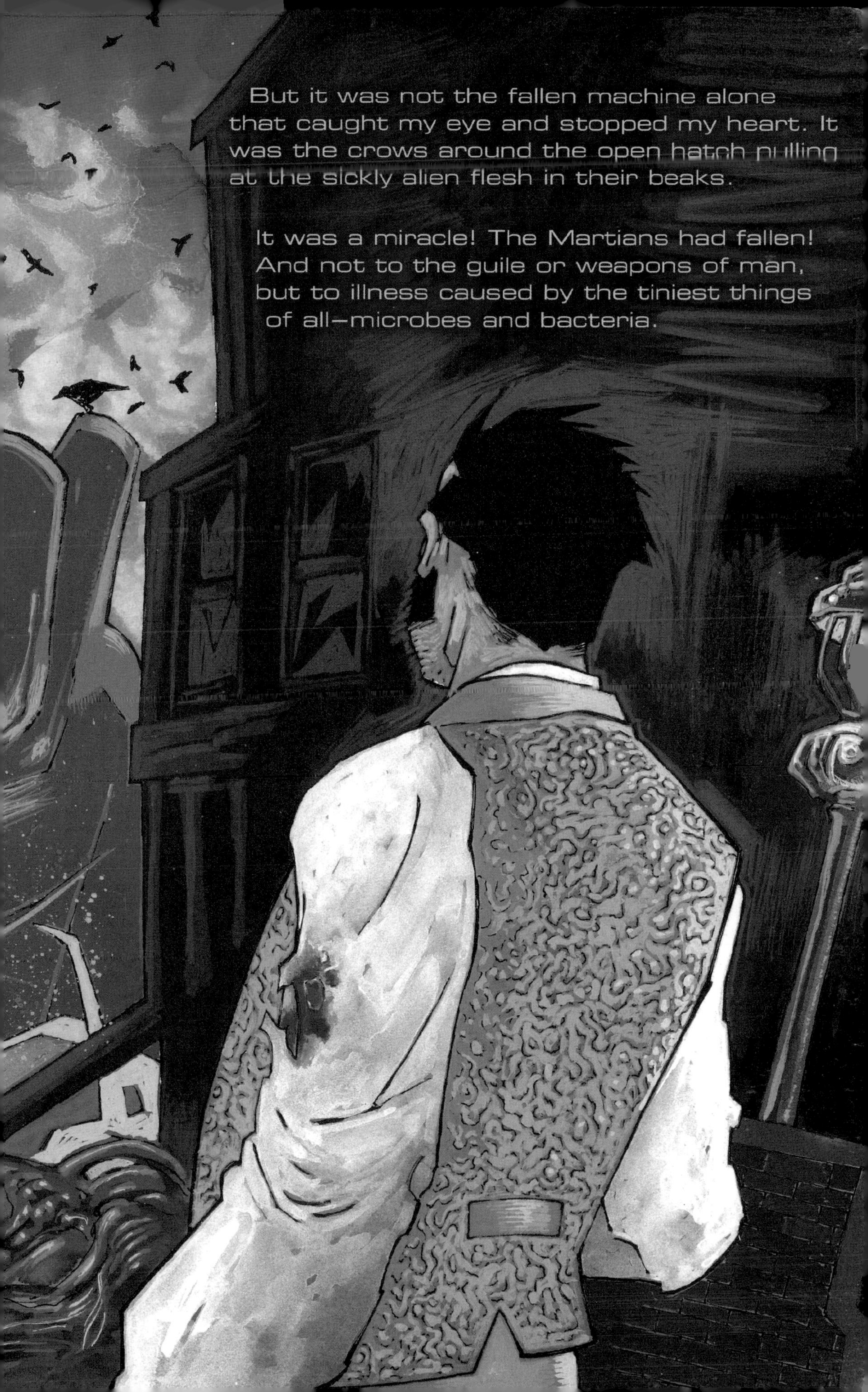
But it was not the fallen machine alone that caught my eye and stopped my heart. It was the crows around the open hatch pulling at the sickly alien flesh in their beaks.
It was a miracle! The Martians had fallen! And not to the guile or weapons of man, but to illness caused by the tiniest things of all—microbes and bacteria.

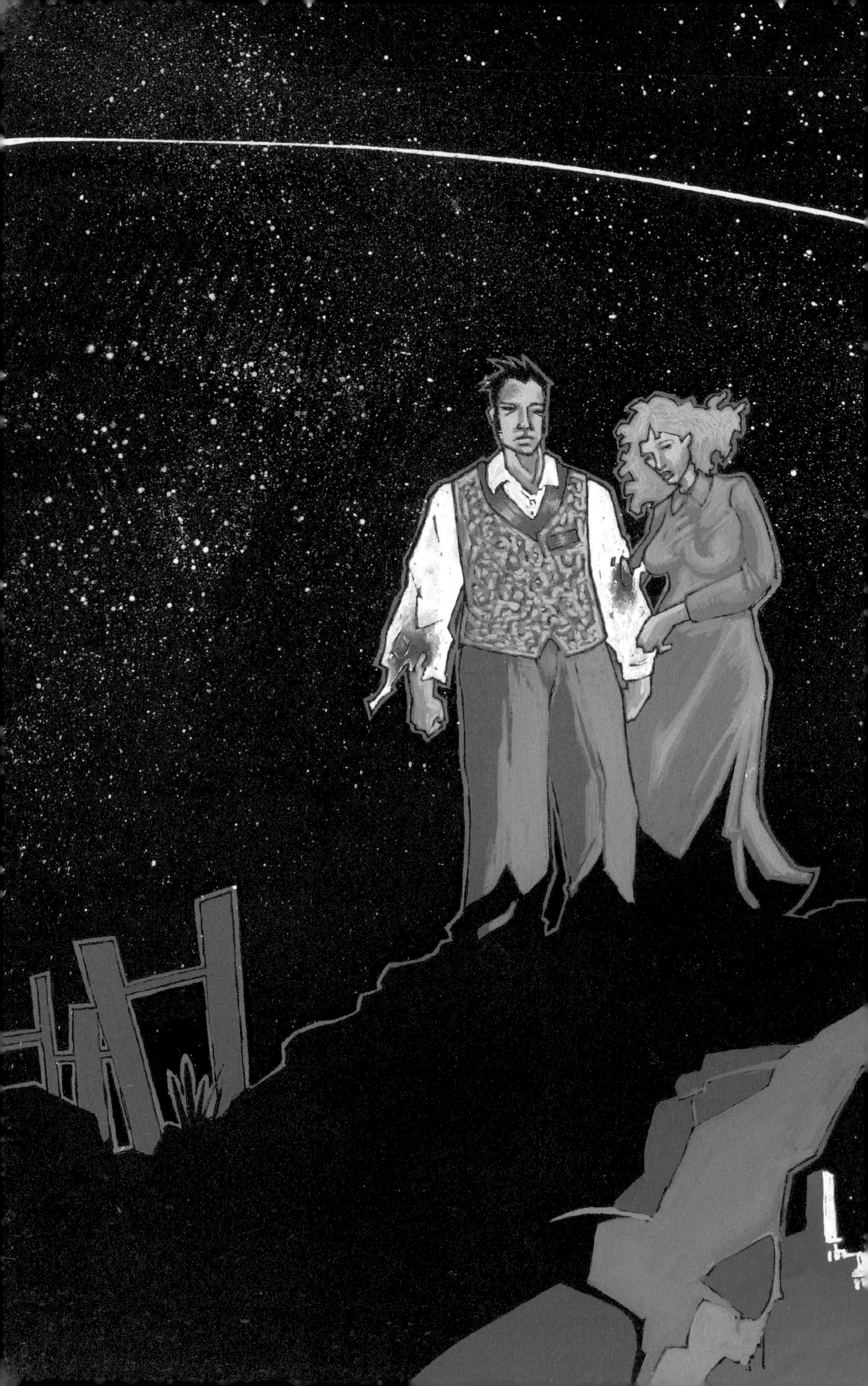

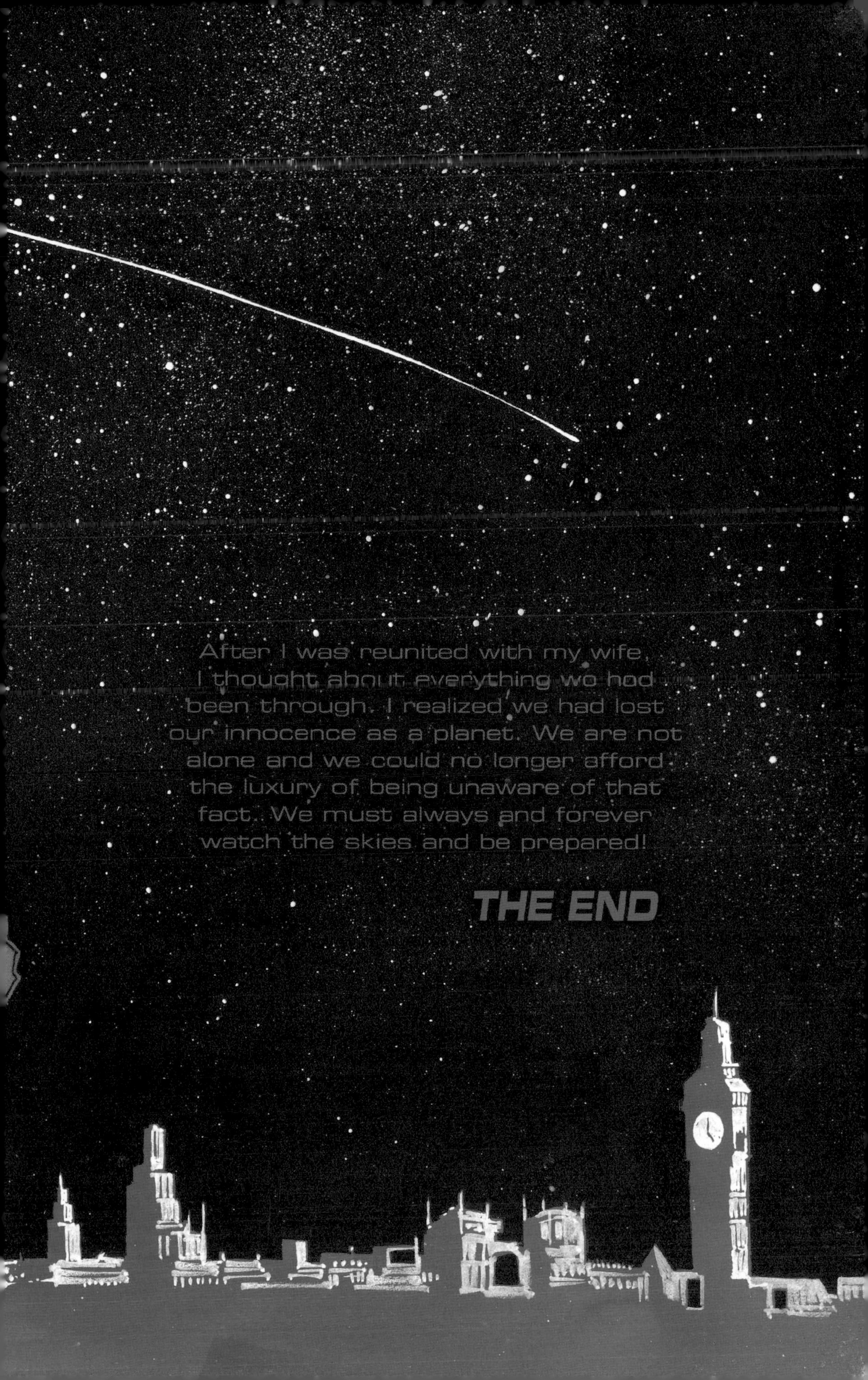
After I was reunited with my wife, I thought about everything we had been through. I realized we had lost our innocence as a planet. We are not alone and we could no longer afford the luxury of being unaware of that fact. We must always and forever watch the skies and be prepared!
THE END

LITTLE BOOK OF HORROR™
DRACULA

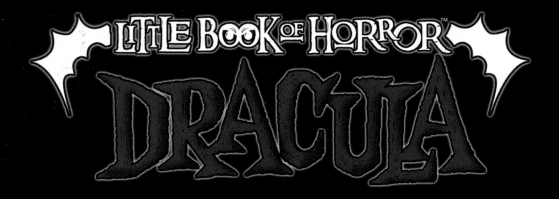

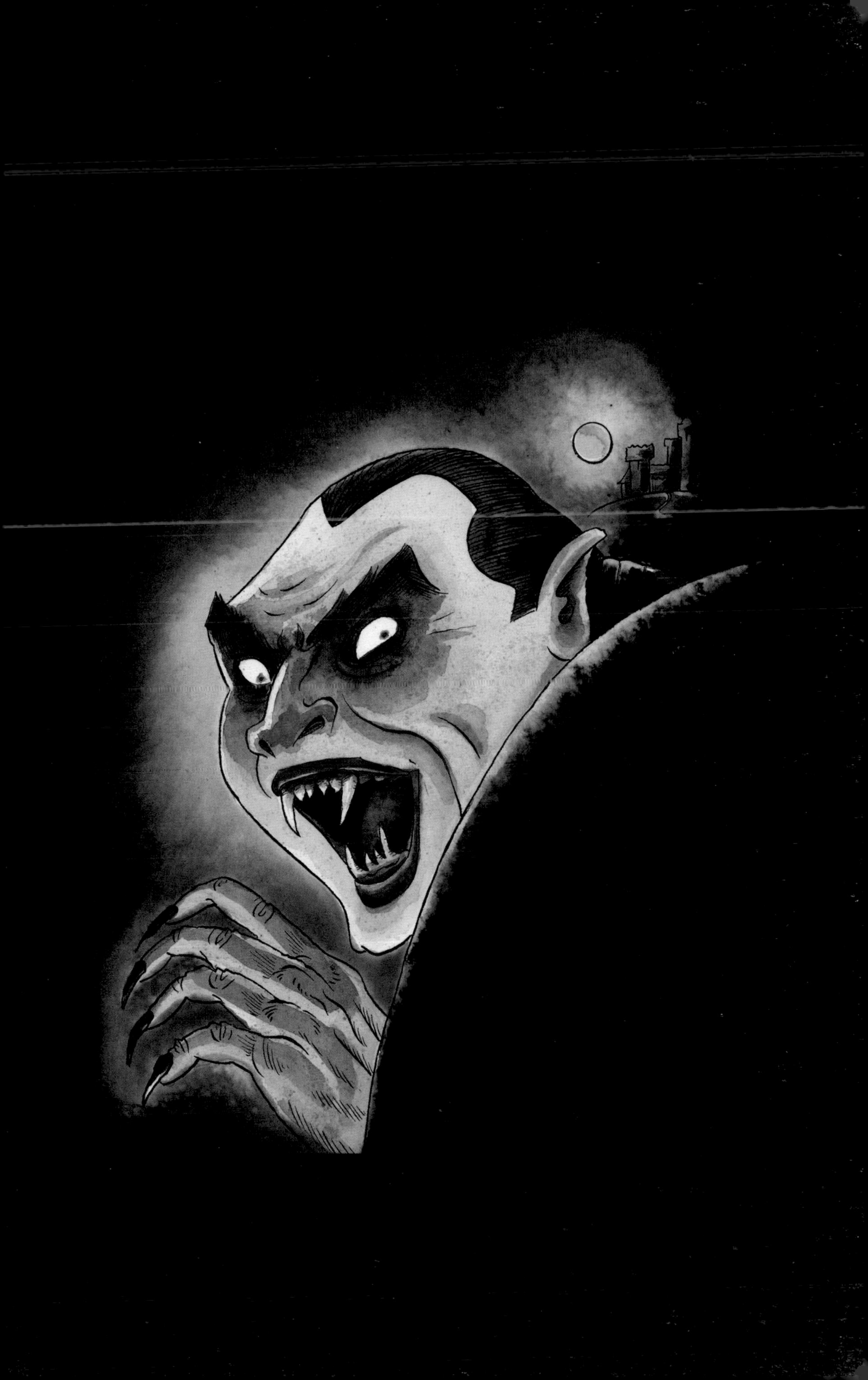

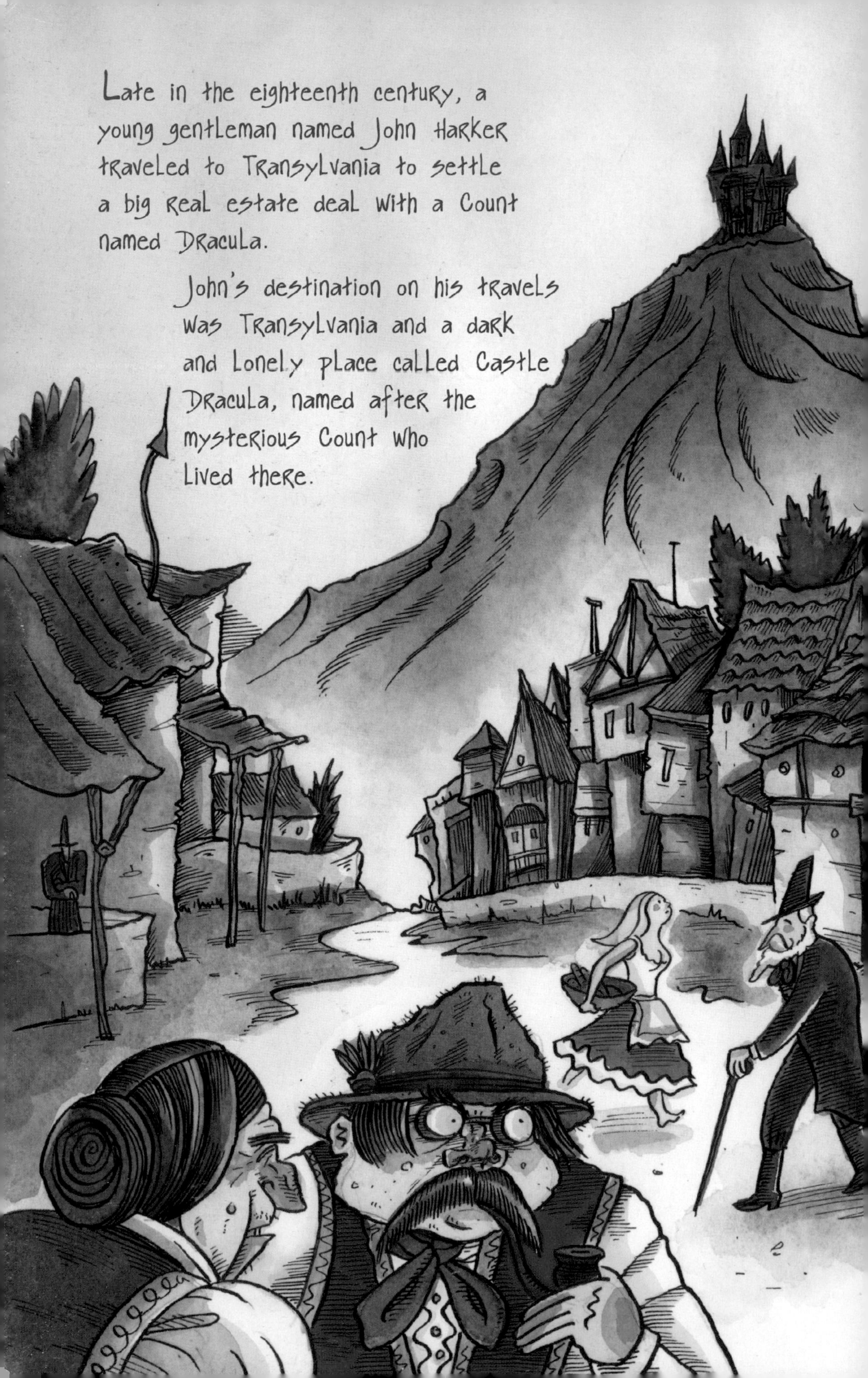
Late in the eighteenth century, a young gentleman named John Harker traveled to Transylvania to settle a big real estate deal with a Count named Dracula.
John's destination on his travels was Transylvania and a dark and lonely place called Castle Dracula, named after the mysterious Count who lived there.

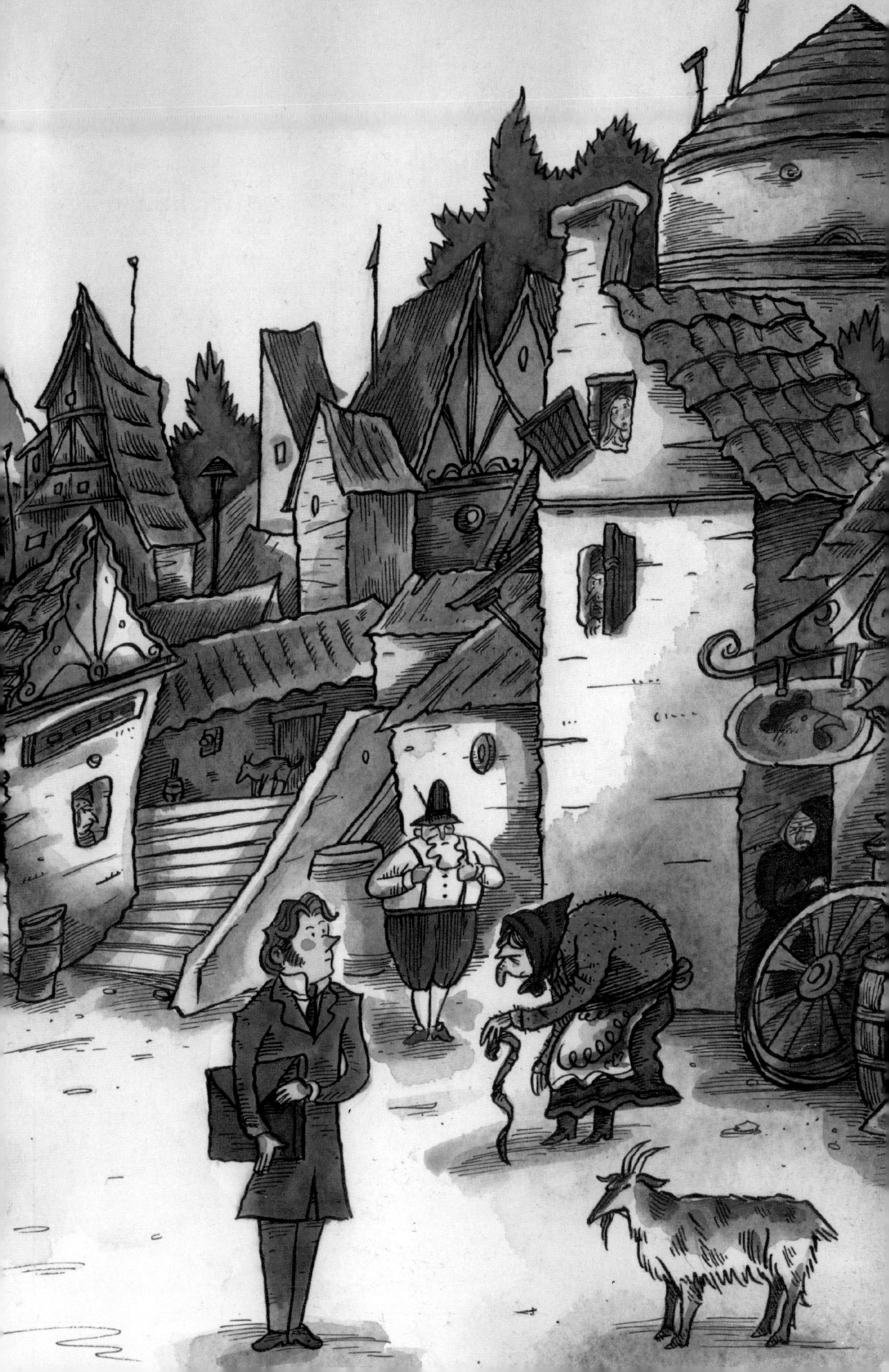

John stopped in a local village for food and directions. The villagers screamed and fainted when John told them his final destination. The villagers told John to stay away from the castle, That the castle was a bad place and no one who ever went there ever returned.

The villagers' warning made John nervous, but he stood to make a great deal of hard cash, so he ignored them and went on to Castle Dracula.

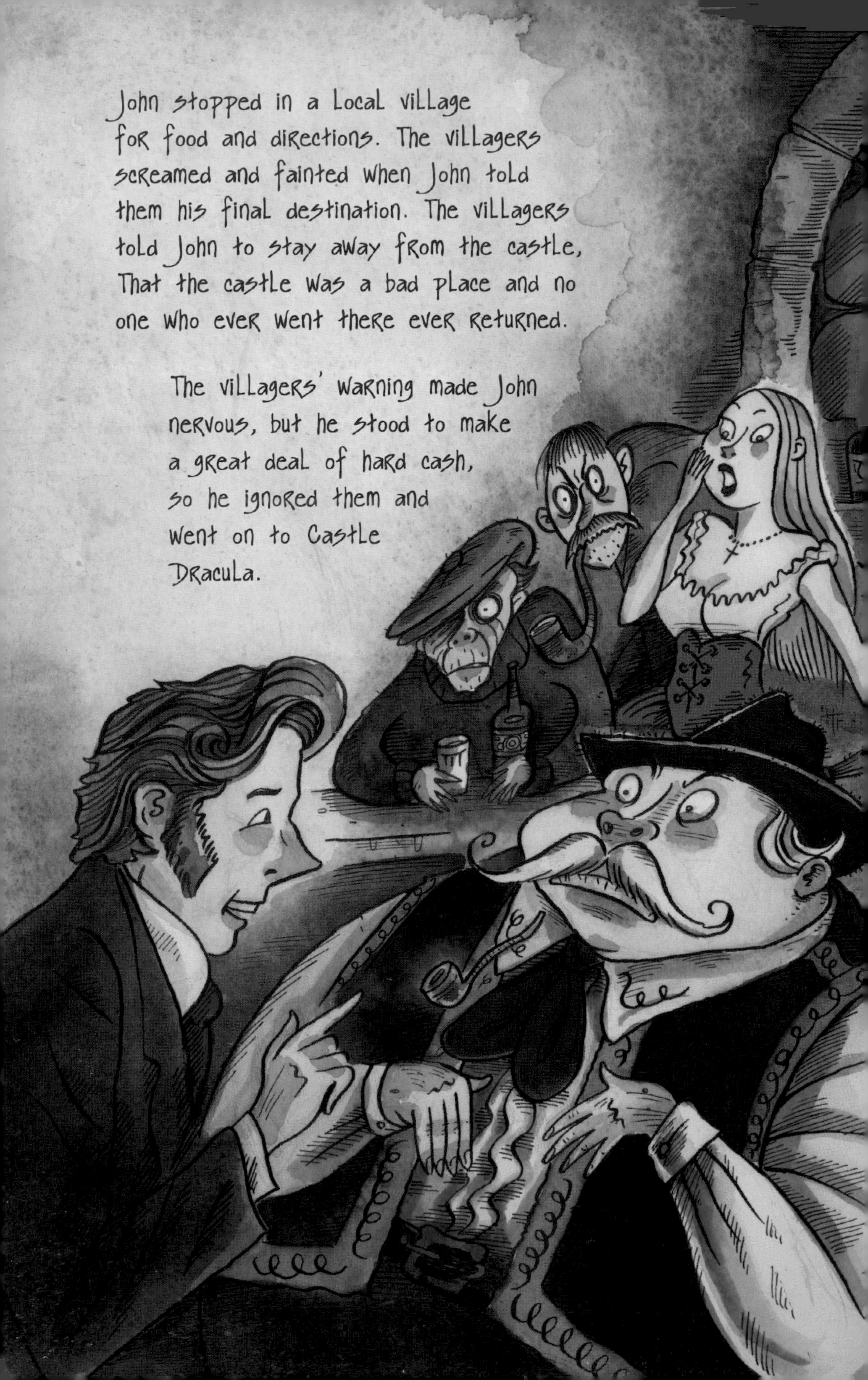

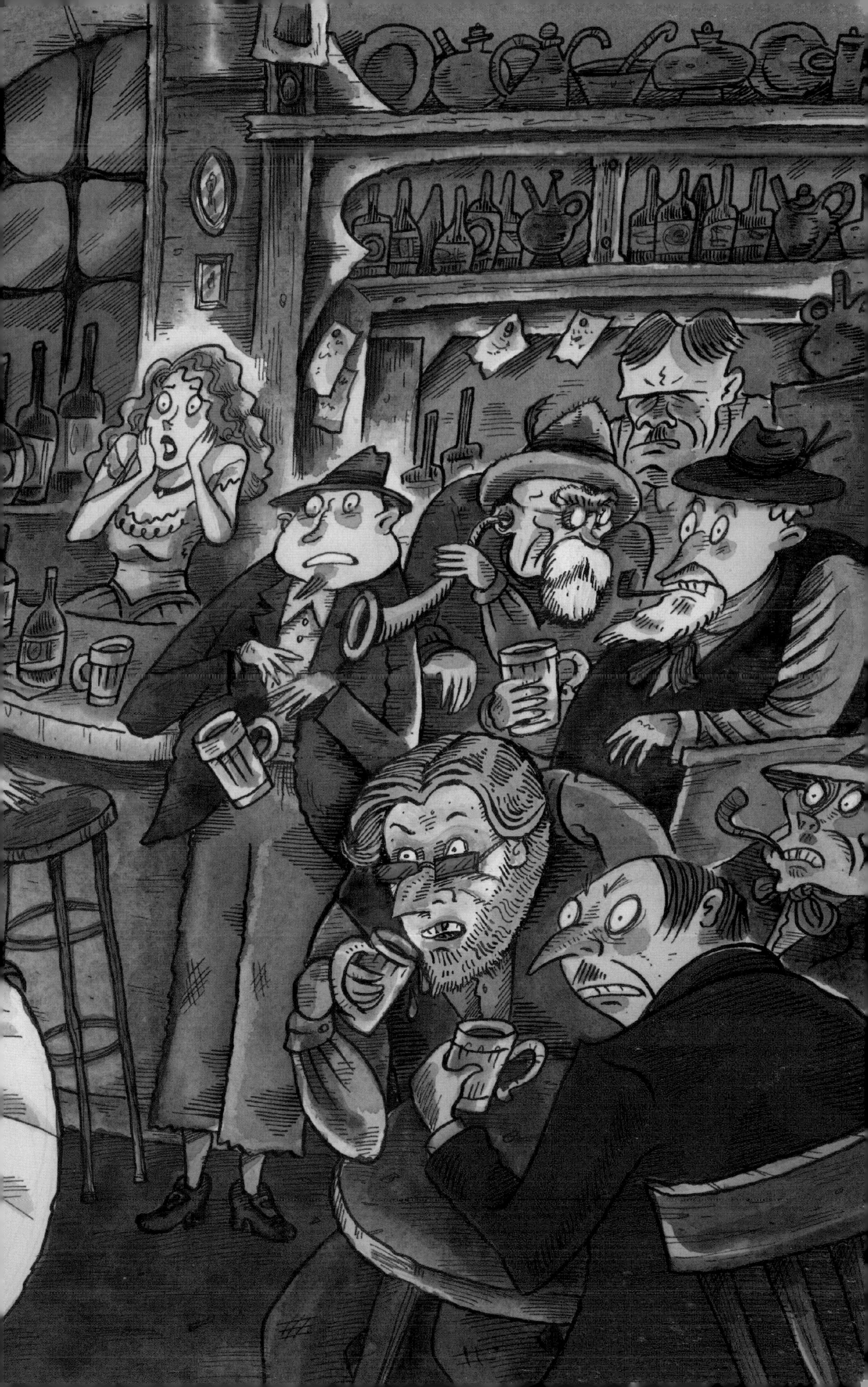

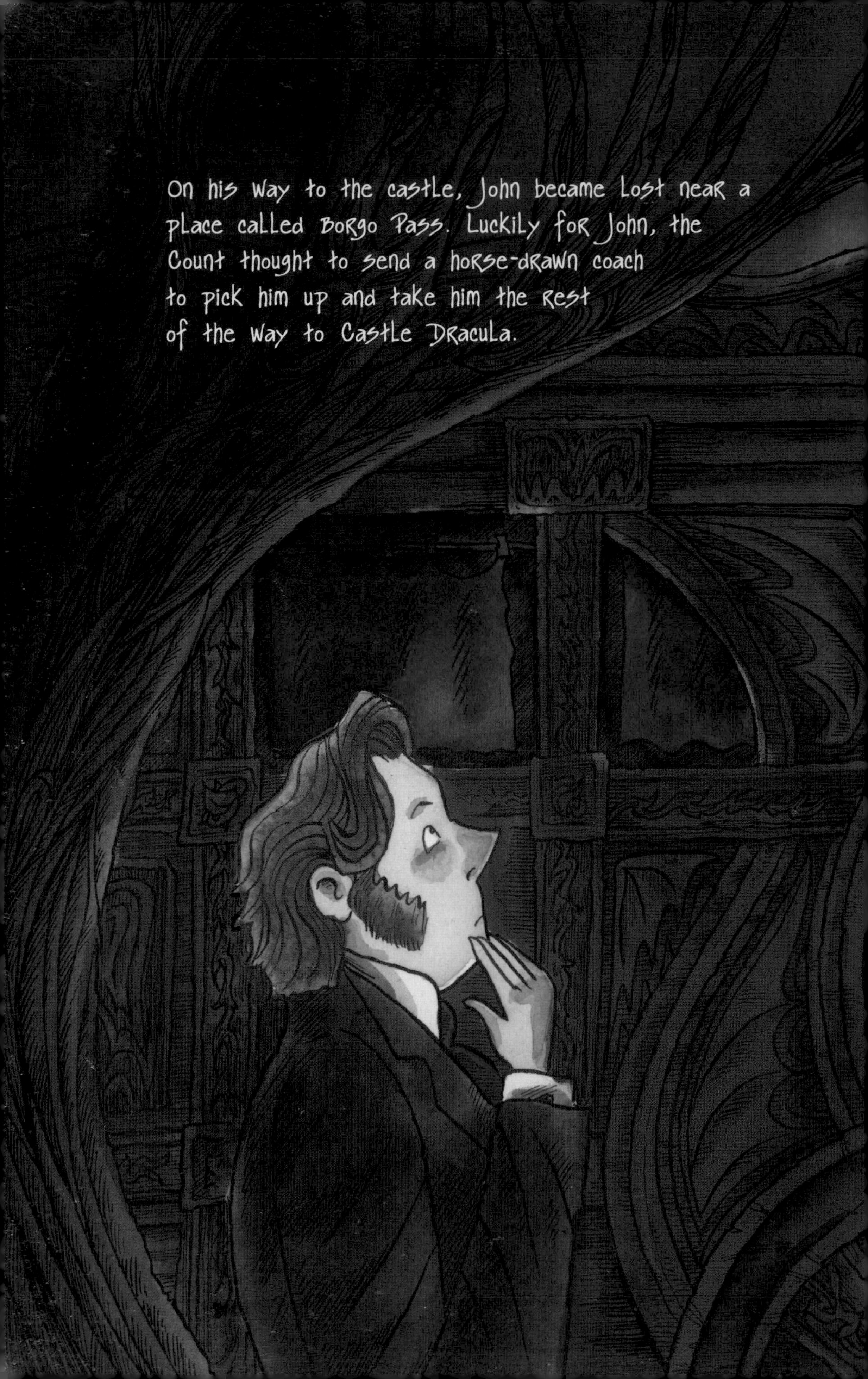
On his way to the castle, John became lost near a place called Borgo Pass. Luckily for John, the Count thought to send a horse-drawn coach to pick him up and take him the rest of the way to Castle Dracula.

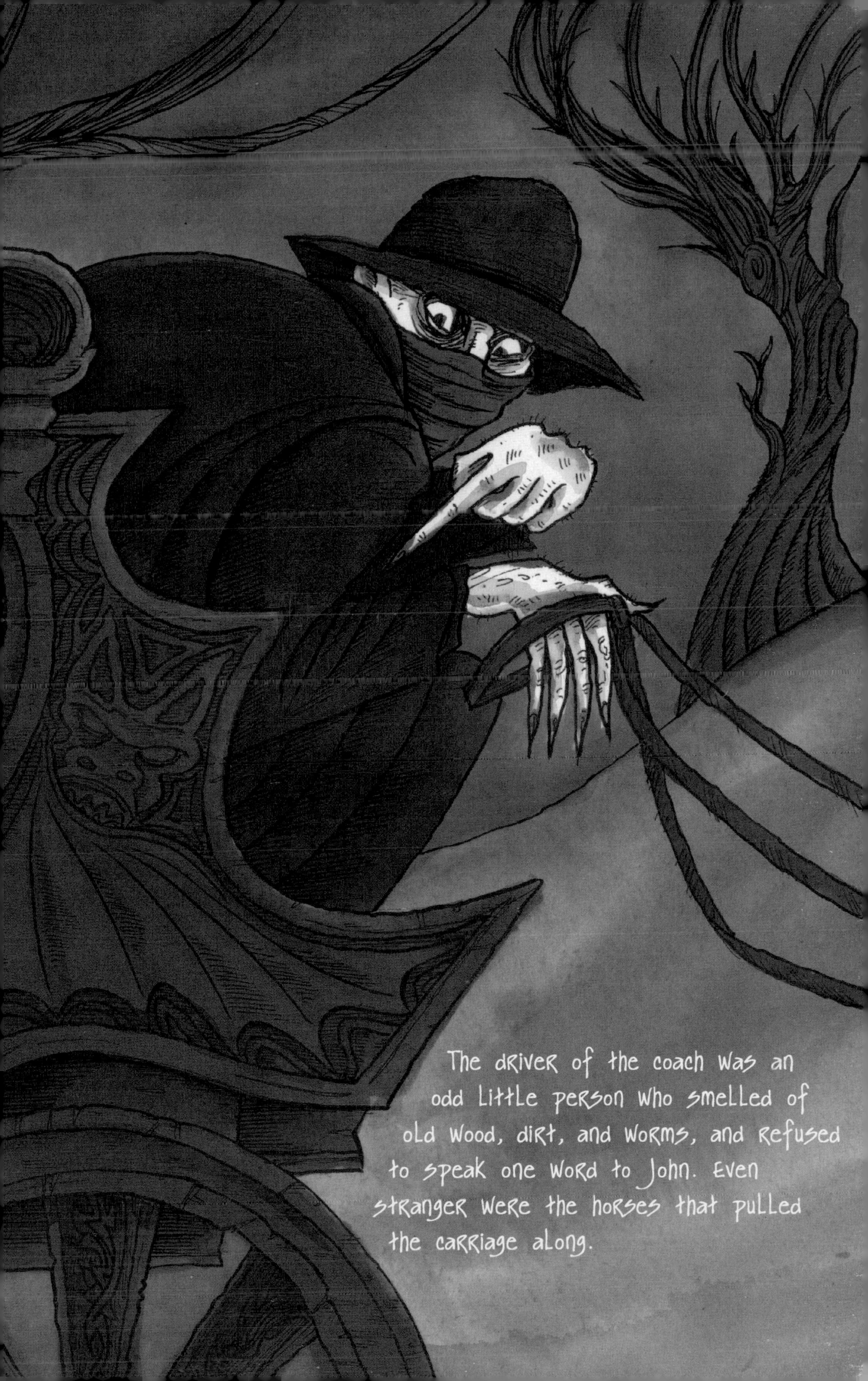
The driver of the coach was an odd little person who smelled of old wood, dirt, and worms, and refused to speak one word to John. Even stranger were the horses that pulled the carriage along.

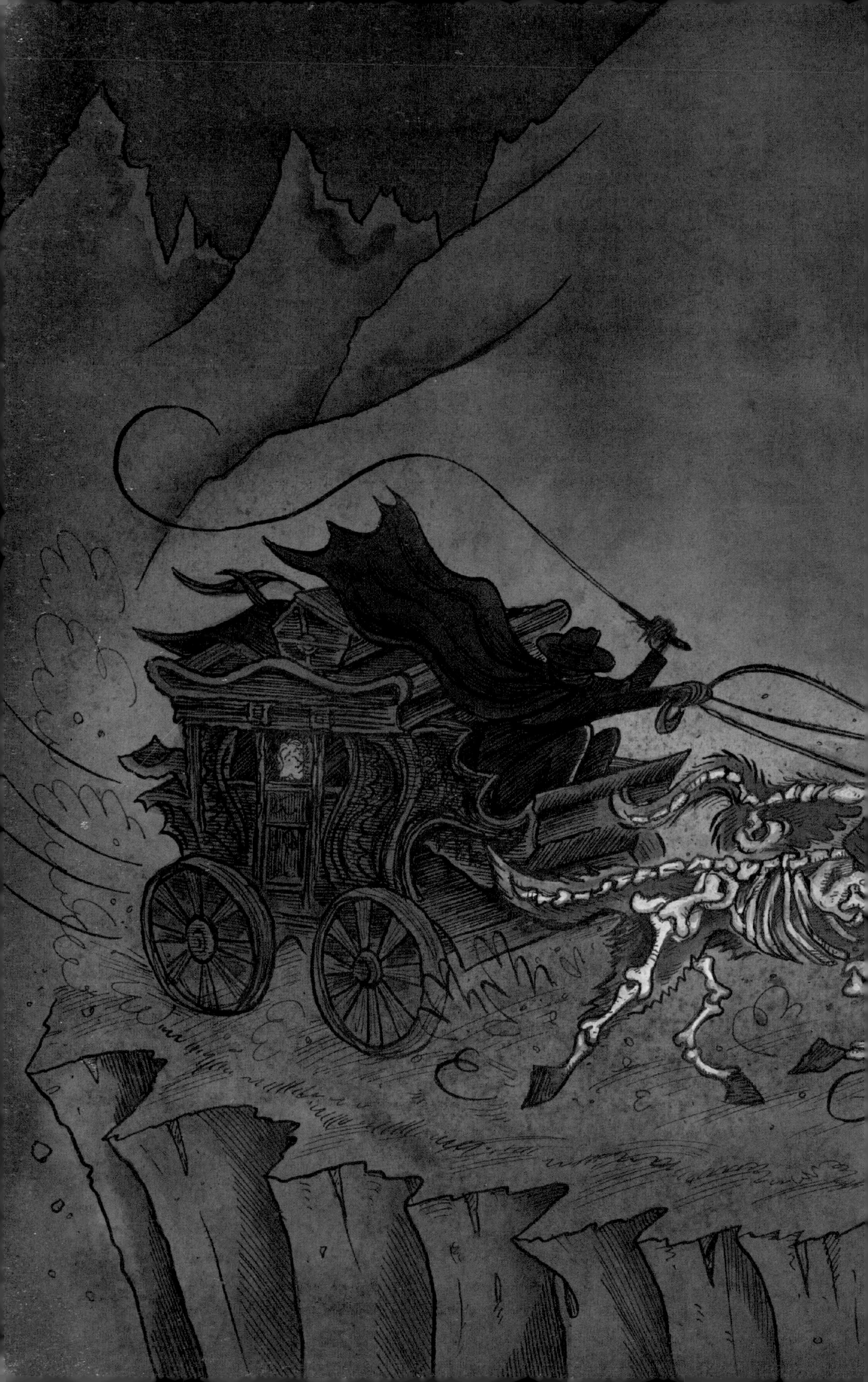

If John were not a human being of sound mind and common sense, he would have said the horses were skeletons. John told himself that the horses must be a rare breed found only in Transylvania. A hairless, skinless, no-organ breed of horse.

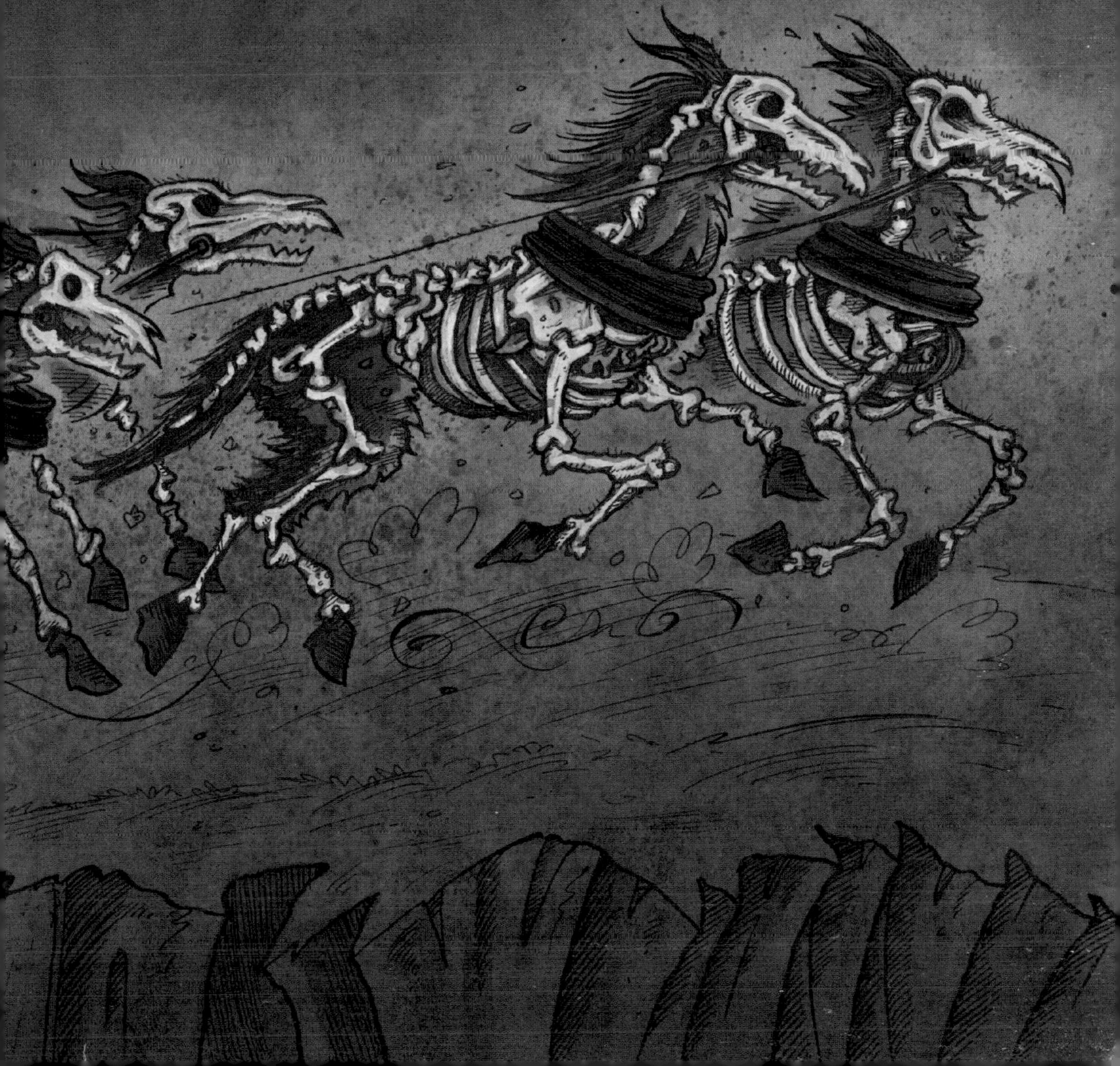

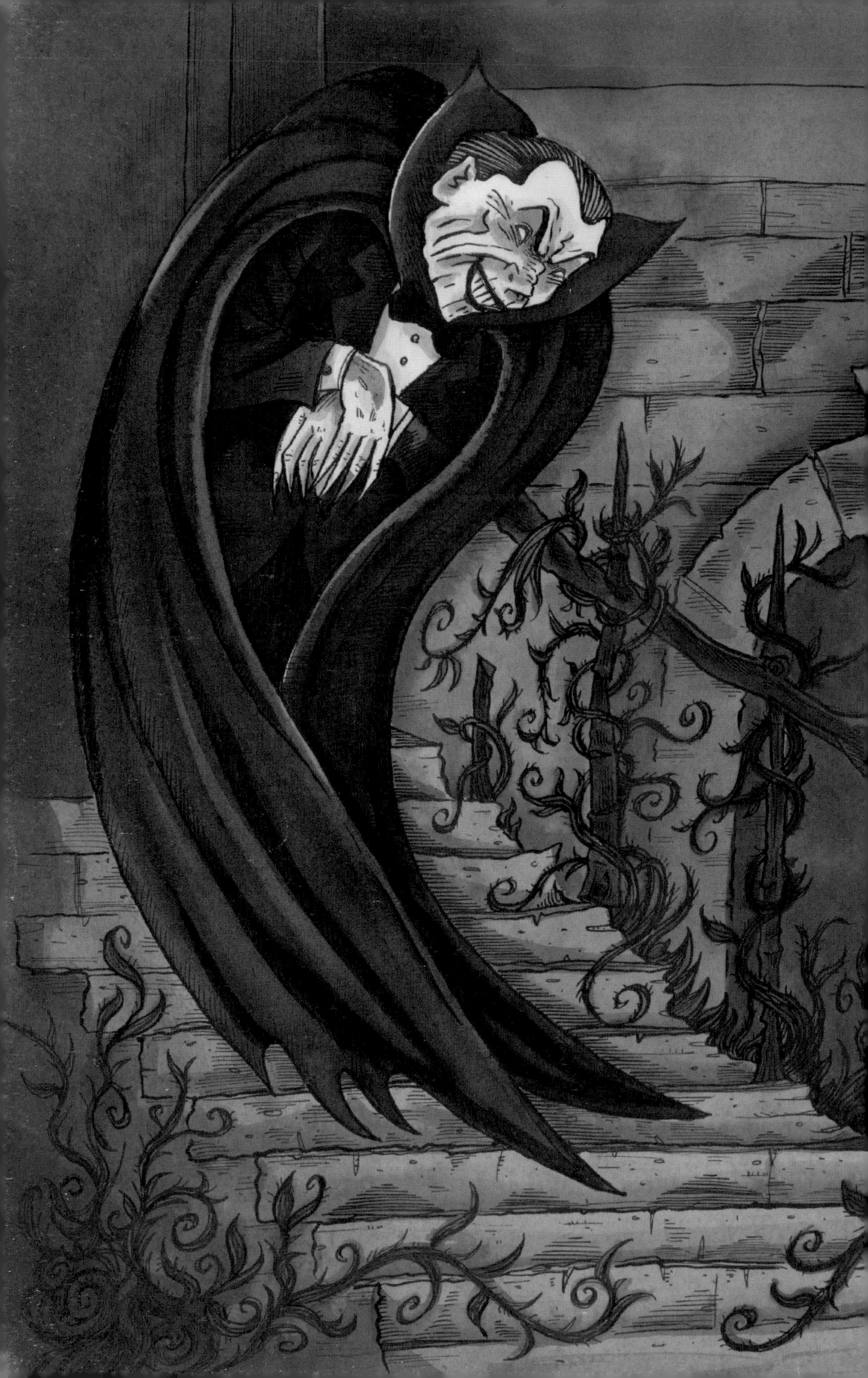

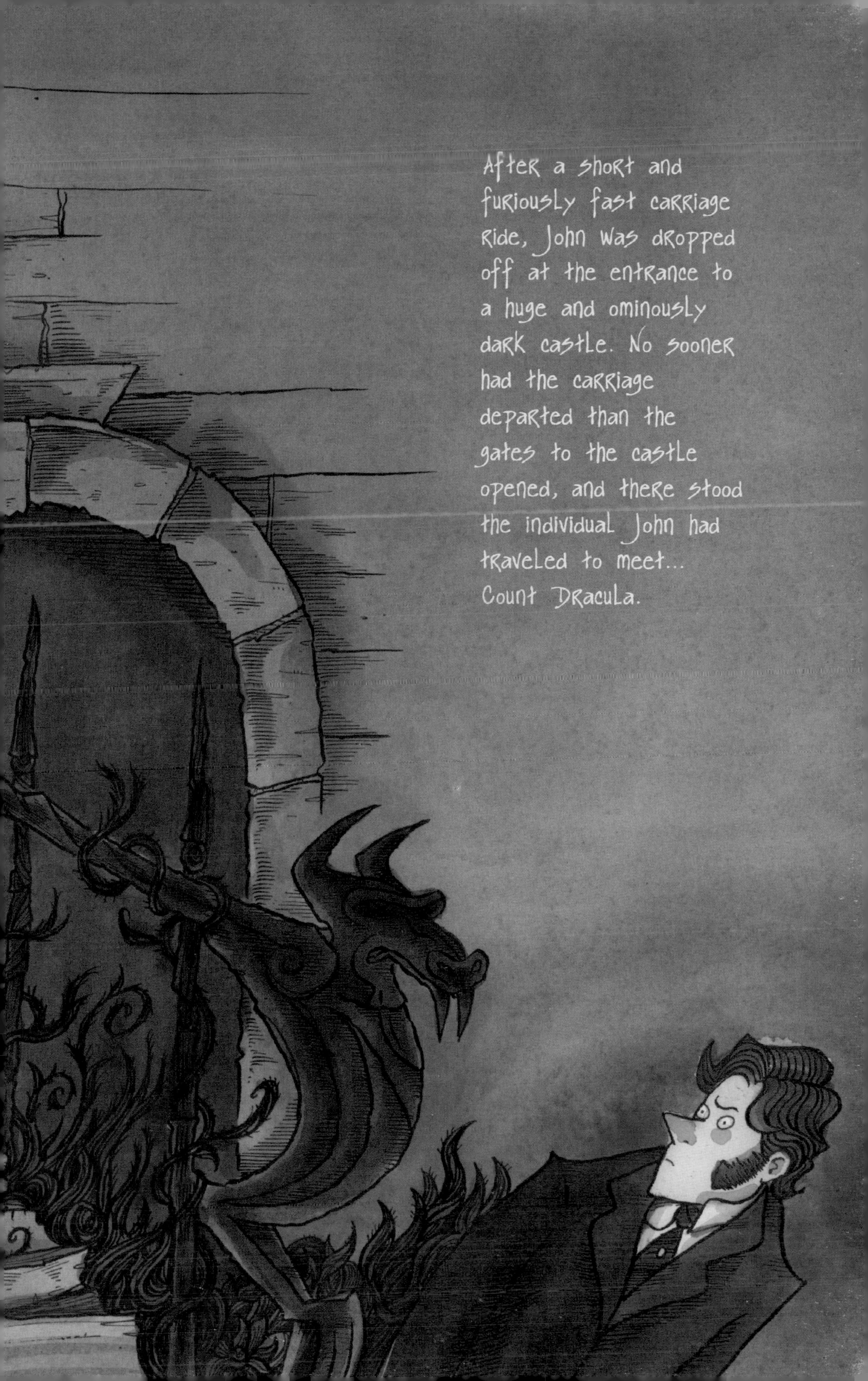
After a short and furiously fast carriage ride, John was dropped off at the entrance to a huge and ominously dark castle. No sooner had the carriage departed than the gates to the castle opened, and there stood the individual John had traveled to meet...
Count Dracula.

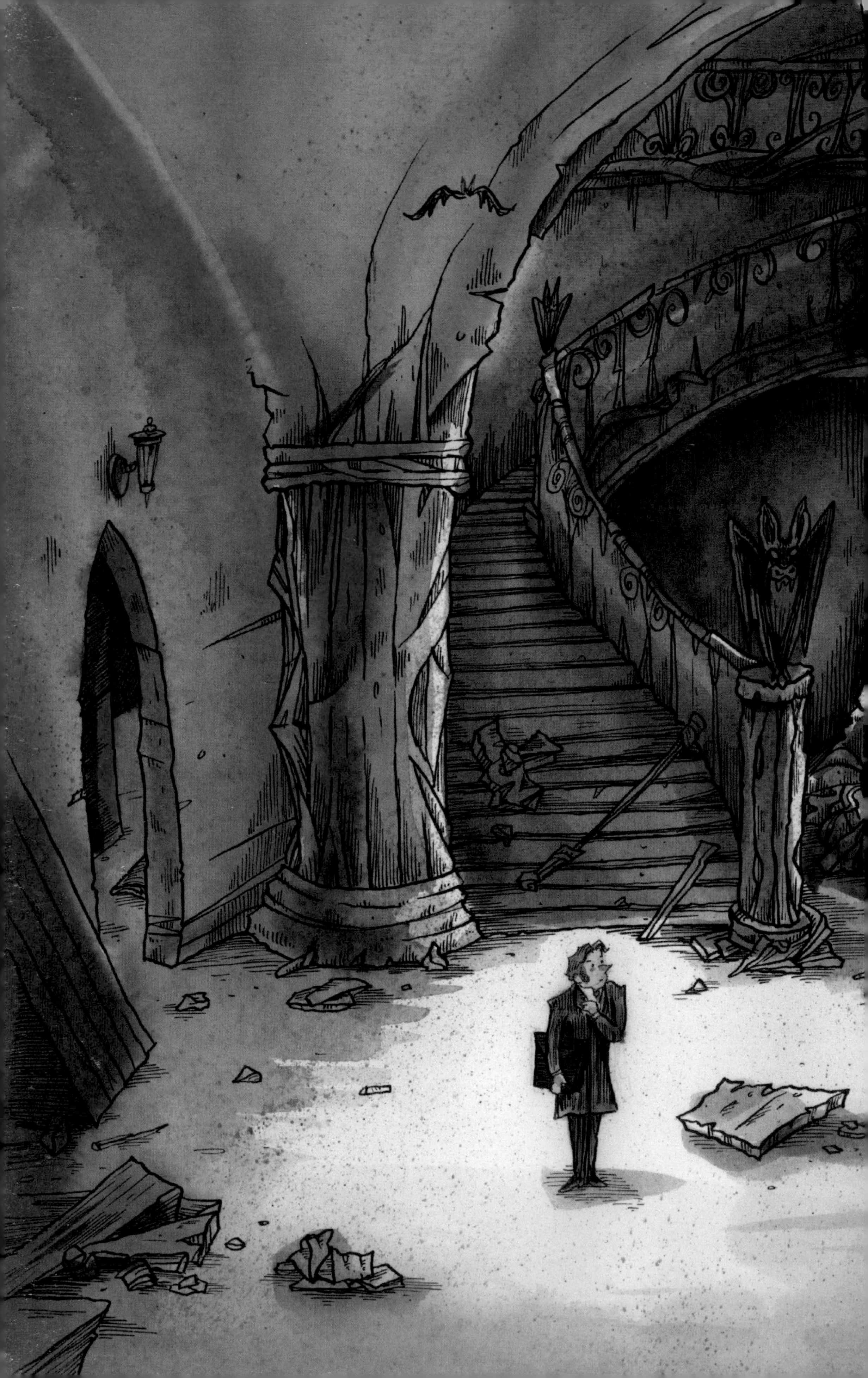

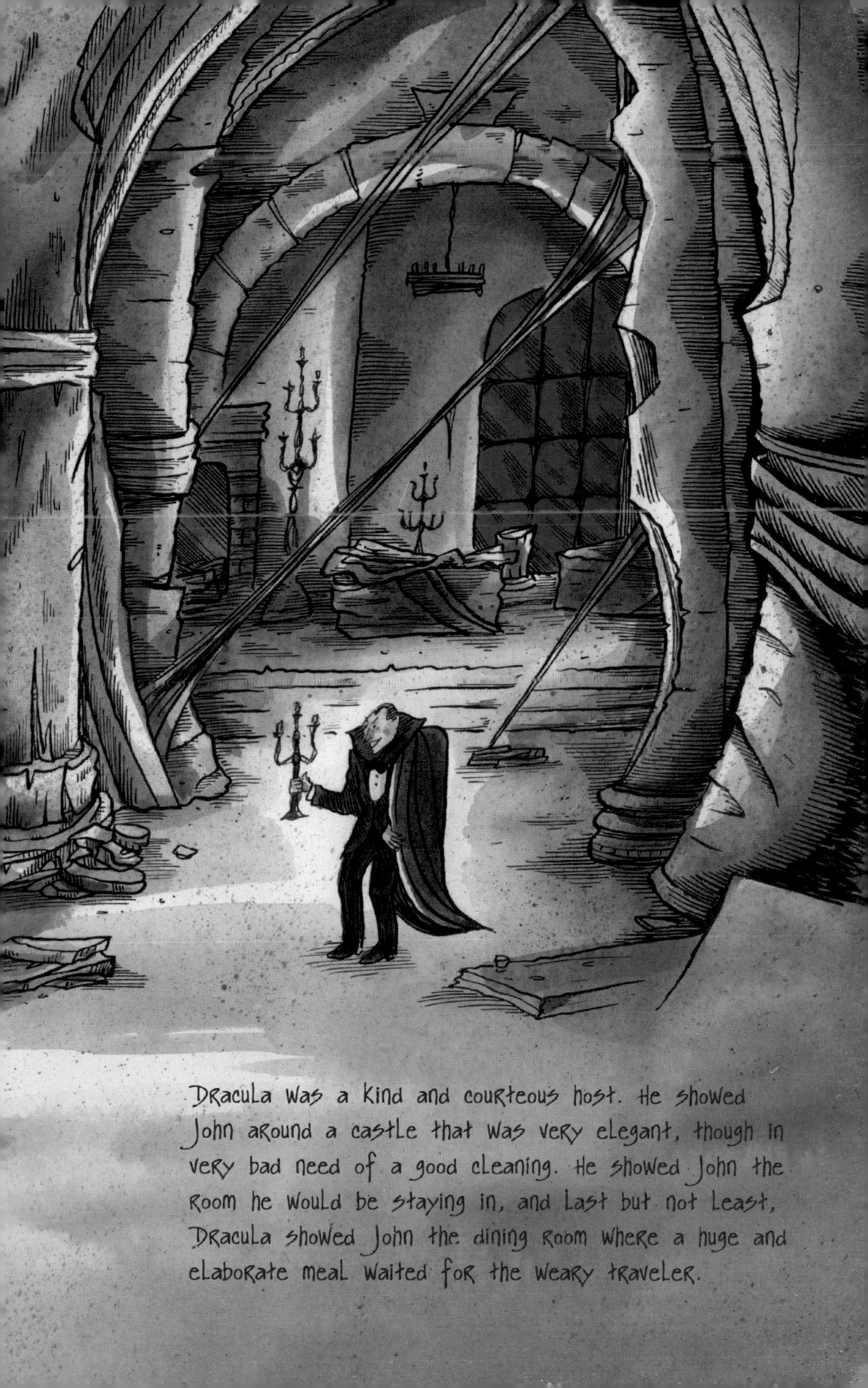

Dracula was a kind and courteous host. He showed John around a castle that was very elegant, though in very bad need of a good cleaning. He showed John the room he would be staying in, and last but not least, Dracula showed John the dining room where a huge and elaborate meal waited for the weary traveler.

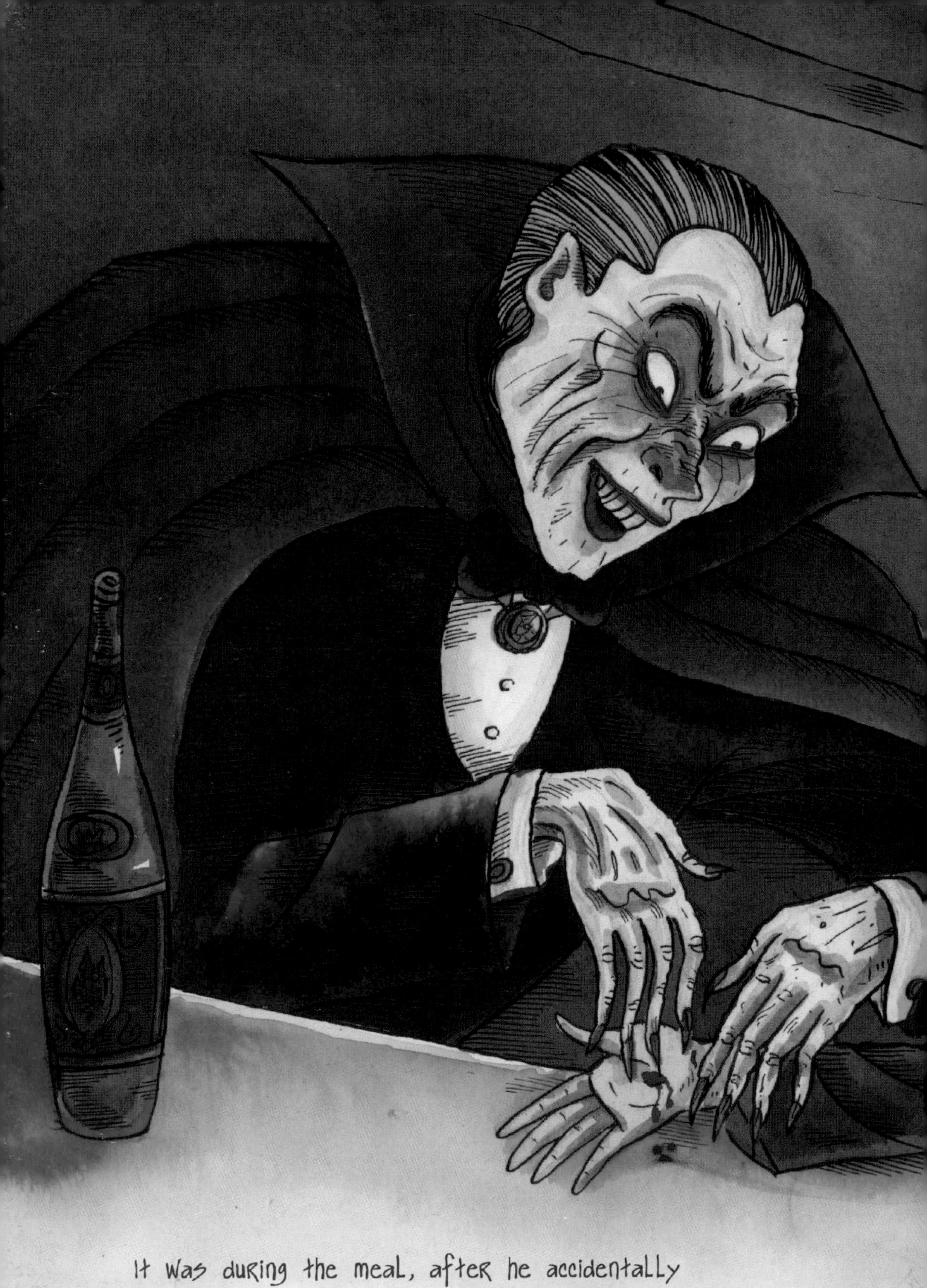

It was during the meal, after he accidentally cut his finger, that John began to suspect that Dracula was more than just an ordinary Count.

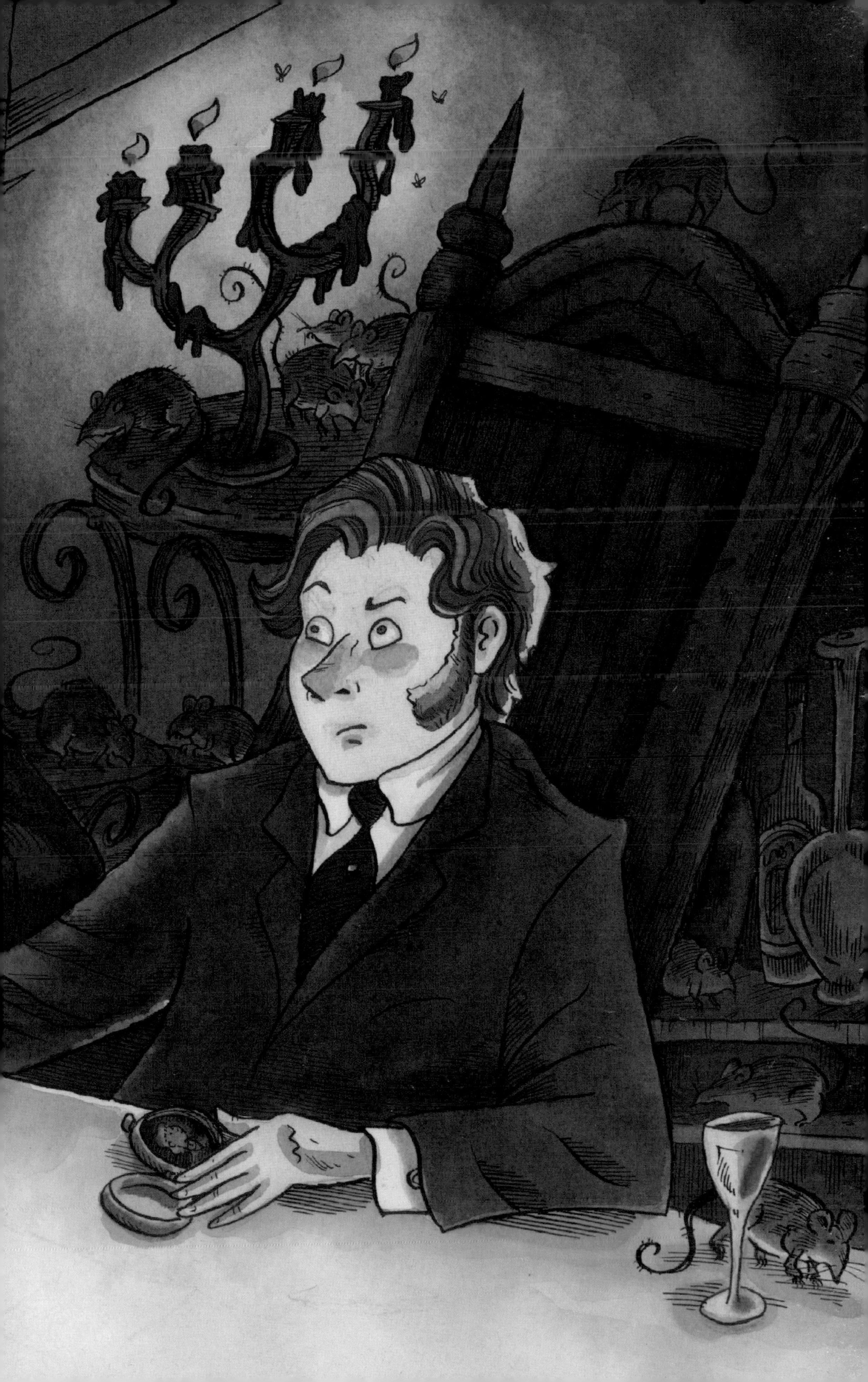

But it was later that same evening that John discovered Count Dracula's terrible secret. The warnings had been true. Dracula was a blood-sucking, sleep-in-his-coffin, turn-into-a-bat vampire!

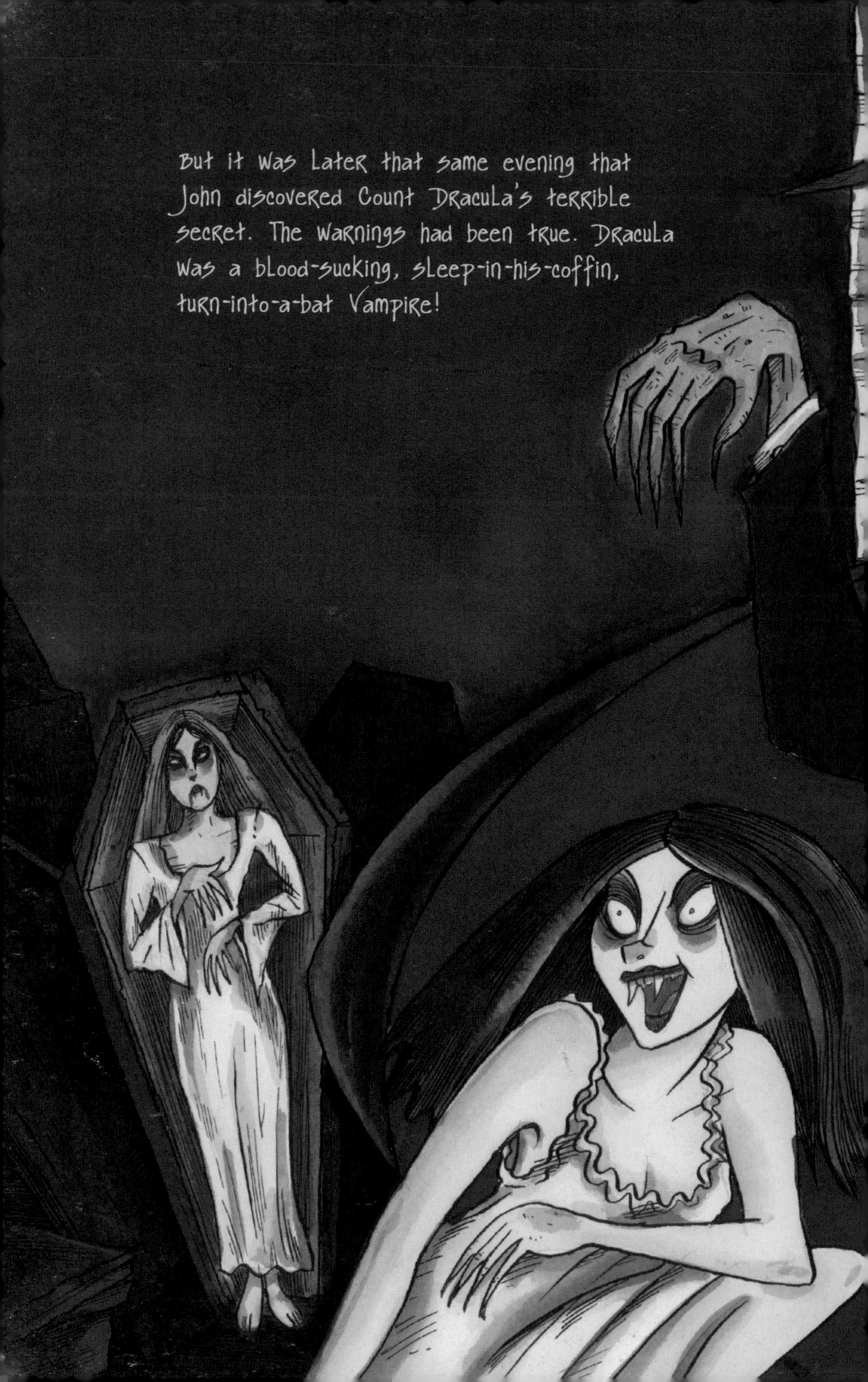

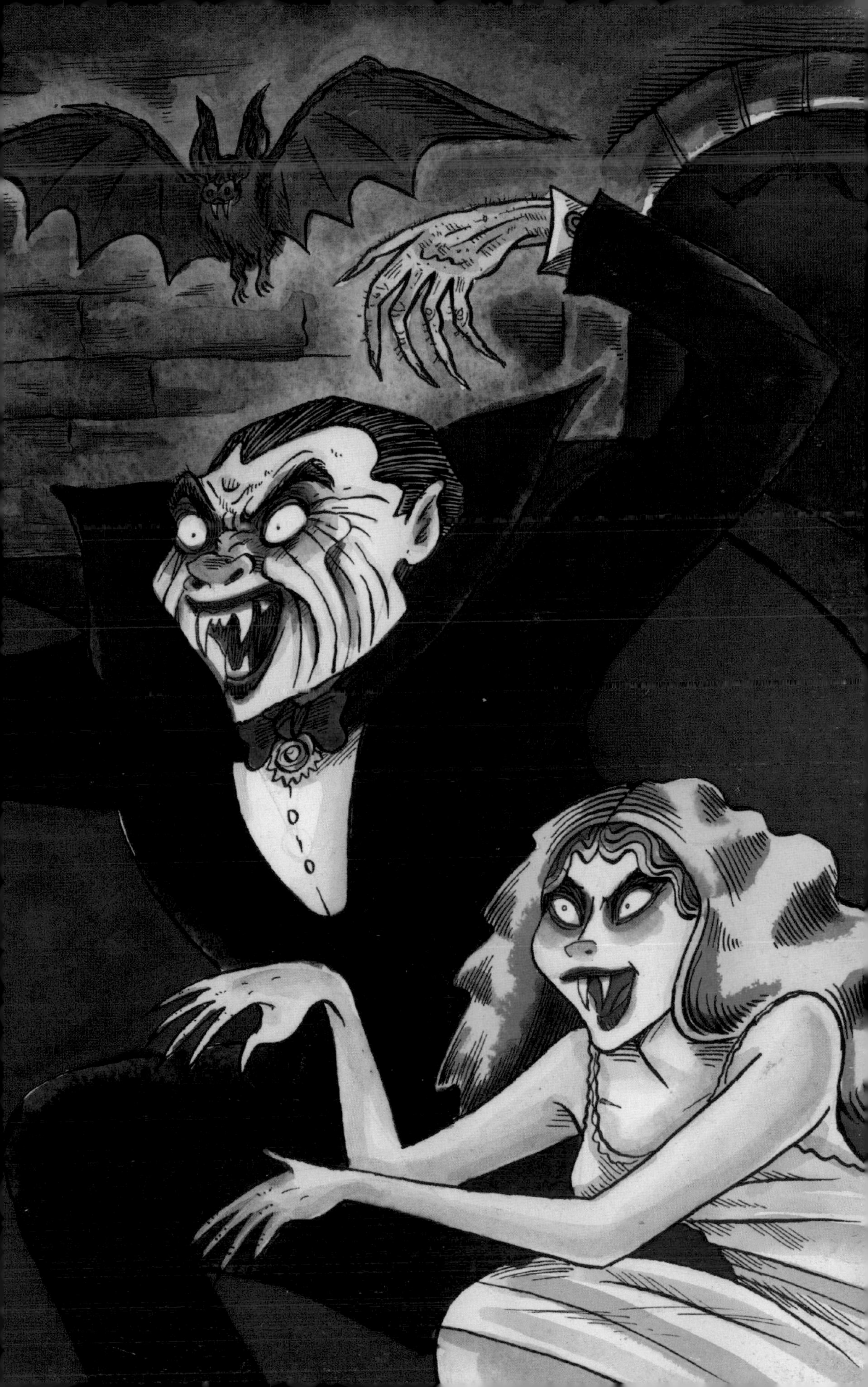

John wished he had listened to the villagers who had tried to warn him about the castle, but it was too late. The Count locked John in a tower high above the ground, and left the castle to spread his evil to John's homeland of England. Dracula was loose in the world, and there was nothing John could do to stop him.

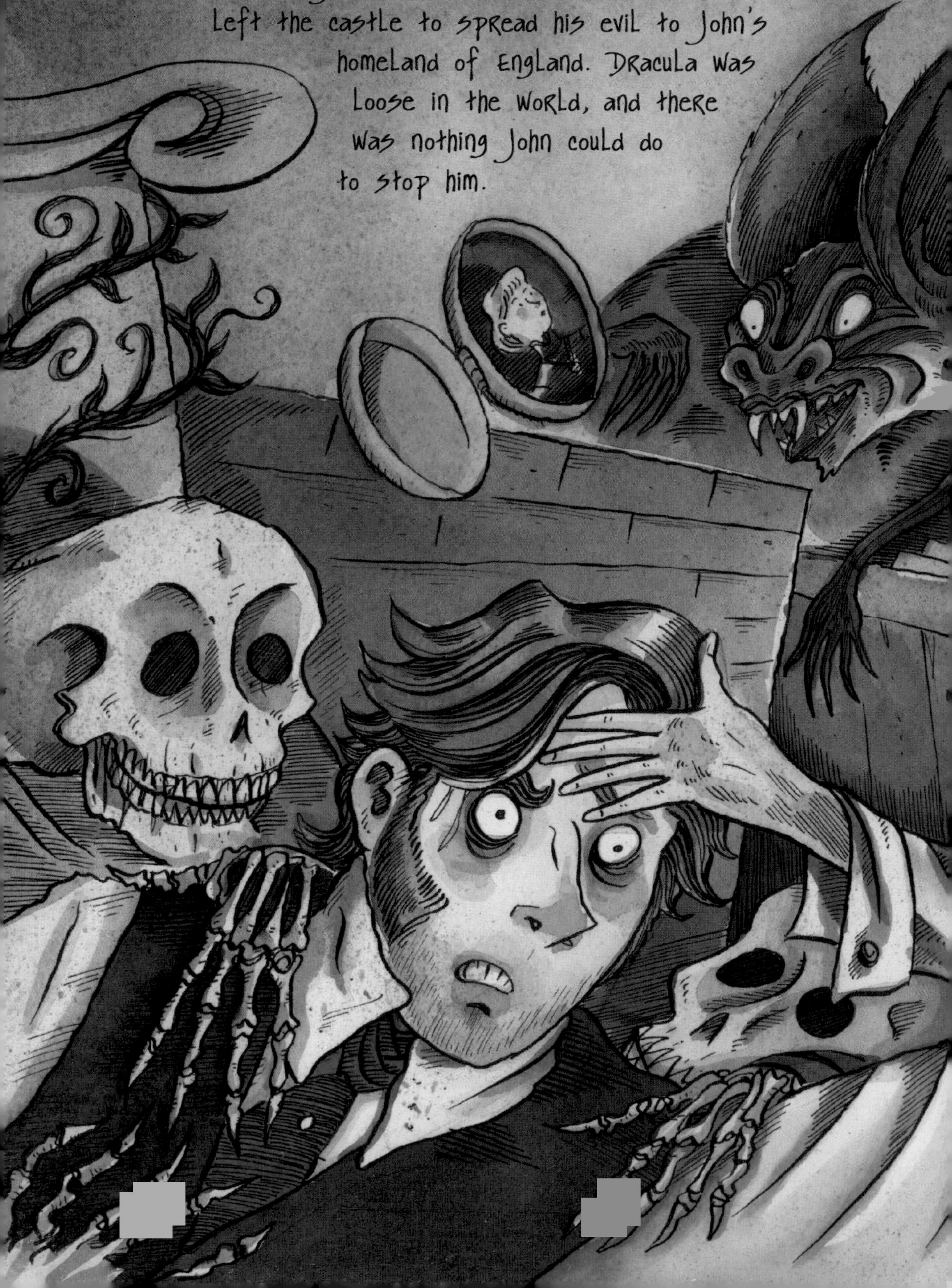

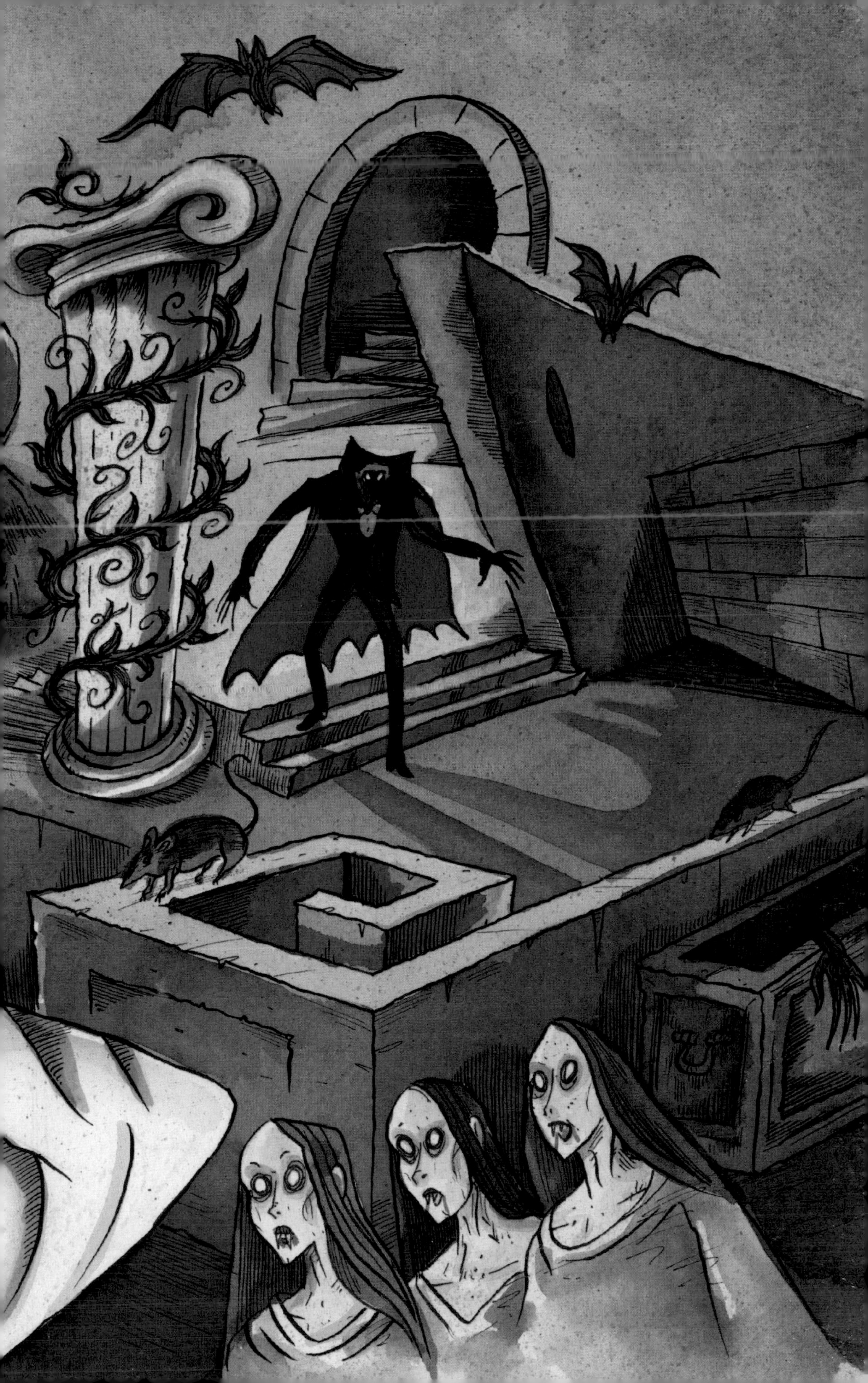

Back in England, Mina worried about her boyfriend, John. It had been a very long time since she had received a letter from him in Transylvania, where he was settling a deal with a Count named Dracula. It was not like John to go so long without writing Mina. She thought this was strange, but it was only the beginning.

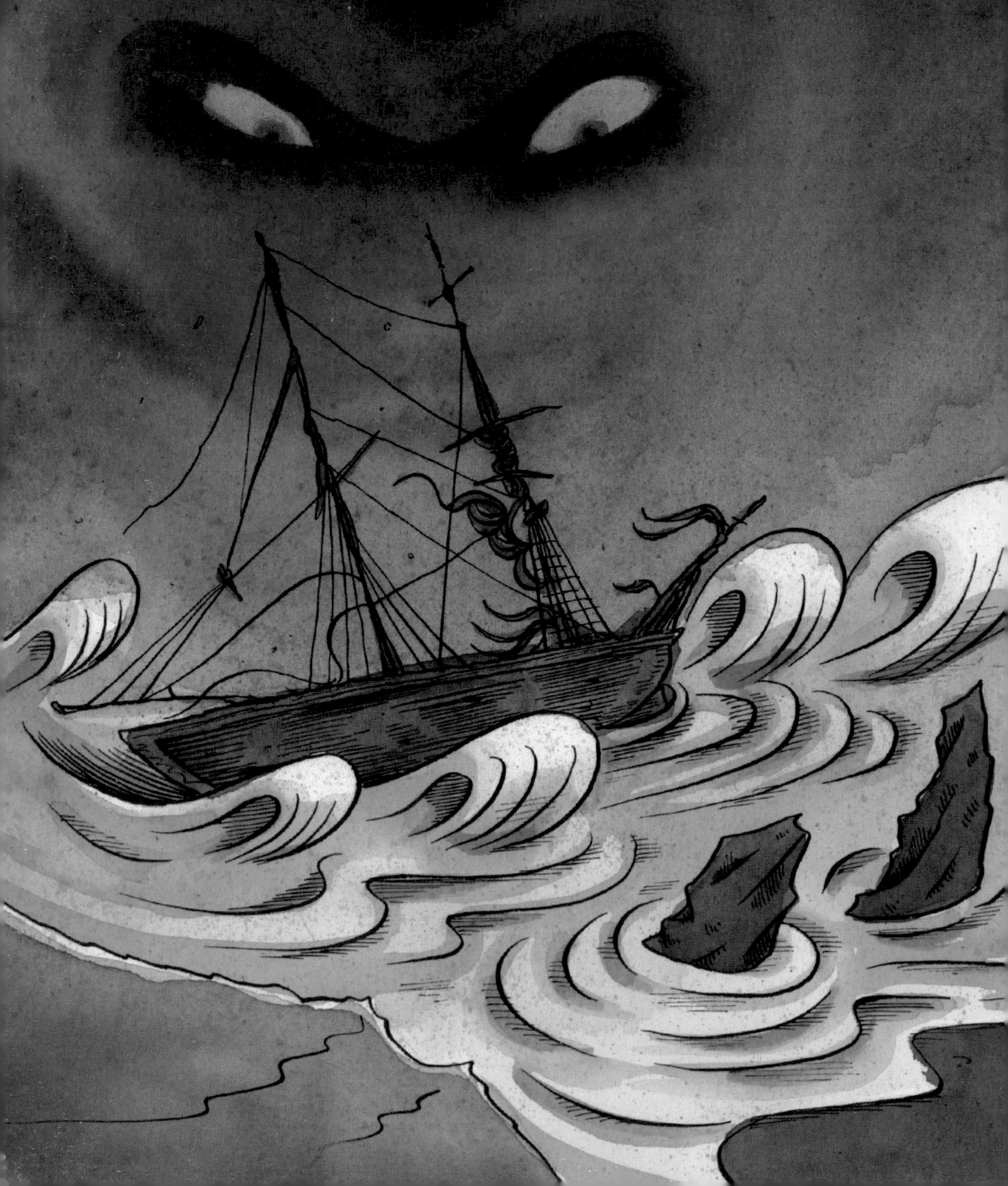

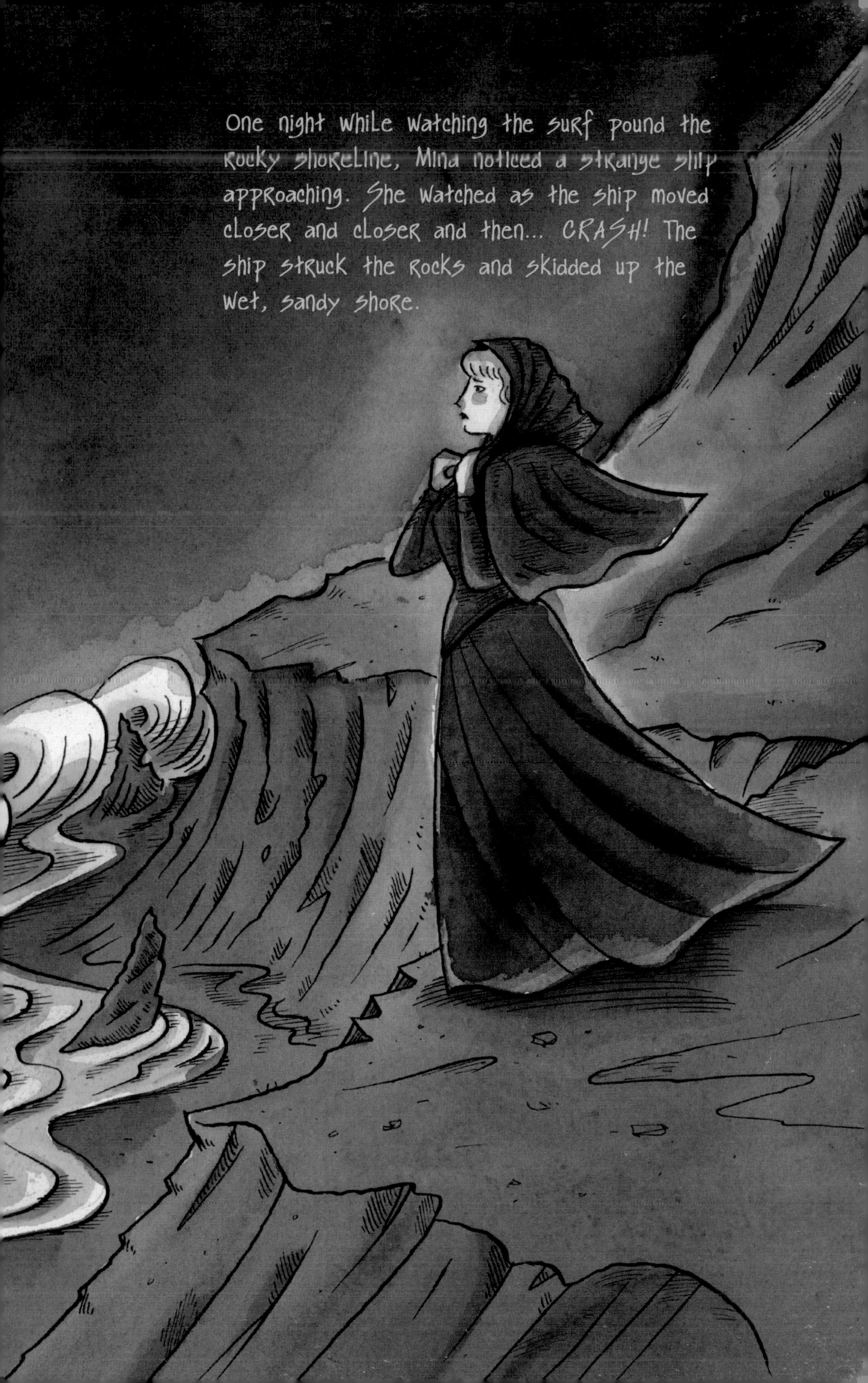
One night while watching the surf pound the rocky shoreline, Mina noticed a strange ship approaching. She watched as the ship moved closer and closer and then... CRASH! The ship struck the rocks and skidded up the wet, sandy shore.

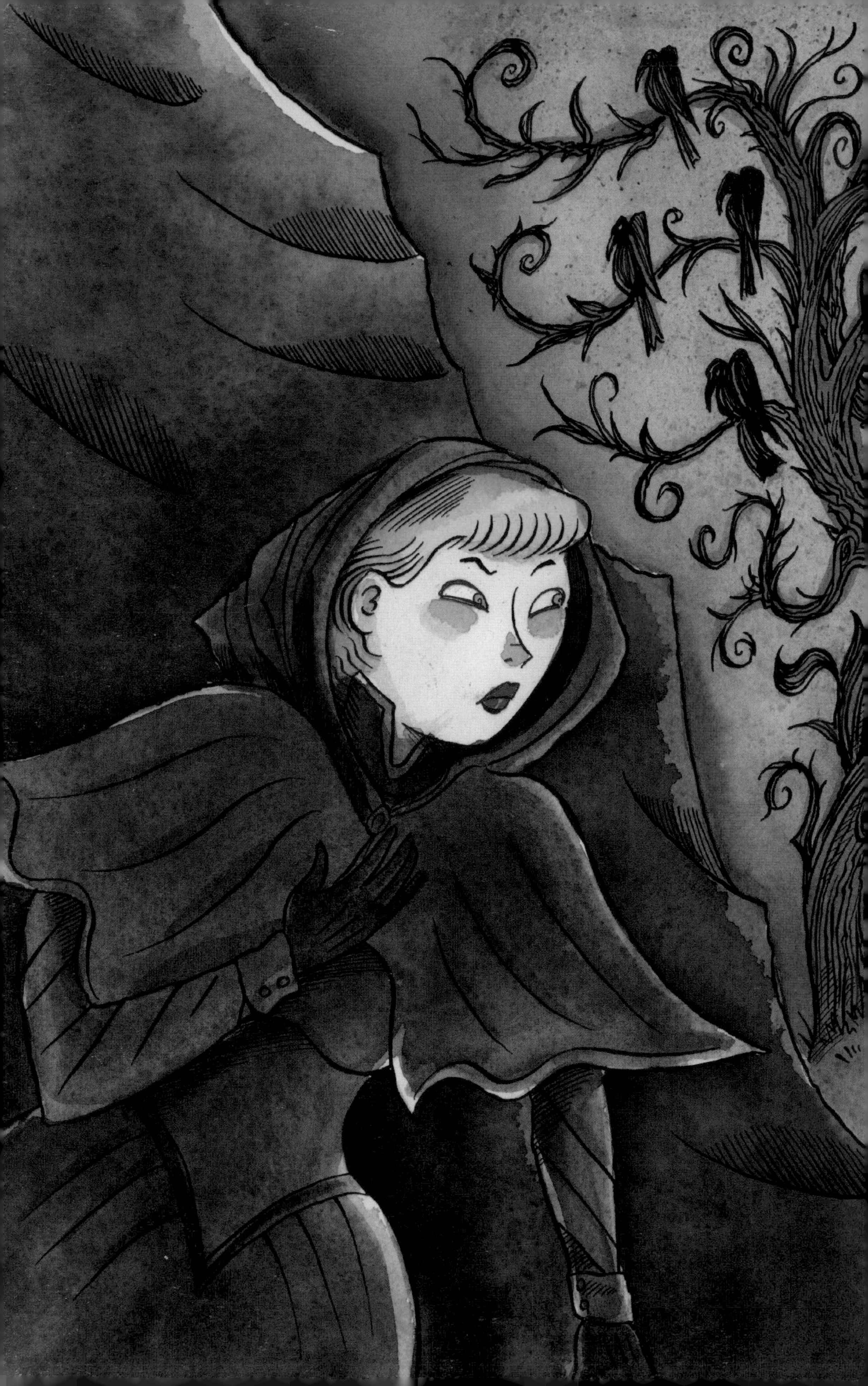

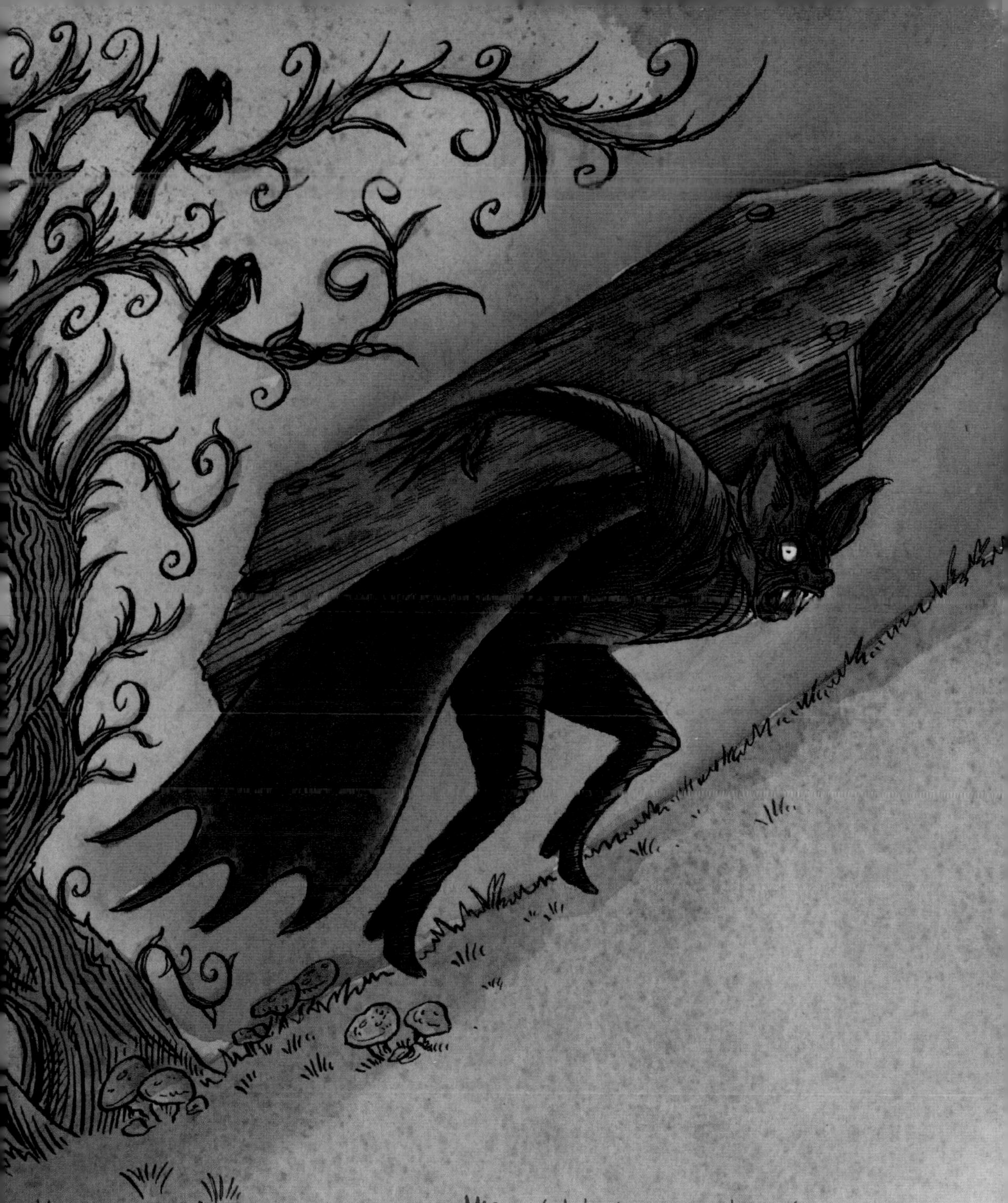

Mina watched as a shadow,
a shape, a thing, scurried
from the shattered boat and
ran into the darkness carrying what
appeared to be a large box atop
his head. It was later that
Mina heard the news. The
entire crew had vanished!

Meanwhile, in Transylvania, John tried over and over to escape from Dracula's Castle without much luck at all, but he would not stop trying until he succeeded. He could not stop because something deep inside told him that his girlfriend Mina was in danger.

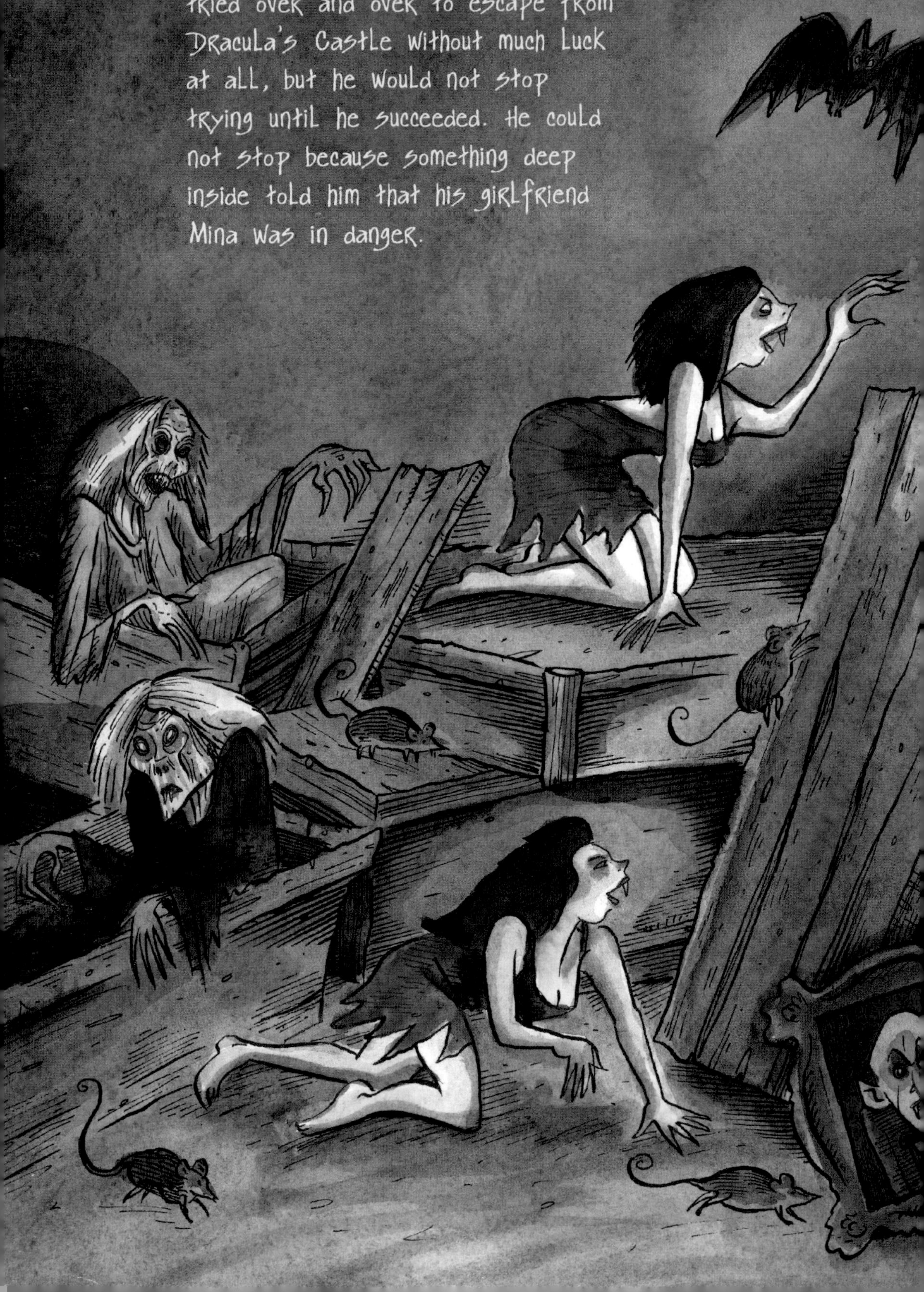

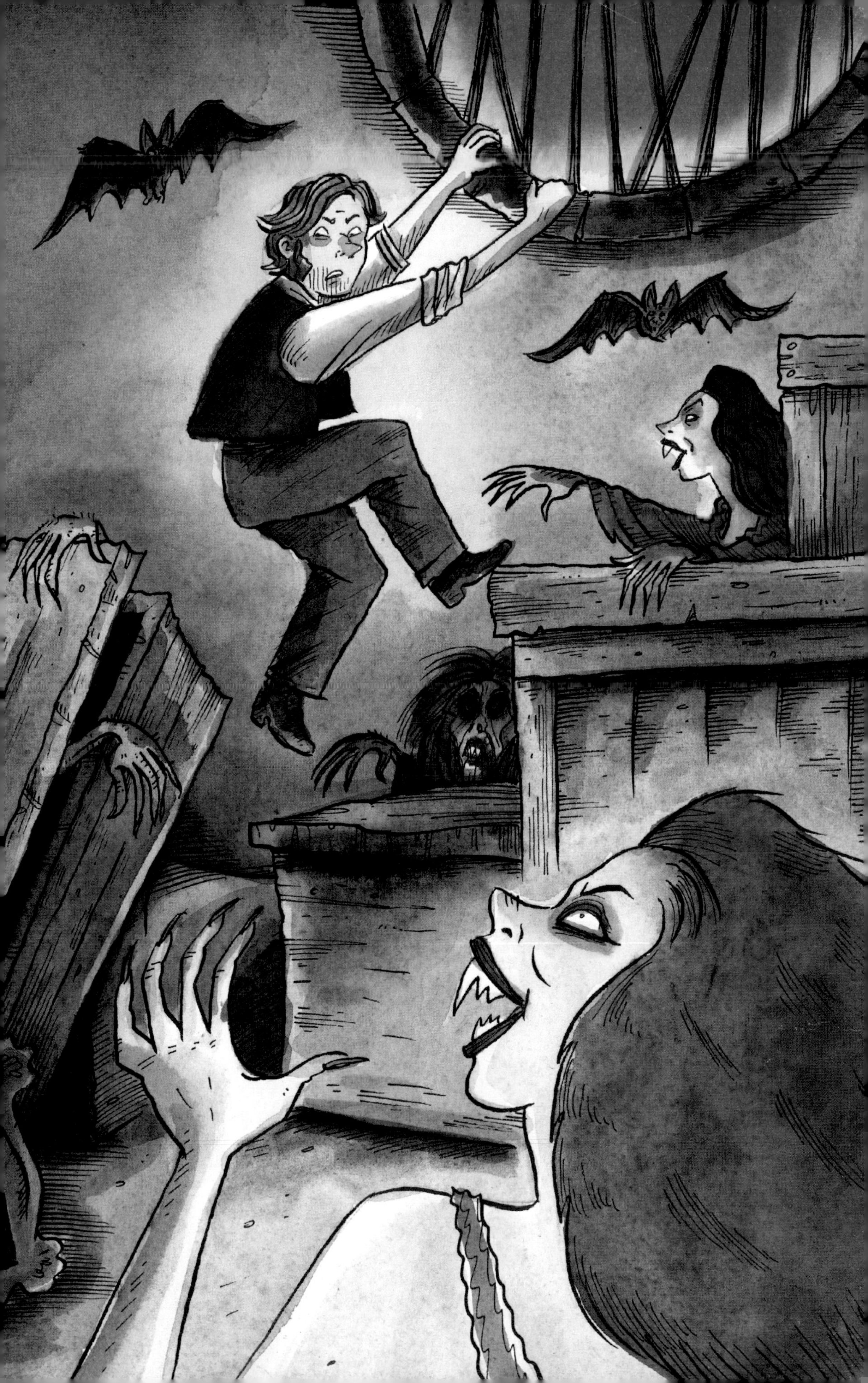

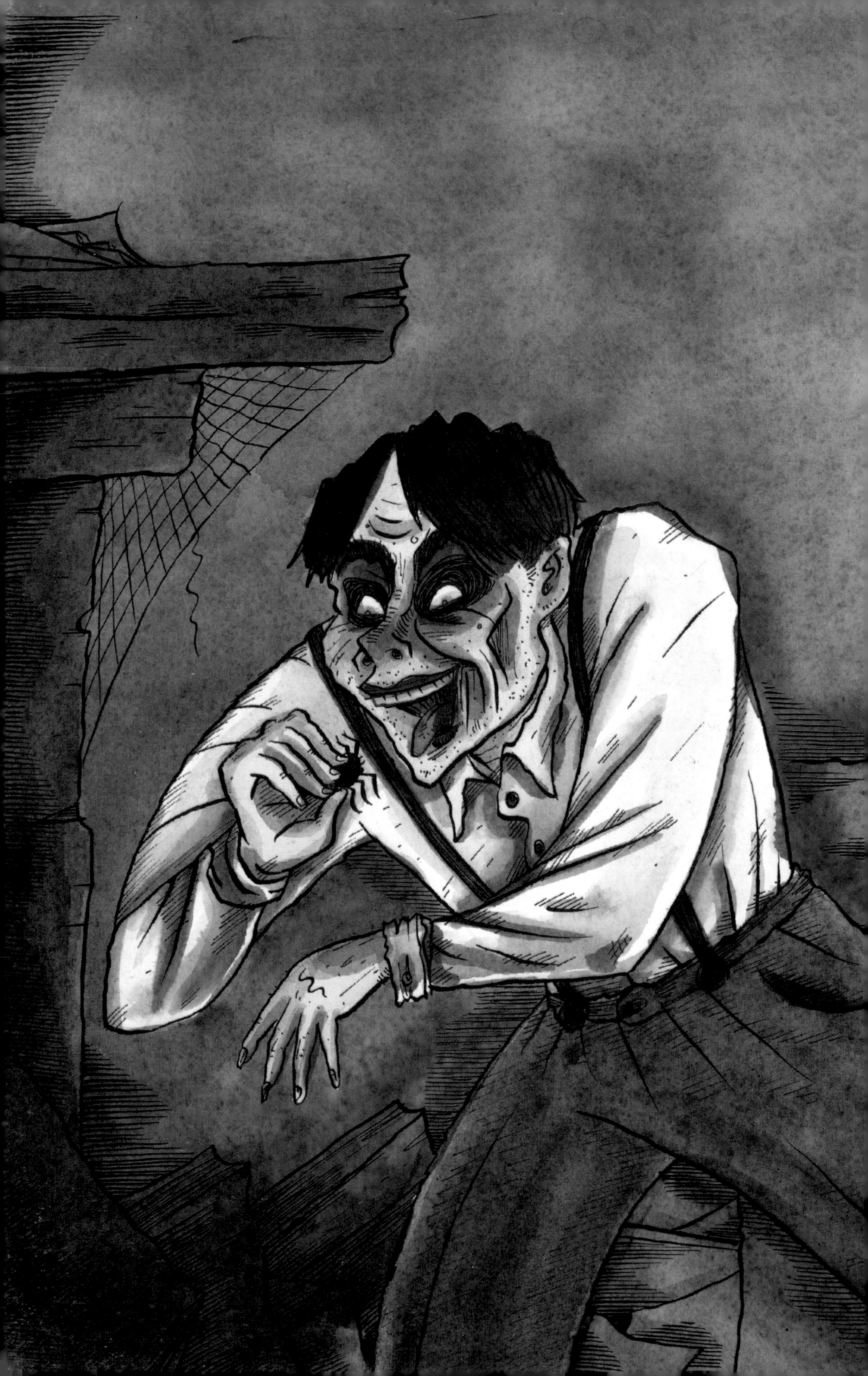

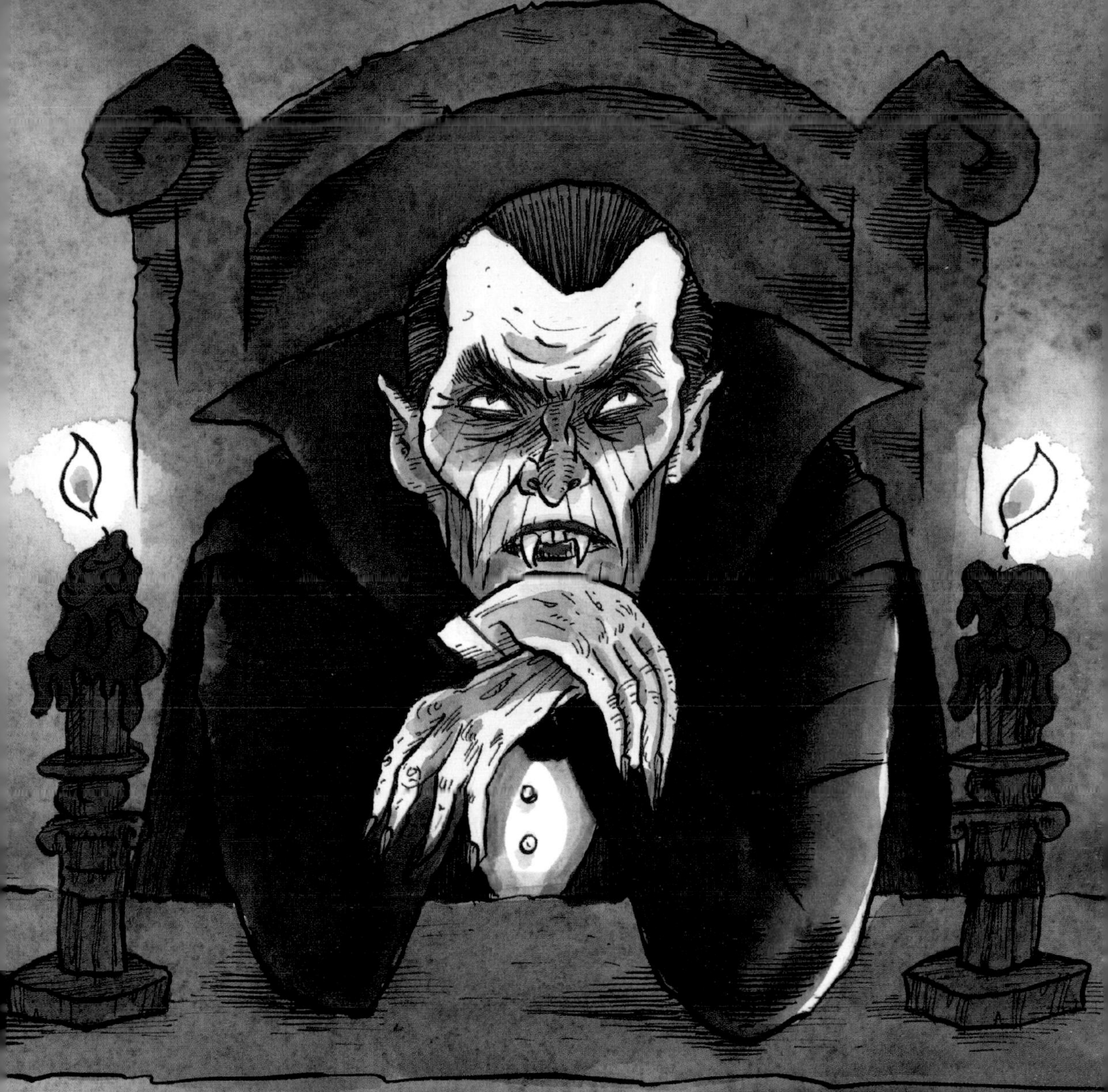

John was right. Dracula, along with his bug-eating assistant, Renfield, had moved into a large and gloomy mansion called Carfax Abbey that was just down the street from Mina's house. It was Dracula's intent to suck the blood out of everyone in England, and his first victim was going to be Mina.

Late at night, while everyone was asleep, Dracula climbed the wall outside Mina's house, crept onto her balcony and into the very room where she slept. Slowly, he moved across the room until he was right beside her bed. Then Dracula bared his pointy fangs and knelt down beside the sleeping Mina and bit her, bit her hard, right in the neck, and sucked her blood!

And night after night, Dracula came to Mina's room, climbed up the wall, crept through her window and drank her blood.

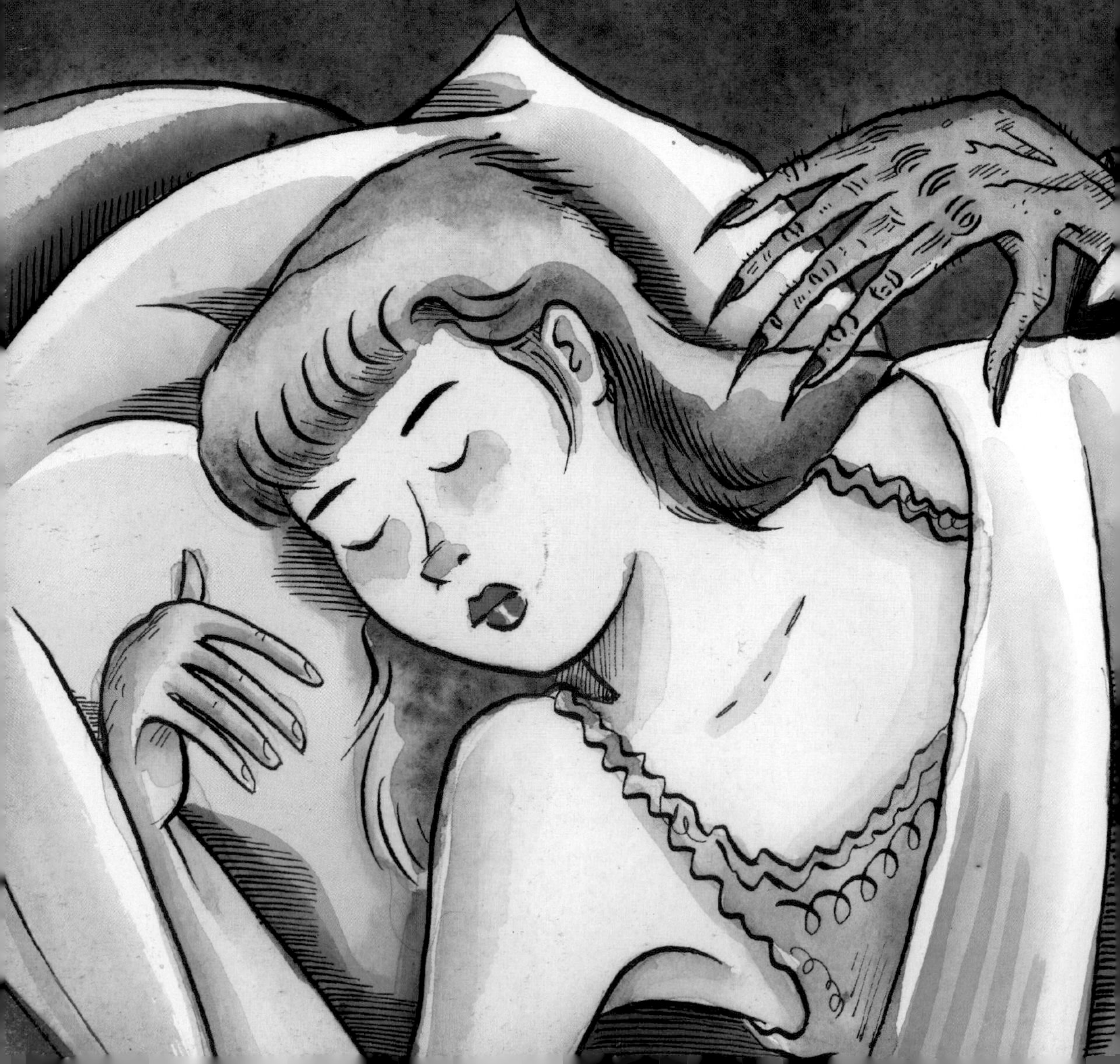

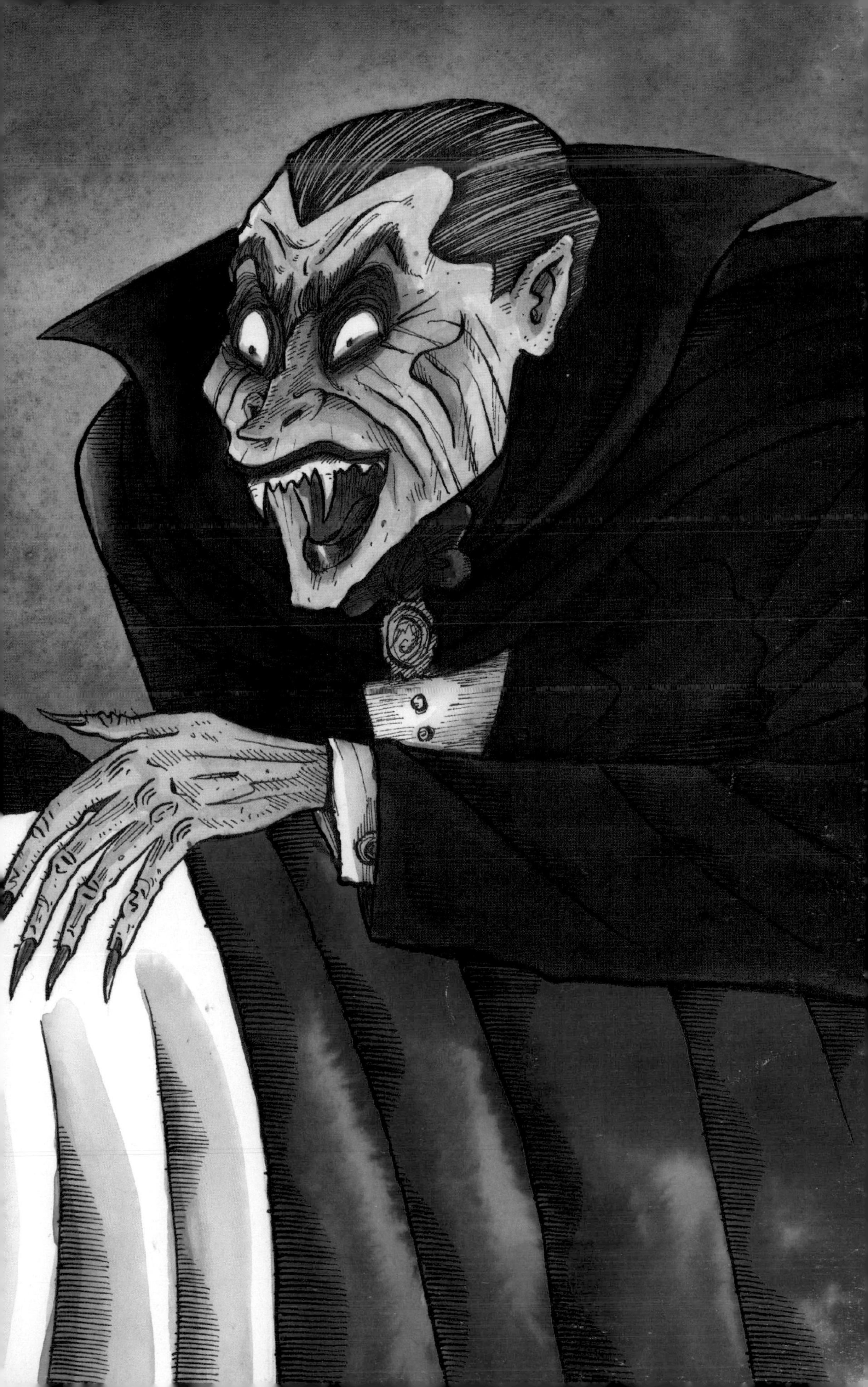

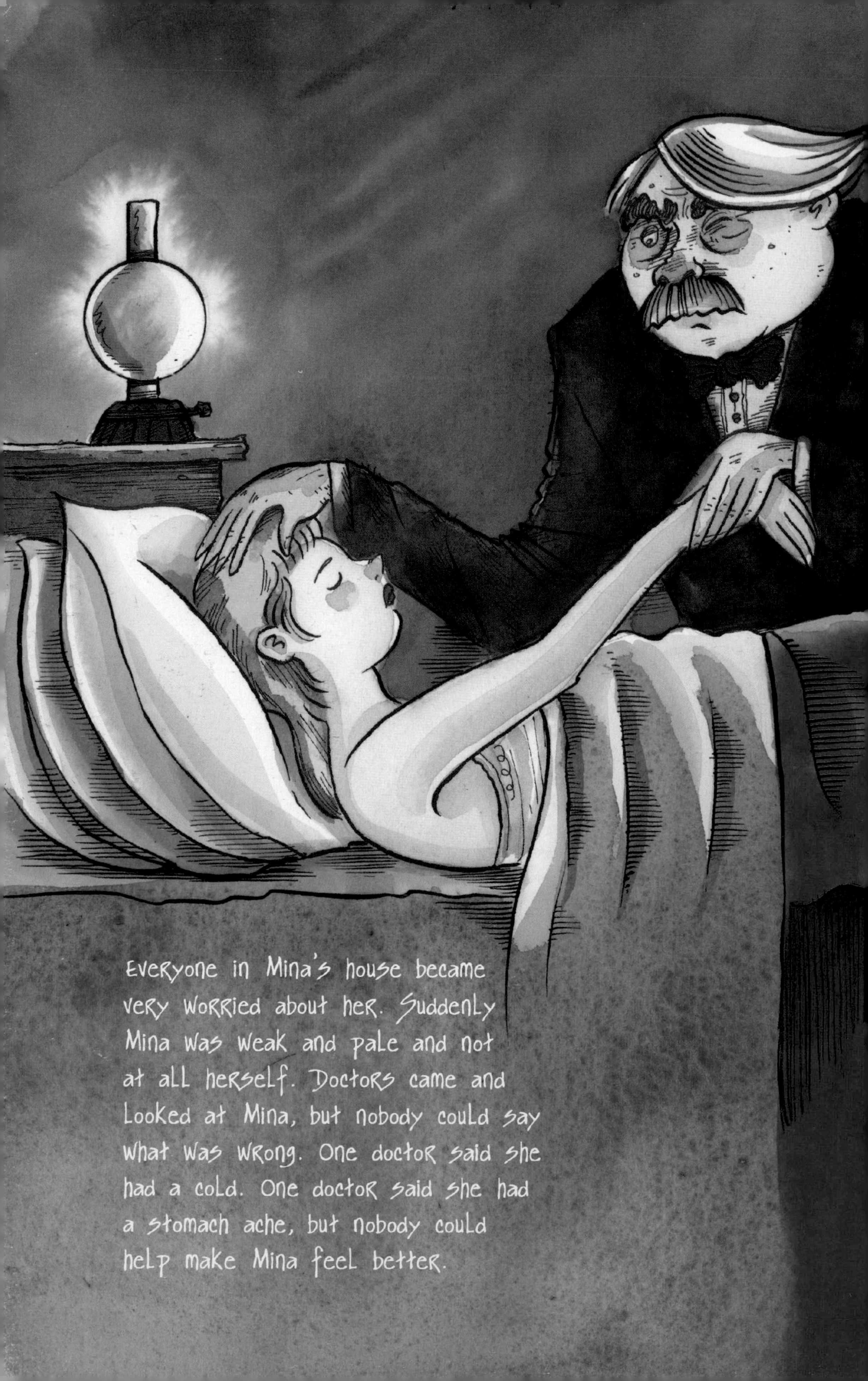

Everyone in Mina's house became very worried about her. Suddenly Mina was weak and pale and not at all herself. Doctors came and looked at Mina, but nobody could say what was wrong. One doctor said she had a cold. One doctor said she had a stomach ache, but nobody could help make Mina feel better.

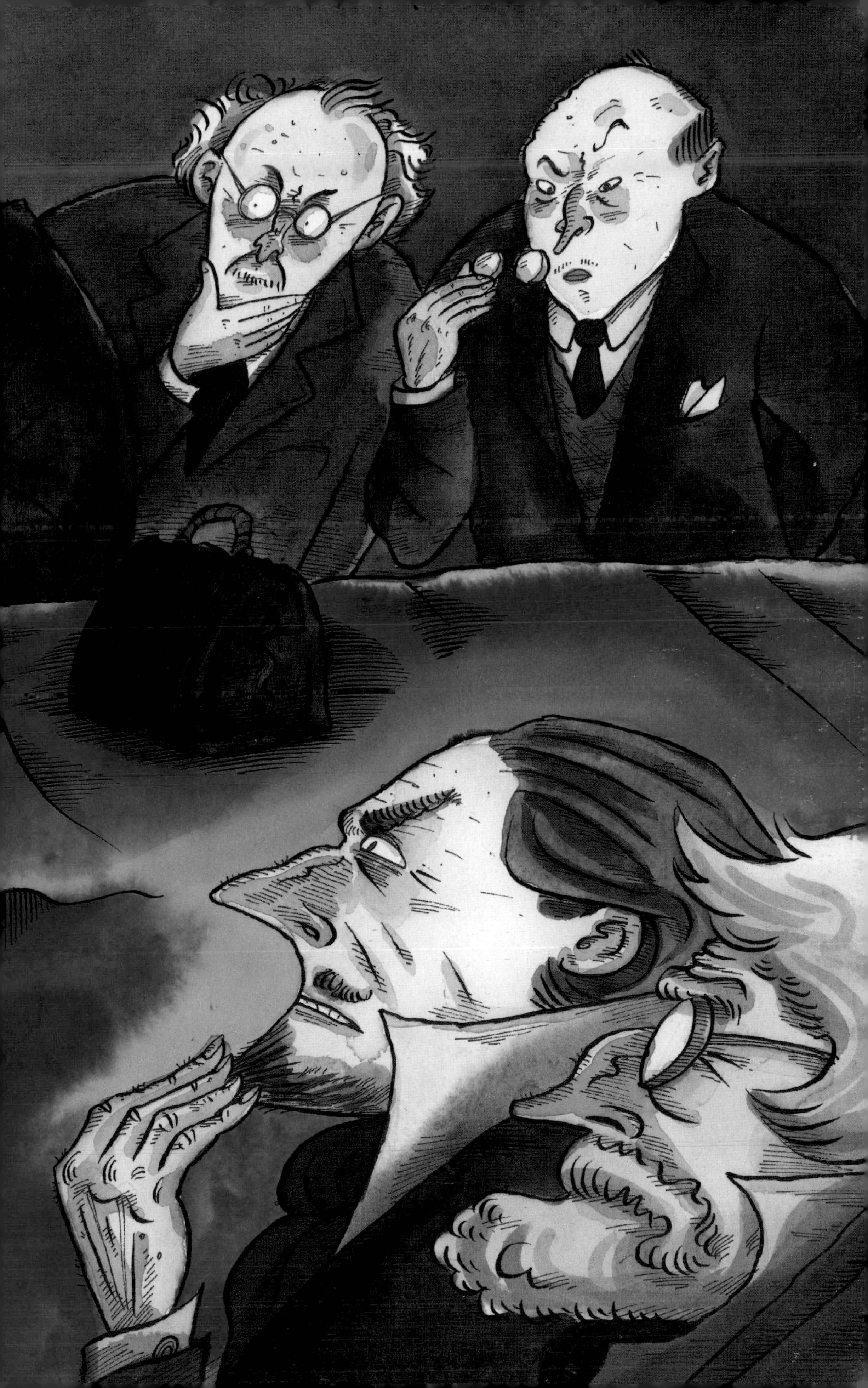

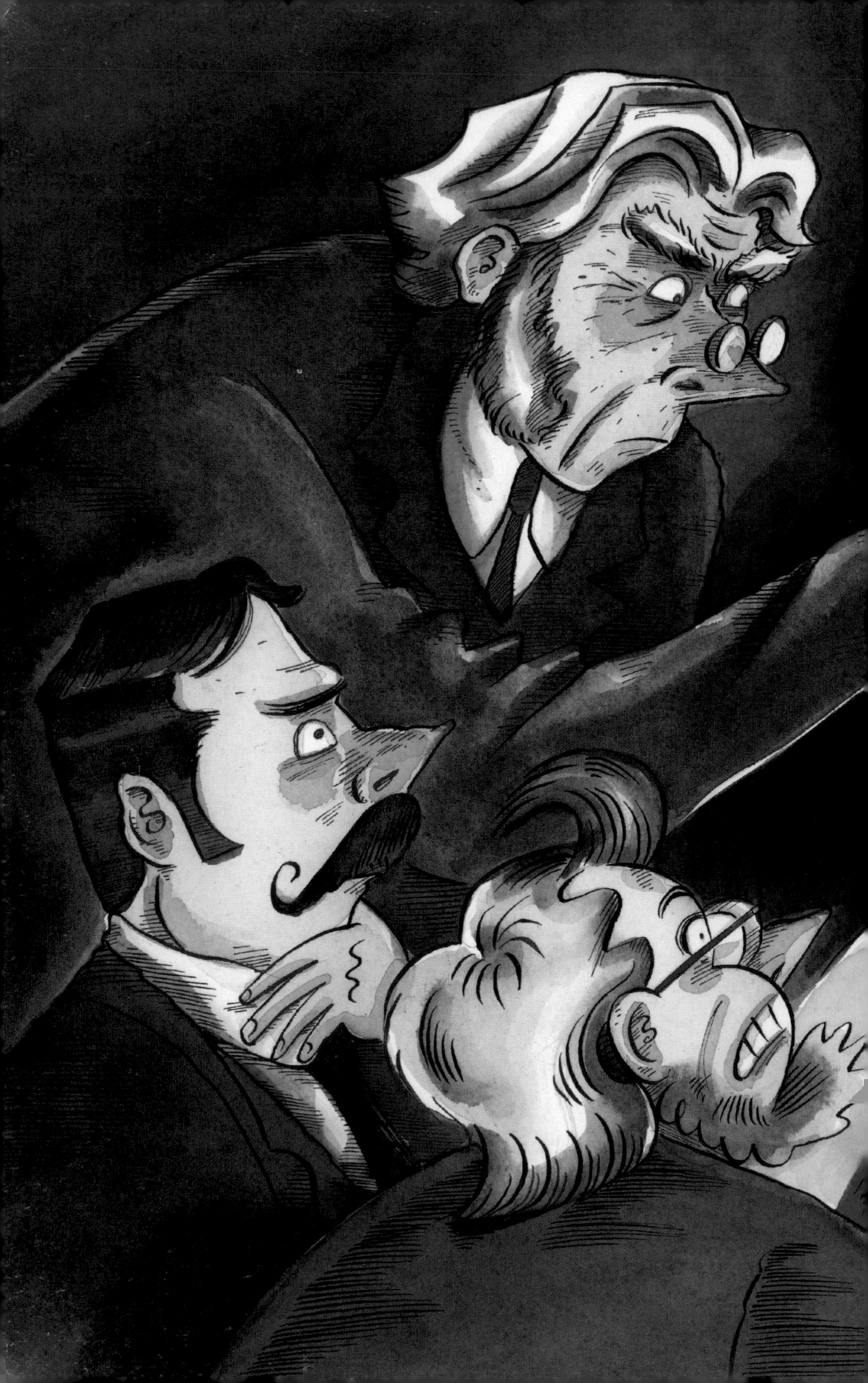

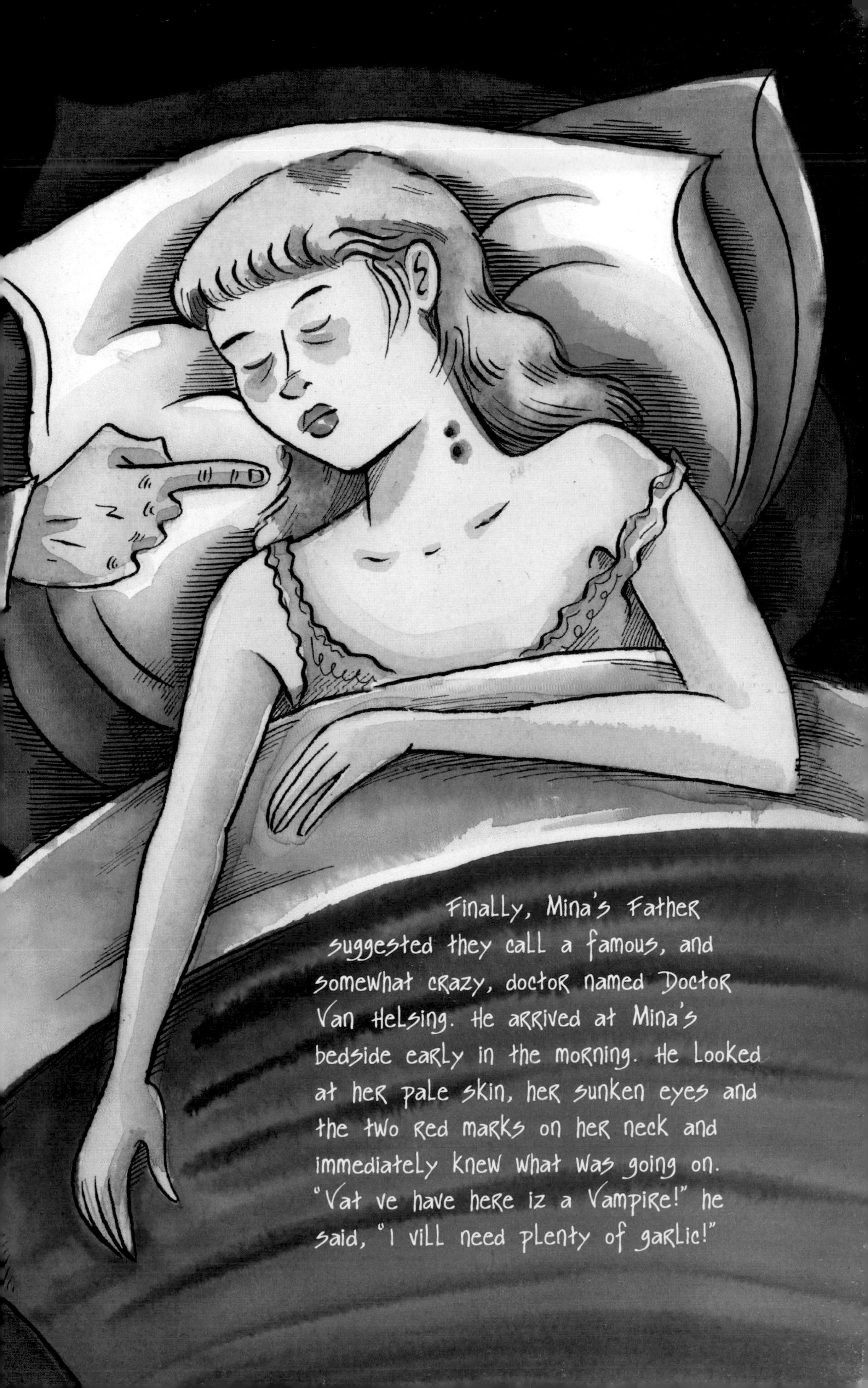

Finally, Mina's Father suggested they call a famous, and somewhat crazy, doctor named Doctor Van Helsing. He arrived at Mina's bedside early in the morning. He looked at her pale skin, her sunken eyes and the two red marks on her neck and immediately knew what was going on. "Vat ve have here iz a Vampire!" he said, "I vill need plenty of garlic!"

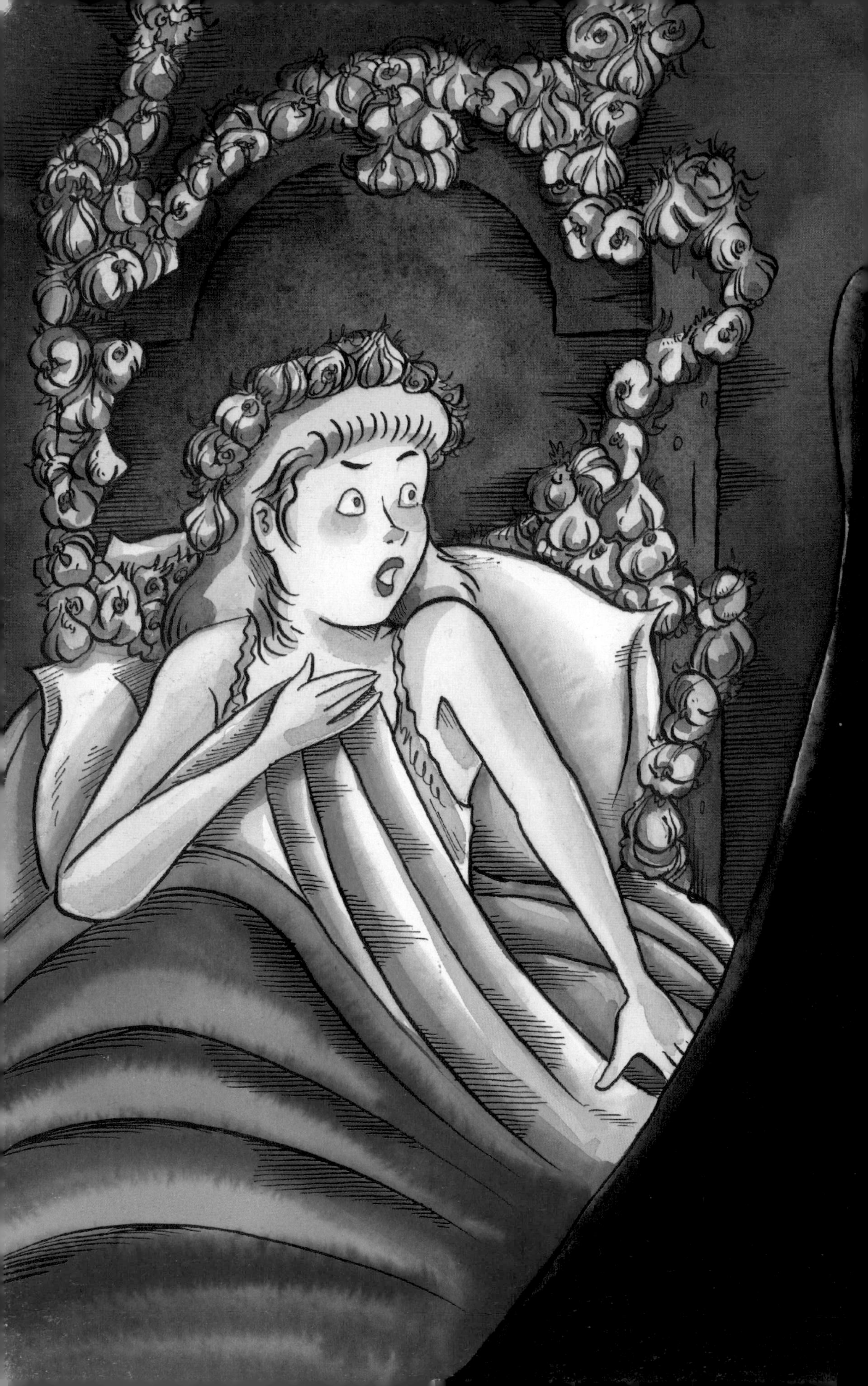

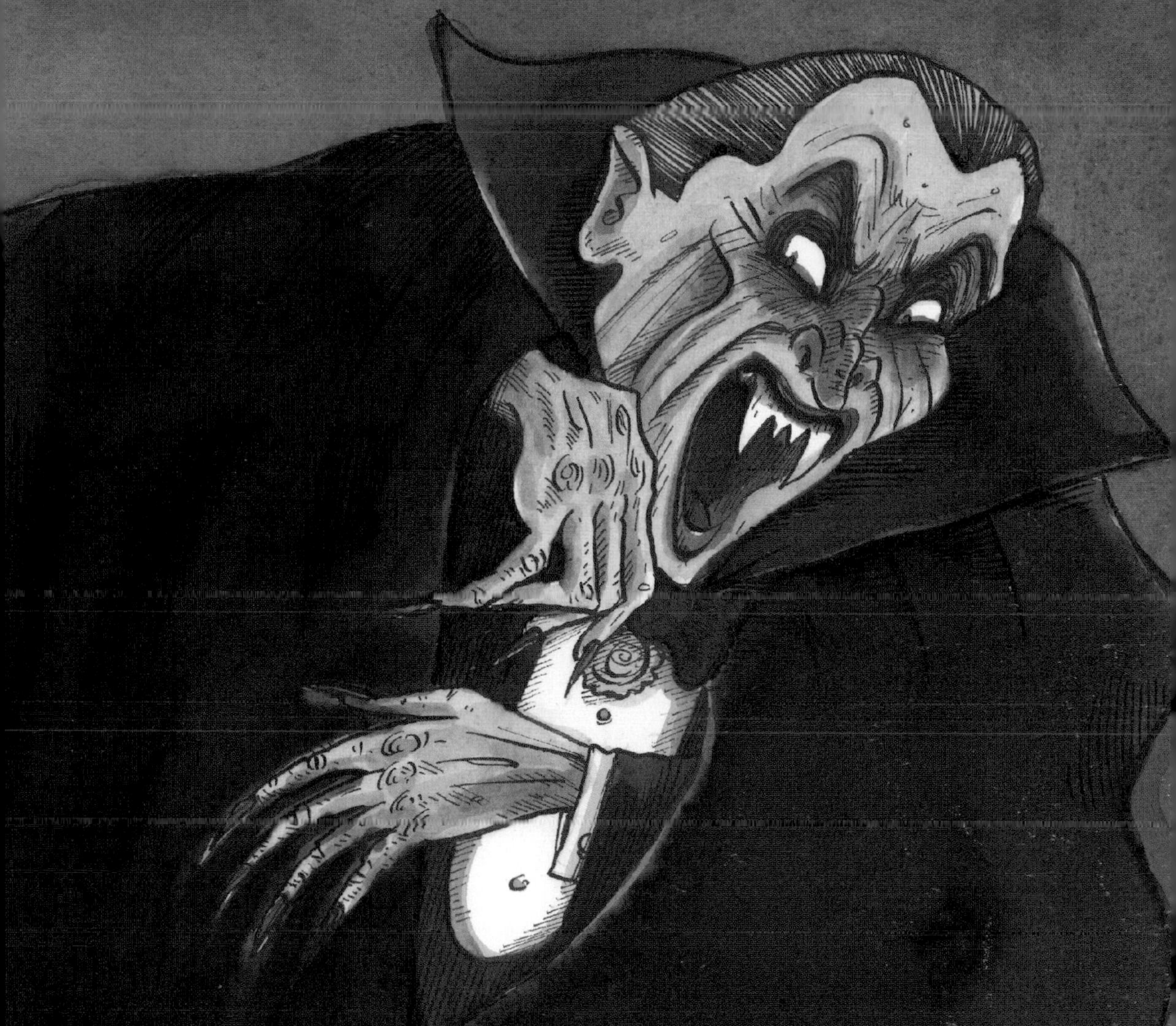

That night, when Dracula climbed the wall outside Mina's room, he crept through the window, and tip-toed to Mina's bed, and a big surprise was waiting for him. Dracula hated garlic, and garlic was everywhere! Garlic was on the bed, and around the door, even in Mina's hair.

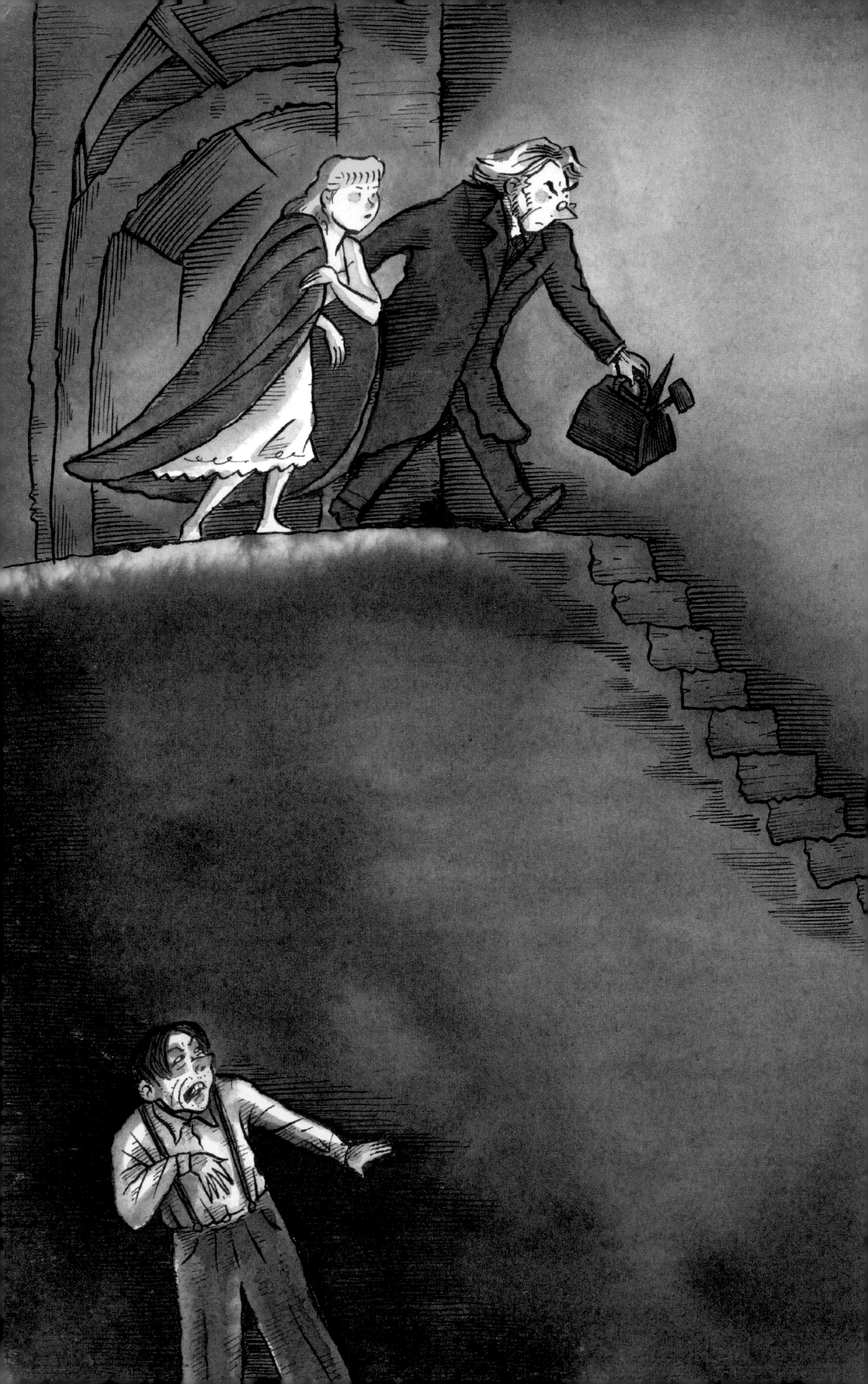

Dracula ran away, but Doctor Van Helsing and Mina chased after him. They chased him all the way back to his new house, Carfax Abbey. They chased him up the stairs and down again, and then they chased him some more.

Outside the dark mansion, the sun had begun to rise, but every time they thought they had the Vampire cornered, he jumped and ducked and hid. At Last, they followed Dracula into his cellar, but when they got there, he had disappeared.

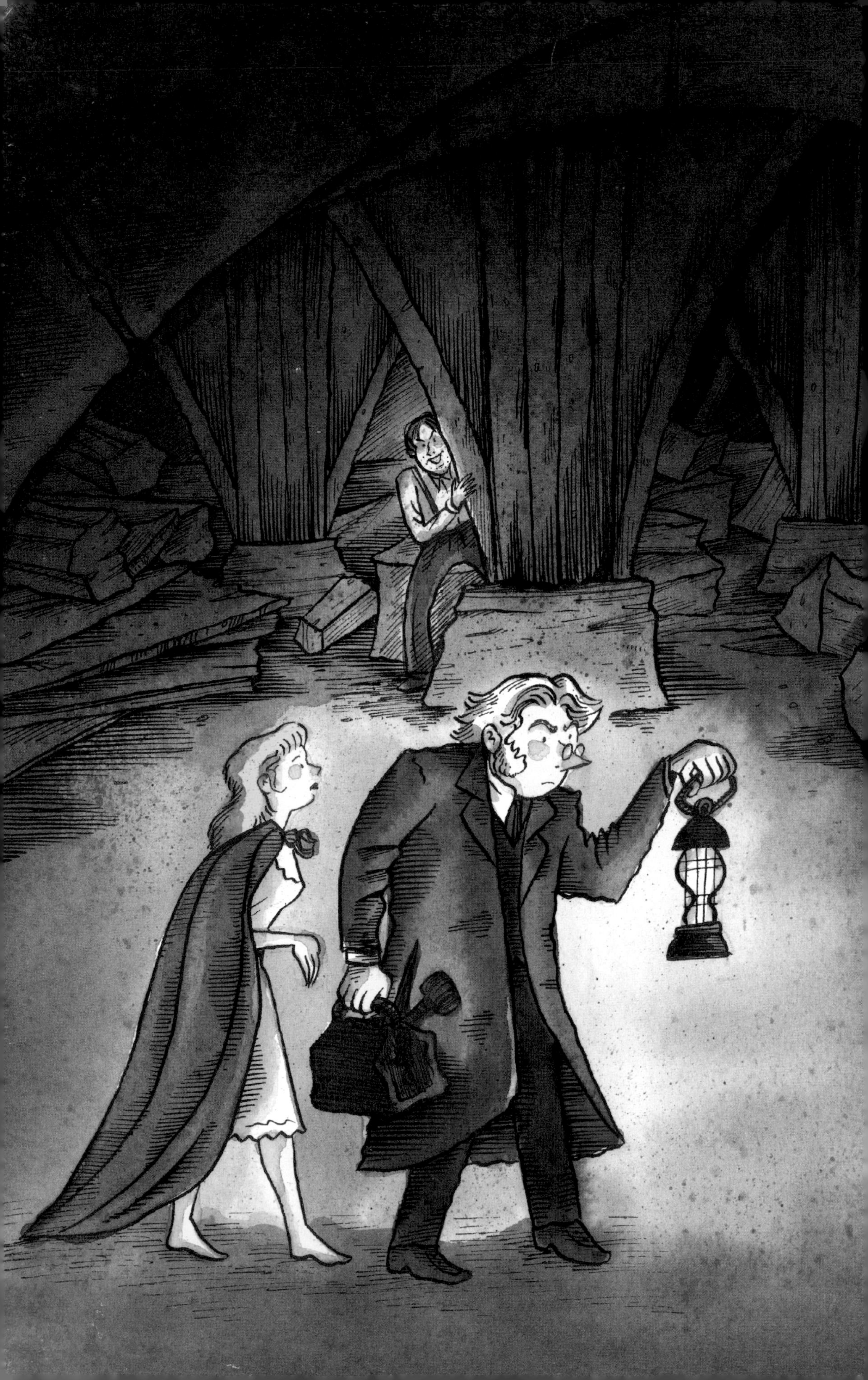

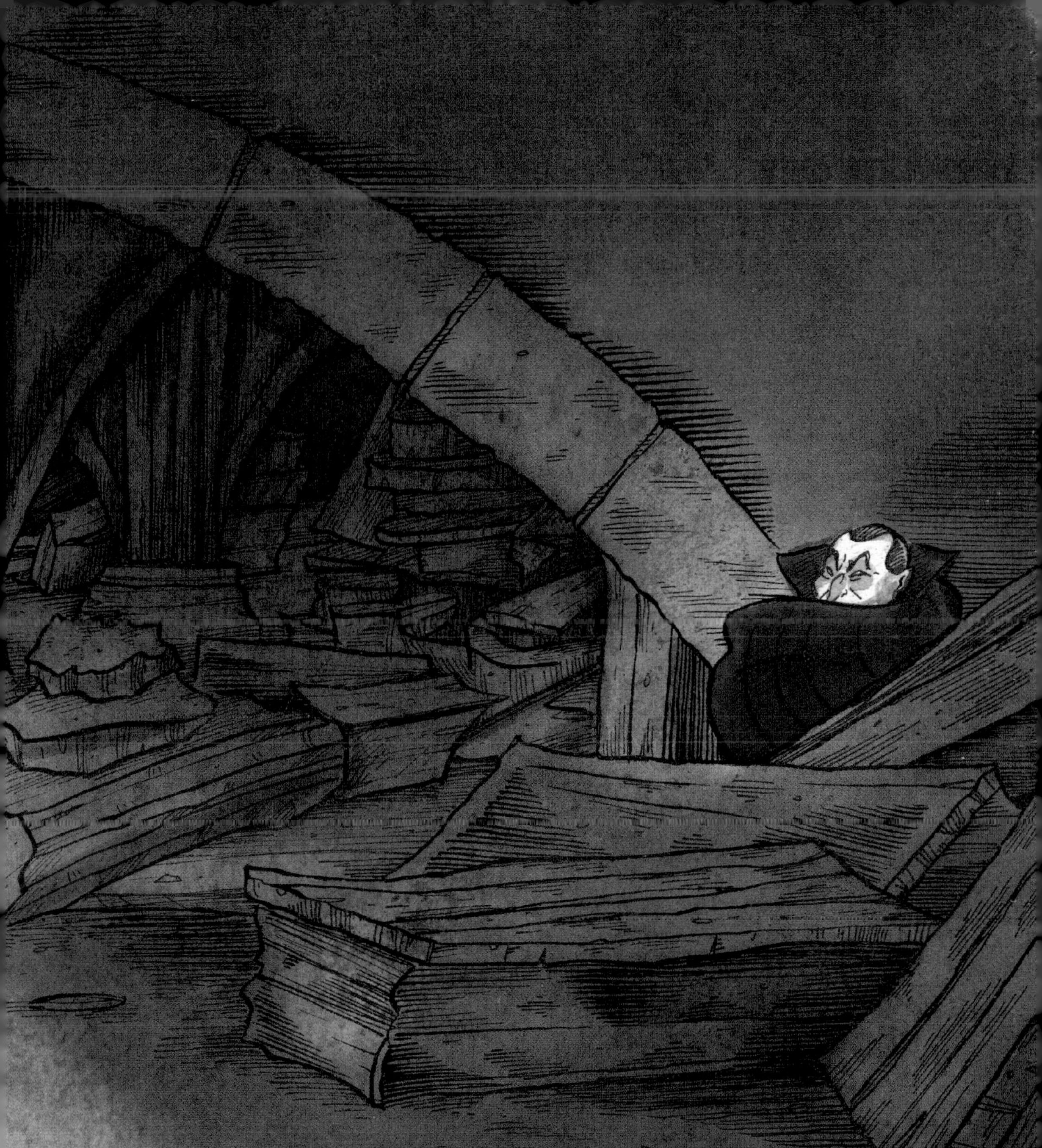

That was when Mina and Doctor Van Helsing realized they had made a very big mistake. They had walked right into a trap! They were in the one room where Dracula was his most powerful. They were in Dracula's Lair, the room in the basement where he slept in his coffin. They were trapped! There was no escape!

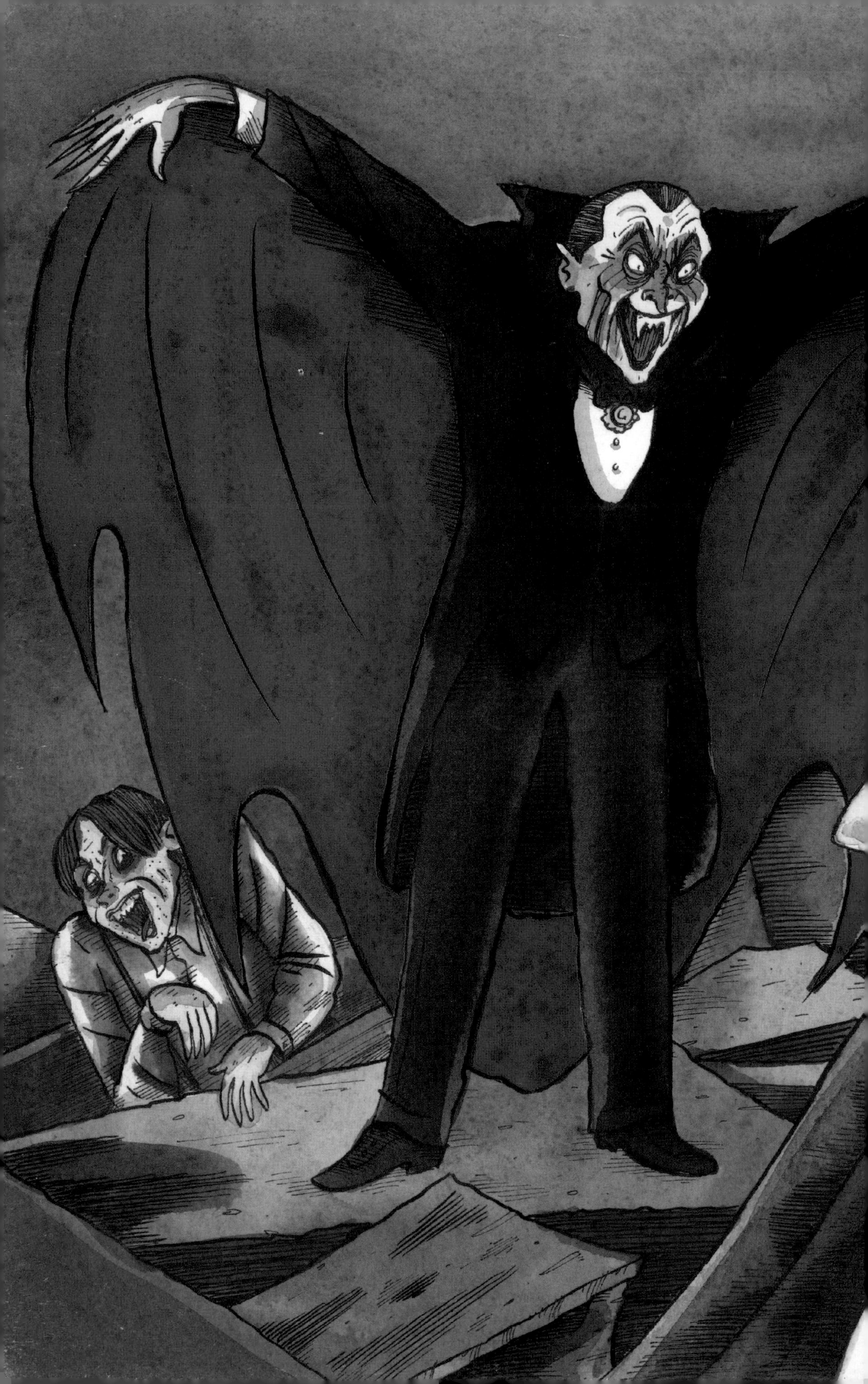

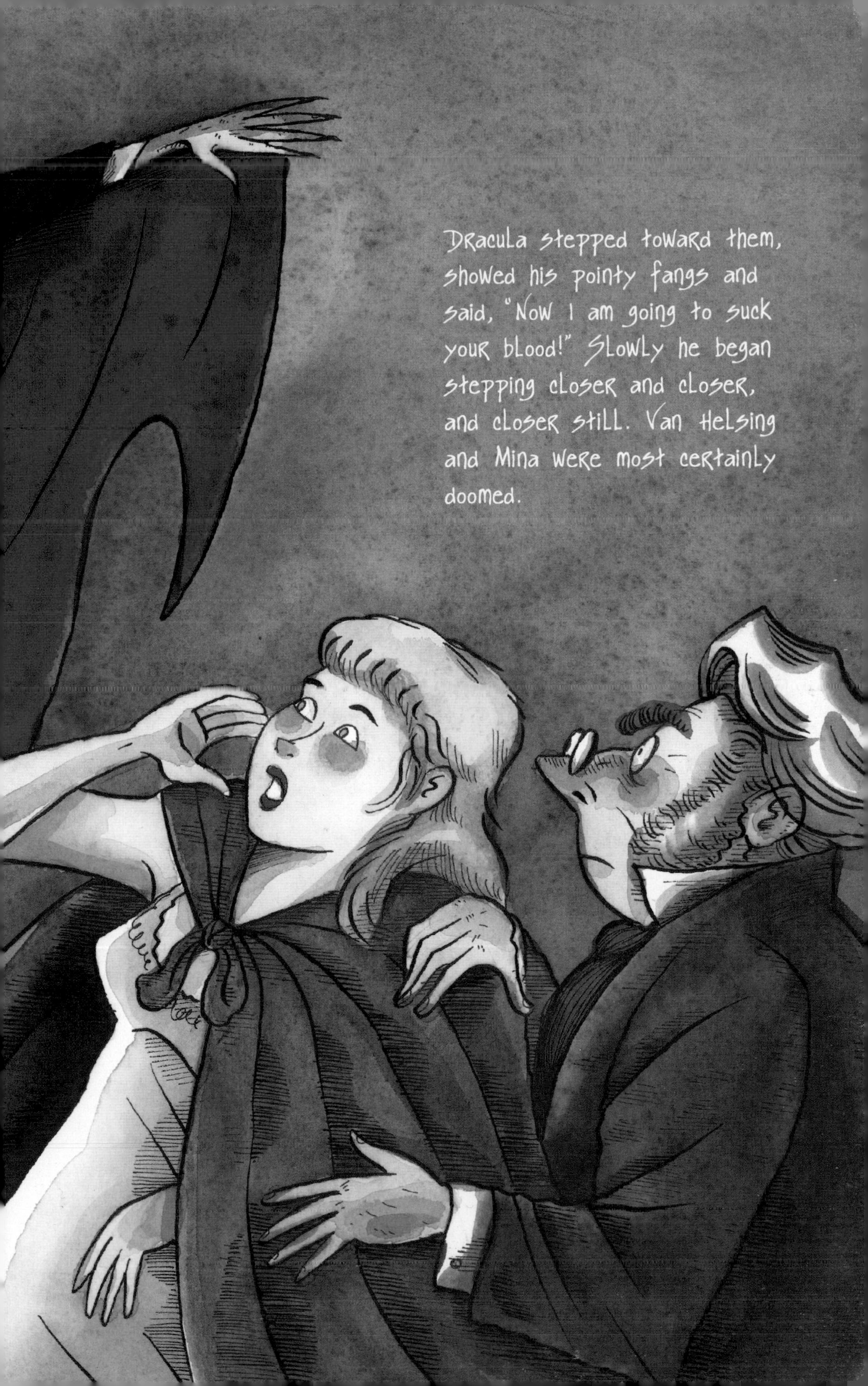

Dracula stepped toward them, showed his pointy fangs and said, "Now I am going to suck your blood!" Slowly he began stepping closer and closer, and closer still. Van Helsing and Mina were most certainly doomed.

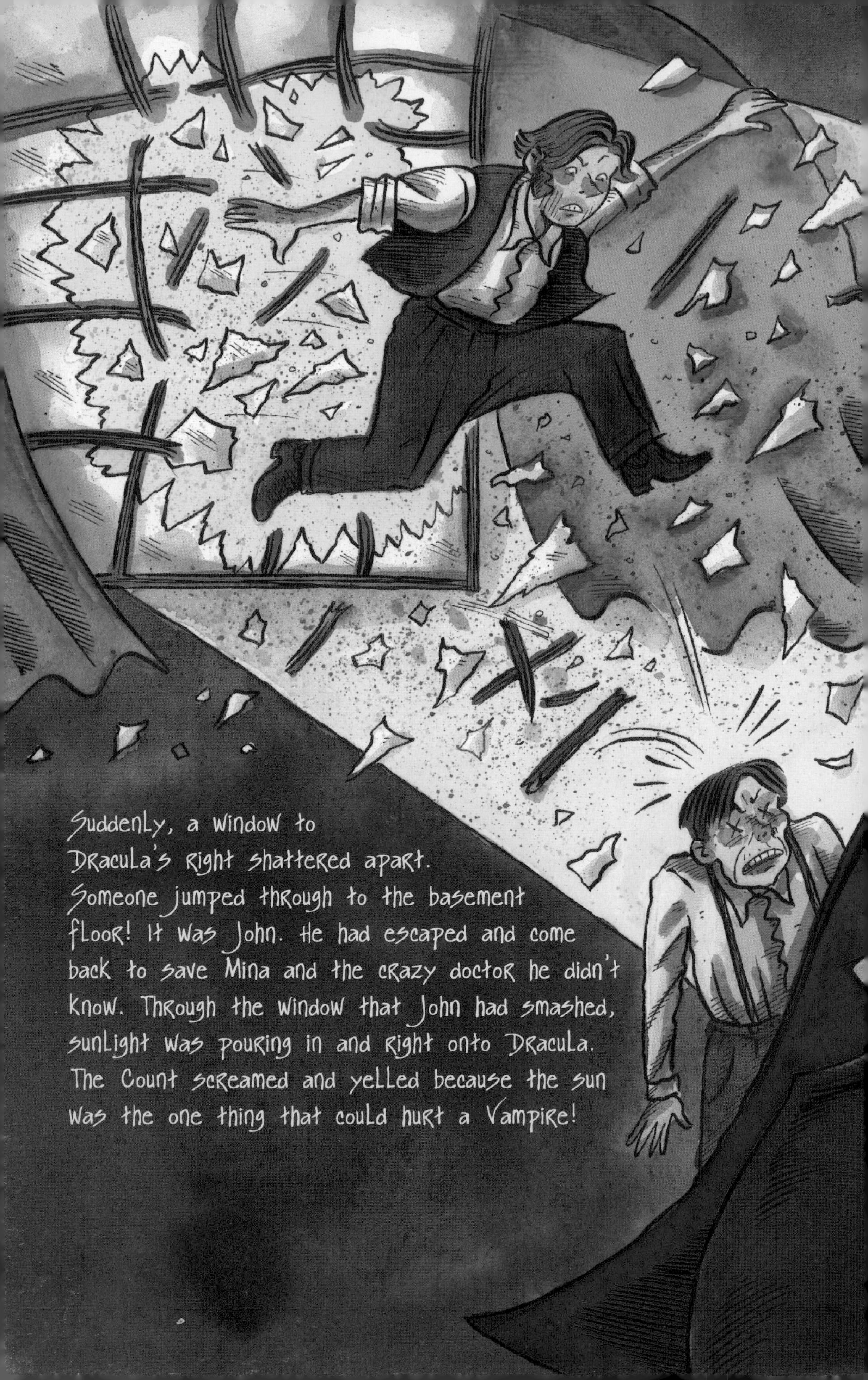
Suddenly, a window to Dracula's right shattered apart. Someone jumped through to the basement floor! It was John. He had escaped and come back to save Mina and the crazy doctor he didn't know. Through the window that John had smashed, sunlight was pouring in and right onto Dracula. The Count screamed and yelled because the sun was the one thing that could hurt a Vampire!

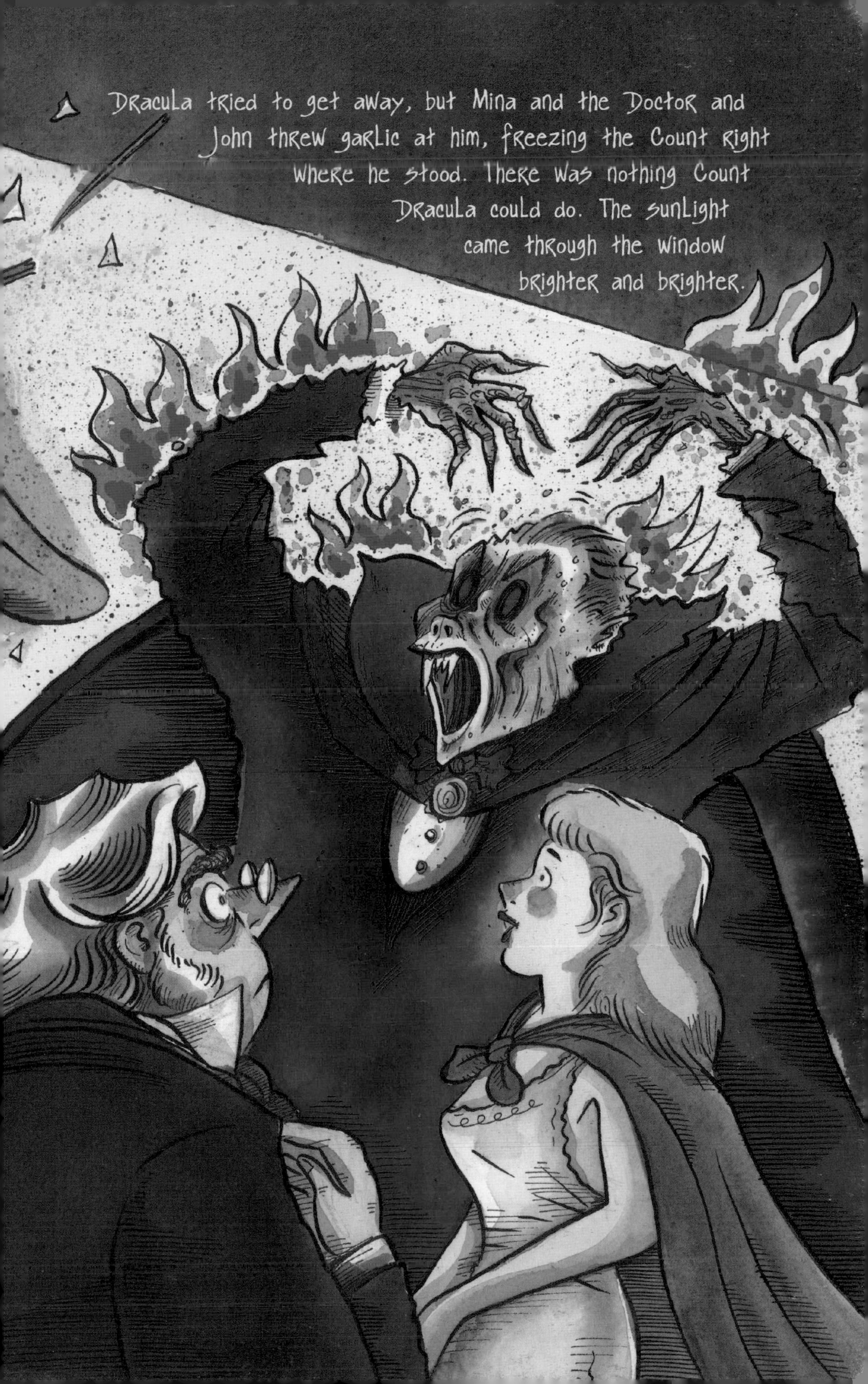
Dracula tried to get away, but Mina and the Doctor and John threw garlic at him, freezing the Count right where he stood. There was nothing Count Dracula could do. The sunlight came through the window brighter and brighter.

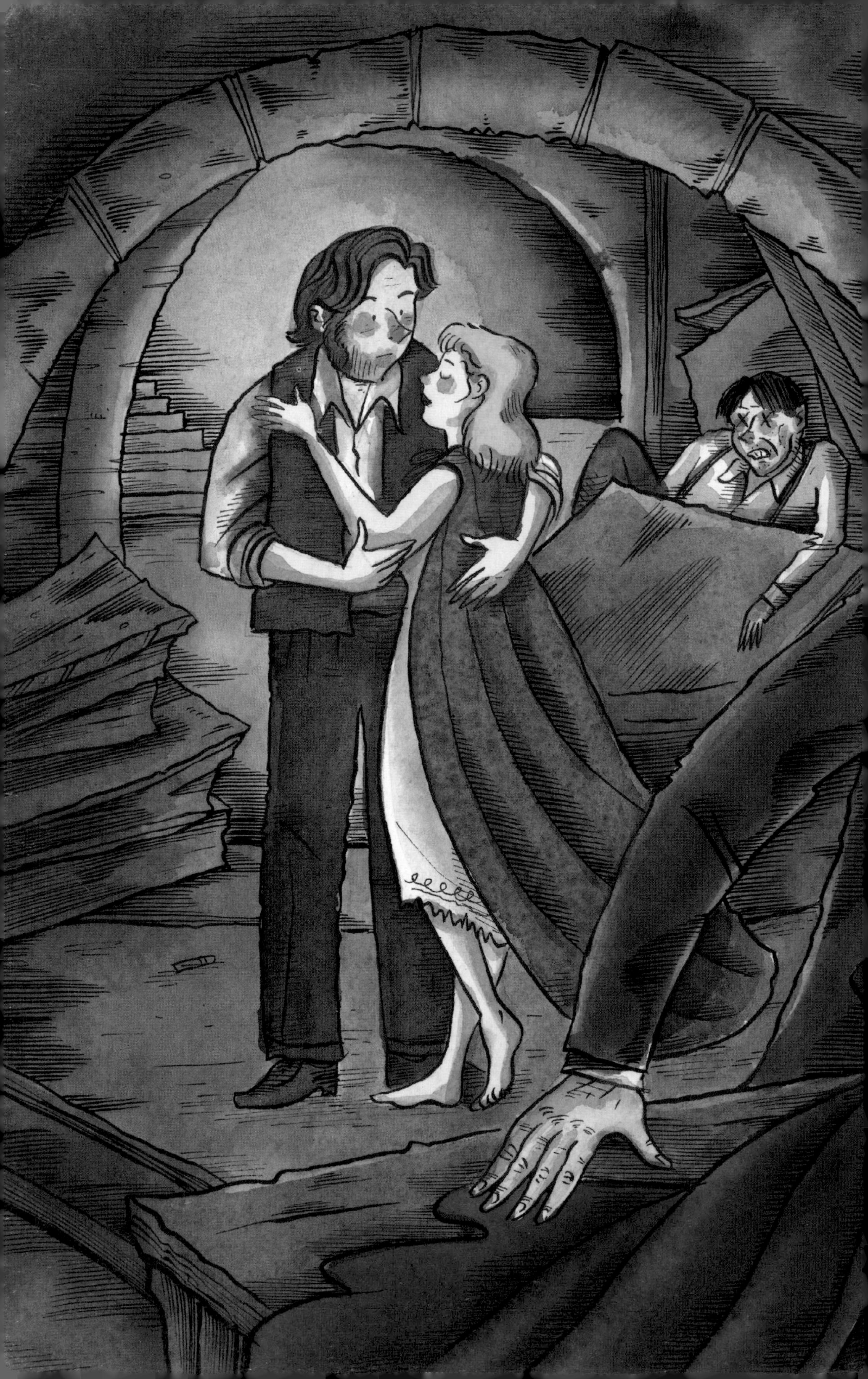

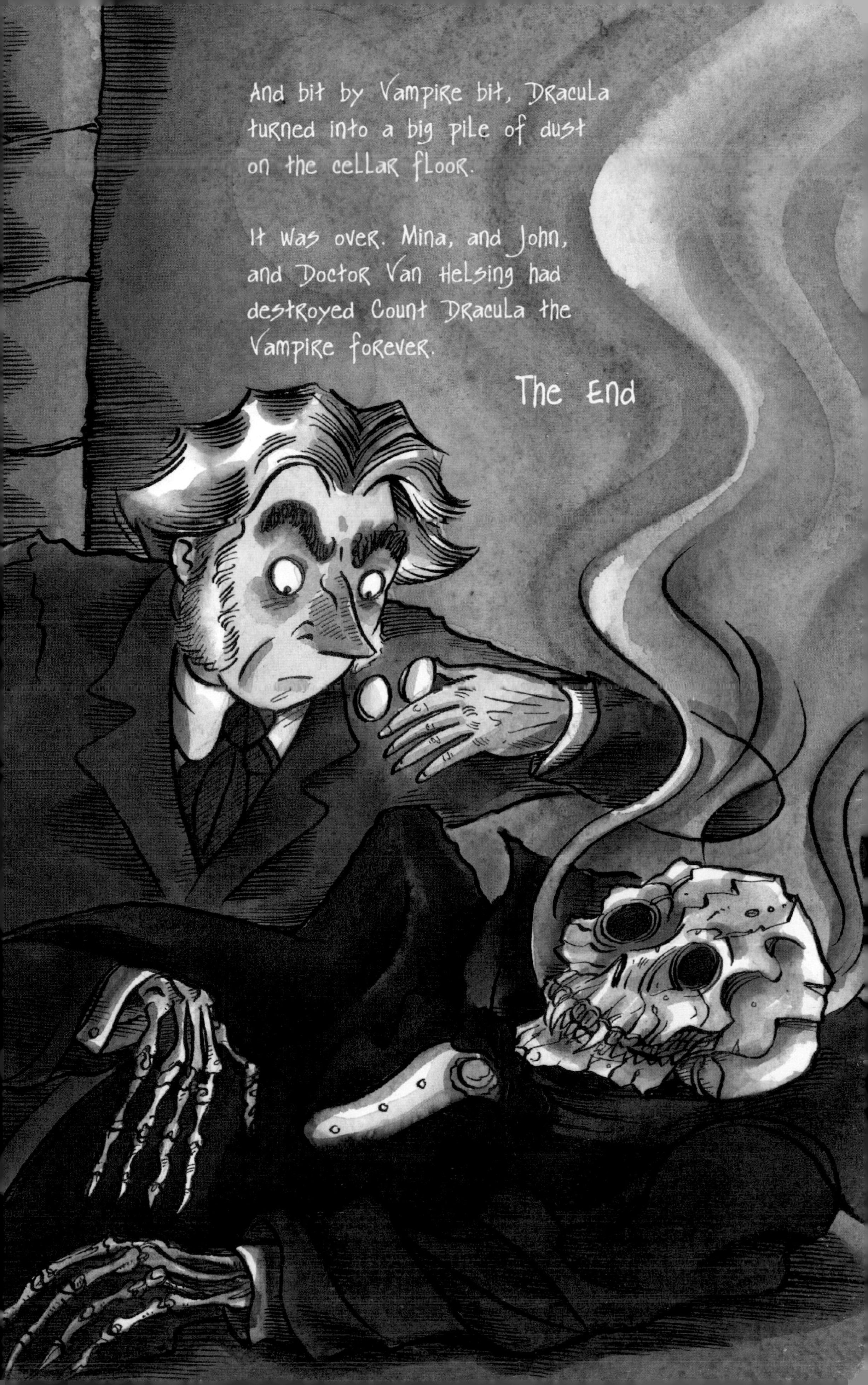
And bit by Vampire bit, Dracula turned into a big pile of dust on the cellar floor.
It was over. Mina, and John, and Doctor Van Helsing had destroyed Count Dracula the Vampire forever.
The End

STEVE NILES

Steve Niles (www.steveniles.com) is one of the writers responsible for bringing horror comics back to the mainstream. Niles is the writer of *Supernatural Freak Machine: A Cal McDonald Mystery*, *Bigfoot* (with Rob Zombie and Richard Corben), *30 Days of Night: Bloodsucker Tales*, and *American Freakshow* for IDW Publishing. Niles also has more Cal McDonald prose novels in the works and recently signed to write *30 Days of Night* prose novels as well.

2002's *30 Days of Night* comic is being developed as a major motion picture, with *Spider-Man 2*'s Sam Raimi producing. Also in production is a *Criminal Macabre* movie for which he will write the screenplay. Niles's *Wake the Dead* and *Hyde* have been optioned by Dimension Films, while Paramount Pictures has optioned the movie rights to *Aleister Arcane*.

Niles got his start in the industry when he formed his own publishing company called Arcane Comix, where he published, edited, and adapted several comics and anthologies for Eclipse Comics. His adaptations include works by Clive Barker, Richard Matheson, and Harlan Ellison. IDW released a hardcover collection of Niles's adaptation of Richard Matheson's *I Am Legend*.

Niles has a wide array of projects due in 2006, including *The Creeper* for DC Comics, *City of Others* with Bernie Wrightson, and more.

Niles lives in Los Angeles.

SCOTT MORSE

Scott Morse (www.scottmorse.com) is the award-winning creator of the graphic novels *Soulwind*, *The Barefoot Serpent*, *Southpaw*, *Spaghetti Western*, and others. In animation, his clients have included Universal, Cartoon Network, Disney, and most recently Nickelodeon, where he served as Art Director on the television series *Catscratch*. He's currently working full-time with Pixar and enjoying life with his family in Northern California.

TED MCKEEVER

Ted McKeever first wrote and illustrated *Transit* and
the Eisner-nominated *Eddy Current* 18 yeas ago. He's
since produced a body of written and illustrated series
such as *Plastic Forks*, *Metropol*, and *Industrial Gothic*, as
well as *Legends of the Dark Night's* "Engines" chapter,
Batman Black and White and Tangled *Web of Spider-man*.
His collaborations include the *Metropolis/Nosferatu/Blue
Amazon* trilogy, and his most recent project, *Enginehead*.

RICHARD SALA

Hooked on all things gruesome and ghastly from an early age, Richard Sala has been drawing shadowy old houses and lurking creatures with fangs and claws since he picked up his first crayon.

Transplanted from California to Chicago at an early age, Sala spent much of his youth in museums and libraries, developing his own vampiric "midnight tan" while the other children were out racing in soap-box derbies and playing stick-ball or whatever children did back in those long ago days of the late 1960s. It was around that time he developed a love (some might say "obsession" —and they might be right) for drawing pictures, which he continues doing to this day.

His books include *Mad Night*, *The Chuckling Whatsit*, *Maniac Killer Strikes Again!*, *Peculia*, and *Peculia and the Groon Grove Vampires*. Visit his web site at www.richardsala.com.

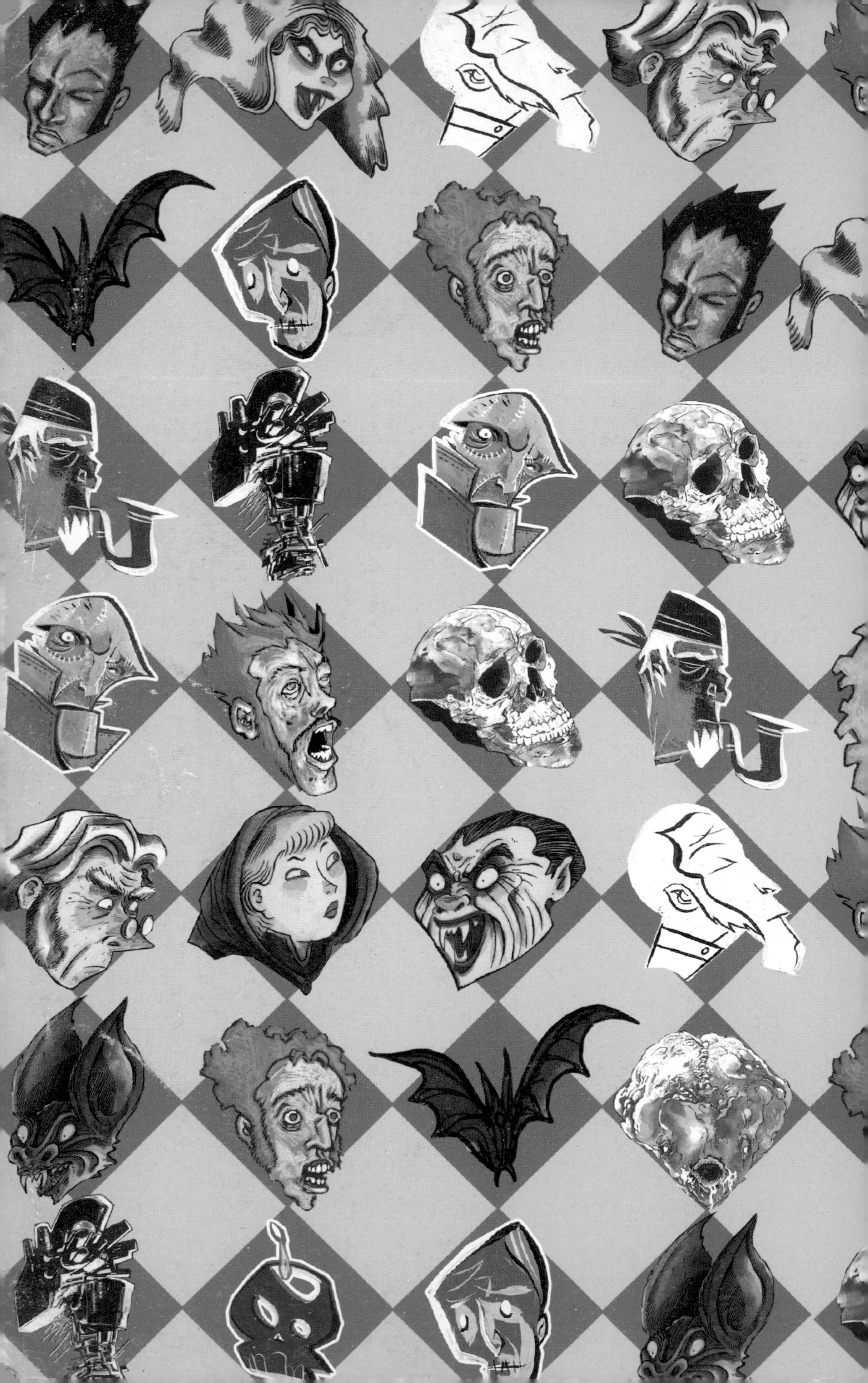